CHRIST OF THE 21ST CENTURY

CHRIST

of the 21st Century

Ewert H. Cousins

ELEMENT

Rockport, Massachusetts ● Shaftesbury, Dorset
Brisbane, Queensland

Published in the U.S.A. in 1992 by
Element, Inc.
42 Broadway, Rockport, MA 01966

Published in Great Britain in 1992 by
Element Books Limited
Longmead, Shaftesbury, Dorset

Published in Australia by
Element Books for
Jacaranda Wiley Ltd
33 Park Road, Milton, Brisbane, 4064

Designed by Roger Lightfoot
Cover design by Max Fairbrother
Typeset by Intype Ltd, London
Printed in the United States of America by
Edwards Brothers, Inc

Library of Congress Cataloging-in-Publication Data
Cousins, Ewert H.
Christ of the 21st century / Ewert H. Cousins.
Includes bibliographical references.
1. Theology–21st century. 2. Christianity–21st century.
3. Spiritual life–Catholic authors. I. Title. II.Title: Christ of the 21st
century.
BX1751.2.C684 1992 230–dc20 91–28368

British Library Cataloguing in Publication Data
Cousins, Ewert H.
Christ of the 21st century.
I. Title
291.4

ISBN 1–85230–276–3

To my late wife Kathryn and my close friend
Robley Whitson, who through the years
constantly encouraged me to write this book.

CONTENTS

ACKNOWLEDGMENTS

Permission has been generously granted to use material published in the following: *Interpreting Tradition: The Art of Theological Reflection*, annual volume of the College Theology Society, 1983, pp. 95–108; *Ebraismo, Ellenismo, Christiancsimo*, Vol. I, (Padova: Cedam, 1985), pp. 115–124; Catholic Theological Society of America *Proceedings*, 25(1981), pp. 124–137; *Cross Currents*, 29(1979), pp. 141–155; *Cross Currents*, 19(1969), pp. 159–177; *Journal of Ecumenical Studies*, 7(1970), pp. 476–498; *Mysticism: Medieval and Modern*, (Salzburg: Institut für Anglistik und Amerikanistik, Universität Salzburg, 1986), pp. 101–108; *Sexual Archetypes, East and West*, (New York: Paragon House Publishers, 1987), pp. 37–50.

INTRODUCTION

In Search of Christ Today

"Who do people say that I am?" (Mark 8:27) This question has echoed through the twenty centuries of Christian history. The gospels describe the scene when Jesus asked the question of his disciples on the way to Caesarea Phillippi in Galilee. It was a turning point in his ministry: He had launched his public teaching, gathered disciples, healed the sick, challenged the Pharisees. What did all this mean? Who was this man? To what extent had he touched the lives of his hearers? What effect would he have on their future, and on the future of the world?

Twenty centuries later, on the eve of the twenty-first century, the question emerges again, at a turning point in world history. In each century each generation of Christians has asked the question: Who is Christ for us today? As Christianity moves into its third millennium, the question surfaces with new urgency and in a setting incalculably more vast than when it was first asked on the hills of Galilee. It resonates now through what twentieth-century scientists know is an expanding universe—through millions of galaxies whose history extends fifteen billion years into the past and unfolds into a future that can be projected only in terms of billions of years. On the planet earth, on the eve of the twenty-first century, the question coincides with the emergence of global consciousness. For the first time since the appearance of human life on our planet, all of the tribes, all of the nations, all of the religions are beginning to share a common history. We can no longer think in terms of Christian history, or even Western history. When Christians raise questions about Christ, they must now ask: How is Christ related to Hindu history, to Buddhist history—to the common global history that the religions are beginning to share? The question is asked not only by professors and students at divinity schools and universities, but by peasants and revolutionaries in Latin America.

The question emerges in an atmosphere far more apocalyptic and

oppressive than that of first-century Palestine. Nuclear holocaust
and ecological pollution threaten life on our planet. More than half of
the world's population groans under economic, social, and political
oppression. What intensifies human problems in our time is that
they are no longer merely local or regional; they have become global
problems calling for global solutions. On the eve of the twenty-first
century, Christians must ask: What is the relation of Christ to these
issues?

This book, then, attempts to raise the question: Who is the Christ
of the twenty-first century? At first glance, the title might appear
bold and even pretentious. How could a single author or a single
book hope to deal with such a topic? If the book were written in
isolation, then these impressions would be justified. But it is not.
Instead, it situates itself in a long tradition of asking the question
raised by Christ in the gospel account and asked continuously
throughout Christian history.

This book would be pretentious if it believed it could answer the
question adequately. Rather, it is an attempt at a partial exploration.
Its significance, if any, lies in the resources it draws into the question-
ing. It does not attempt to ignore the spiritual and intellectual
resources of the centuries. It will not leap from the New Testament
to the late twentieth century and cut the mystery of Christ to fit the
limits of contemporary Western culture. Rather it will draw from the
resources of tradition from Origen, Gregory of Nyssa, Augustine,
Bernard of Clairvaux, Bonaventure, Dante, and Eckhart. While
drawing from tradition, it will not treat tradition as a static heritage.
Rather, it will suggest how tradition must be transformed in order
to be a dynamic force in the twenty-first century.

If it is not audacious to ask the question of Christ at the present,
is it not a mark of hubris to ask it about a century that has not yet
dawned? The future itself imposes this task on us—not out of our
pride but to make us humble before the task. Since the sixties and
seventies, the future has become a dimension of our present. Like
it or not, we must discern where history is moving. We have not
yet developed sophisticated ways of doing this, but do it we must—
willingly and humbly. It is in this spirit that I risk all inadequacies
and failures of a primitive attempt to deal with theology and spirituality in what will increasingly be its new dimension.

This book is about the Christ of faith. Its title makes this clear.
It does not join the quest for the historical Jesus, although it is not
oblivious of that quest. Rather it takes its cue from Peter's response
to Jesus. When Jesus asked, "Who do people say that I am," Peter
answered, "You are the Christ." Implicitly, this has been the
response of the Christian tradition since the time of Paul and the

early Christian communities that stand behind the gospels of Mark, Matthew, Luke, and John. It has been the response of the patristic, medieval, Reformation, and modern Christian communities.

If it is difficult—even impossible—to contact the Jesus of history, it may seem equally beyond our reach to have access to the Christ of faith. Fortunately, however, this is not the case. For the Christ of faith lives in the consciousness of the Christian community—in its long and cumulative history. There are numerous witnesses to this Christ mystery: liturgy, hymns, prayers, and meditations, contemplative and mystical experiences, creeds and theological reflection.

Is there a method that will enable us to penetrate into that Christ mystery? This book is largely a search for such a method. It is an application of the method to the mystery of Christ. As we will see in the subsequent chapters, this method grounds itself in religious or spiritual experience and will attempt to describe that experience in its depth and inner structures.

The method that unfolds in the book has three strands: historical, theological, and prophetic-projective. The book begins by exploring the history of consciousness in a non-theological fashion, by describing the transformation of consciousness that occurred in the first millennium B.C.E. In the light of this historical study, it turns to the present and attempts a prophetic projection of the future based on past and present trends. Then it enters the context of Christian theology, attempting to retrieve the classical theological and spiritual tradition, and moves toward a constructive theology for the future.

The contents of the book represent the work of many years and are the expression of ideas that have been presented as talks and papers at conferences, a number of which have appeared in print as articles. They have been reworked and drawn into a thematic whole. In retrospect I have become aware that this book has been writing itself over the past years, although I was not always aware of it as an organic progress.

In drawing from the history of theology, the book makes no claim to be comprehensive. The classical writers I have chosen are those in whom I have worked. Another author, addressing similar themes, might have chosen other resources. I have not marshaled texts from Scripture to illustrate or support my claims, in part because this has not been an area of my specialization. Yet in drawing from the history of Christian theology and spirituality, I realize that the authors I have selected were themselves solidly grounded in Scripture and that foundation permeates their thought.

I want to take this occasion to express my gratitude to all who have contributed to the process that has led to this publication. They are far too numerous to mention by name: my many colleagues in the academic world, my teachers, and students. I owe a special debt of gratitude to my children—Hilary, Sara, and Emily—who have not only provided a supportive environment, but have enriched me with their discussion and their own creative inquiry. I would like to single out Richard Payne, who through many years has been a close friend, collaborator, and editor. He has encouraged and guided me not only in this, but in many other related projects as well. Many of the ideas of this book have been discovered and explored in dialogue with him. I am deeply grateful also to Anna Harrison, who especially over the last two months of work on the book has generously devoted her time and talents to every level of the manuscript: its content, structure, style, and countless editorial details. The book could not have reached completion at this time without her invaluable contributions. Finally, I wish to express my gratitude to Carolyn Gonzales, my typist for over twenty years. In a number of cases she had typed an earlier version of material in the book before the days of computers. At this point I have been fortunate to share in her highly developed skills in computer technology.

I

Religions on the Eve of the 21st Century

As we begin to explore the Christ of the twenty-first century, we must become conscious of our viewing point. Where will we stand in order to perceive the dimensions of the emerging mystery of the Christ of the future? First, we must not isolate Christ from culture. Although we will concentrate on the mystery of Christ from theological and spiritual perspectives, we must not abstract these from culture. We must not view the mystery exclusively from theology or spirituality, but within the fabric of human life as a whole. Since prehistoric times, religion has played a formative role in human society. It shaped the burial customs of primitive tribes and inspired their art on the walls of caves. As nations and empires emerged, religion provided a cosmic vision for social and political institutions. Throughout history, religion has been a wellspring of cultural creativity. Much of the great art of the world—architecture, sculpture, painting, music and literature—has been religious in inspiration and function. Religion has preached justice, brotherhood, universal peace. It has defused hatred, deflected aggression, and humanized society, disciplining conduct and evoking noble actions through lofty ideals. Yet religion has a dark side. It has launched wars and persecutions, has justified slavery, discrimination, and oppression, and has blocked the advance of knowledge. It has been used, both consciously and unconsciously, as a tool for social, political and economic exploitation. Throughout its long history, religion has revealed its paradoxical nature. At its best, it is a most creative force in culture; at its worst, it can be distorted to destroy the very ideals it espouses.

There is another paradox in the relation of religion and culture. Religion focuses on the transcendent, the otherworldly, the divine realm, while culture grounds itself in the concrete, the material, the humanistic and artistic, in the social, political, economic dimensions of human existence. Religion claims to transcend culture, to stand in opposition to culture, to escape from culture. Yet even in its flight from culture, religion is shaped by culture, and in turn, shapes culture. When it flees from the world, as in monasticism, it indirectly influences the world economically and politically. Even in secular societies, religion is not absent. Although dormant for decades, religious energies can suddenly erupt or, remaining submerged, they may exercise a prolonged influence, masked in secular guise.

In view of the pervasiveness of religion in culture and in view of its potential for both creativity and distortion, it would be disastrous to ignore the relationship of religion and culture. It would be especially disastrous at this moment in history when culture is being transformed into a global reality, when issues are being transposed from a national to a global level. At this period the religions of the world, which throughout their long histories have been embedded in specific cultures, must simultaneously relate to each other globally and direct their mission to the common problems of the human race as a whole.

THE RELIGIOUS PHENOMENON

How, then, can we approach religions on the eve of the twenty-first century? Certainly within culture as a whole, as we observed above. But we must do more than that. We must view both religions and culture in a process, not merely statically, frozen in the past or present. Rather we must observe how religions have emerged out of their past into the present, but most of all we must discern the dynamics of the process through which they are moving into the future. To do this, we must disengage ourselves from any particular culture or religion, situating ourselves at a viewing point from which we can see clearly both cultures and religions in a global perspective. In doing this we will be like the astronauts who travelled into outer space and looked back on the earth. What they saw overwhelmed them! For the first time in history, human beings actually saw the earth as a whole. They saw the earth's clouds, oceans and continents, it is true, but not as discrete elements; nor did they behold merely a limited horizon as when standing on the earth's surface. Rather they saw the earth as an interrelated, organic whole—a single globe of remarkable beauty and unity. It is striking that at the very moment in history when culture is becoming globalized, we have obtained our first sense impression of the earth as a single globe. This image of the beautiful blue globe, shining against the black background of the universe, moving in its orbit in space can concretely symbolize the emergence of global consciousness on the eve of the twenty-first century.

From our astronaut's position, then, what do we observe? The most visible phenomenon from this vantage point is the convergence of disparate cultures into an organic whole and the emergence of global consciousness. This has been brought about by the increase of population and the development of communication through industrialization and technology. This convergence does not necessarily lead to a flattening of cultures by levelling them to a least common denominator. If intelligently directed, it can bring about an enormous enrichment, which retains and even intensifies diversity in the midst of unity. Through complementarity, polar elements in cultures can reinforce each other and lead to a much more complex reality than can be achieved by individual cultures in isolation. Emerging out of this complexity, and yet transcending it, is the most characteristic quality of the contemporary phenomenon: the development of global consciousness. With this new dimension of consciousness, each person will be aware of belonging primarily to the entire globe — not merely to an ethnic group, tribe, or nation, but directly to the whole.

From our astronaut's point of view, what do we observe as the religious phenomenon? First we see the meeting of world religions. Just as cultures are converging, so are the world religions, in a way that is unprecedented in history. For the first time, religions are meeting on a global scale and in an atmosphere of understanding, appreciation, and mutual enrichment. In this context there has emerged the dialogue of world religions. As the religions of the world encounter each other, a new and complex form of religious consciousness is being born. In the dialogue, the partners enter into the structures of consciousness of the others and return enriched to their own. This experience of mutual enrichment broadens the horizons of the various religions, contributing to the process of transformation into global consciousness.

From our vantage point, we observe a second dimension of the contemporary religious phenomenon. The secular forces which have brought about global consciousness have also led to the secularization of culture, chiefly in the West, but in varying degrees throughout the world. Through secularization cultures are being emptied of their religious heritage. Thus the religious phenomenon manifests a process of both fulness and emptiness. By sharing their values in the dialogue of religions, the various traditions are mutually supported, enriched and fulfilled. At the same time, however, these very religious values are being stripped away by the process of secularization, which focuses on the pragmatic rather than the ritualistic, on the social, political, and economic dimensions of human existence rather than the spiritual. Yet these secular values have a spiritual dimension which must be acknowledged by the religions as a basis for support and cultivation.

From this astronaut's point of view, then, we will explore more in detail the religious phenomenon on the eve of the twenty-first century. To do this we will extend our gaze not only across space, but also back in time to observe how the religions were shaped in their historical development. First, I will examine the transformation of consciousness that occurred in what has been called the Axial Period of history: during the first millennium B.C.E. when the great religions as we know them came into existence. Secondly, I will explore the present period, on the eve of the twenty-first century, which I designate as a Second Axial Period, whose characteristic is the emergence of global consciousness. Thirdly, I will make some observations on the Christ of the twenty-first century in the light of the Second Axial Period.

THE AXIAL PERIOD

From our astronaut's perspective we have seen how religions and cultures are caught up in a process leading to global consciousness. Let us now transport ourselves back in history to another period when the world religions were fundamentally shaped in their present form. If we were to look at the earth from our distant vantage point during the first millennium B.C.E., we would observe another remarkable phenomenon. From the period between 800–200 B.C.E, peaking about 500 B.C.E, a striking transformation of consciousness occurred around the earth in three geographic regions, apparently without the influence of one on the other. If we look at China, we will see two great teachers, Lao-tze and Confucius, from whose wisdom emerged the schools of Chinese philosophy. In India the cosmic, ritualistic Hinduism of the Vedas was being transformed by the Upanishads, while the Buddha and Mahavira ushered in two new religious traditions. In the same geographic region, Zoroaster emerged in Persia describing the struggle between good and evil. If we turn our gaze farther west, we observe a similar development in the eastern Mediterranean region. In Israel the Jewish prophets— Elijah, Isaiah, and Jeremiah—called forth from their people a new moral awareness. In Greece Western philosophy was born. The pre-Socratic cosmologists sought a rational explanation for the universe; Socrates awakened the moral consciousness of the Athenians; Plato and Aristotle developed metaphysical systems.

It was Karl Jaspers, the German philosopher, who some 40 years ago pointed out the significance of this phenomenon in his book *The Origin and Goal of History*.[1] He called this period from 800–200 B.C.E. the Axial Period because "it gave birth to everything which, since then, man has been able to be." It is here in this period "that we meet with the most deepcut dividing line in history. Man, as we know him today, came into being. For short, we may style this the 'Axial Period'."[2] Although the leaders who effected this change were philosophers and religious teachers, the change was so radical that it affected all aspects of culture; for it transformed consciousness itself. It was within the horizons of this form of consciousness that the great civilizations of Asia, the Middle East, and Europe developed. Although within these horizons many developments occurred through the subsequent centuries, the horizons themselves did not change. It was this form of consciousness that was spread to other regions through migration and explorations, thus becoming the dominant, though not exclusive, form of consciousness in the world. To this day, whether we have been born and raised in the culture of China, India, Europe, or the Americas, we bear the structure of consciousness that was shaped in this Axial Period.

What is this structure of consciousness and how does it differ from pre-Axial consciousness? Prior to the Axial Period the dominant form of consciousness was cosmic, collective, tribal, mythic, and ritualistic. This is the characteristic form of consciousness of primal peoples whose cultures provided a substratum throughout the world for the later civilizations and which survive to this day in tribal groups. Between these traditional cultures and the Axial Period there emerged great empires in Egypt, China, and Mesopotamia, but these did not yet produce the full consciousness of the Axial Period.

The consciousness of the tribal cultures was embedded in the cosmos and in the fertility cycles of nature. Thus there was established a rich and creative harmony between primal peoples and the world of nature, a harmony which was explored, expressed, and celebrated in myth and ritual. Just as they felt themselves part of nature, so they experienced themselves as part of the tribe. They had no sense of independent identity apart from the tribe. It was precisely the web of interrelationships within the tribe that sustained them psychologically, energizing all aspects of their lives. To be separated from the tribe threatened them with death, not only physical but psychological as well. However, the fusion of their identity with the collectivity did not extend beyond their own tribe, for they often looked upon other tribes as mean and hostile. Yet within their tribe they felt organically related to their group as a whole, to the life cycles of birth and death and to nature and the cosmos.

The Axial Period ushered in a radically new form of consciousness. Whereas primal consciousness was tribal, Axial consciousness was individual. "Know thyself" became the watchword of Greece; the Upanishads identified the *atman*, the transcendent center of the self. The Buddha charted the way of individual enlightenment; the Jewish prophets awakened individual moral responsibility. This sense of individual identity, as distinct from the tribe and from nature, is the most characteristic mark of Axial consciousness. From this flow other characteristics: consciousness that is self-reflective, analytic, and that can be applied to nature in the form of scientific theories, to society in the form of social critique, to knowledge in the form of philosophy, to religion in the form of mapping an individual spiritual journey. This self-reflective, analytic, critical consciousness stood in sharp contrast to primal mythic and ritualistic consciousness. When self-reflective *logos* emerged in the Axial Period, it tended to oppose the traditional *mythos*. Of course, mythic and ritualistic forms of consciousness survive in the post-Axial Period even to this day; but they are often submerged, surfacing chiefly in dreams, literature, and art.

Although Axial consciousness brought many benefits, it involved loss as well. It severed the harmony with nature and the tribe. Axial persons were in possession of their own identity, it is true, but they had lost their organic relation to nature and community. They now ran the risk of being alienated from the matrix of being and life. With their new powers, they could criticize the social structure and by analysis discover the abstract laws of science and metaphysics, but they might find themselves mere spectators of a drama of which in reality they were an integral part.

The emergence of Axial consciousness was decisive for religions, since it marked the divide in history where the great religions emerged and separated themselves from their primal antecedents. The great religions of the world as we know them today are the product of the Axial Period. Hinduism, Buddhism, Taoism, Confucianism, and Judaism took shape in their classical form during this period; and Judaism provided the base for the later emergence of Christianity and Islam. The common structures of consciousness found in these religions are characteristic of the general transformation of consciousness effected in the Axial Period.

The move into Axial consciousness released enormous spiritual energy. It opened up the individual spiritual path, especially the inner way in which the new subjectivity became the avenue into the transcendent. It allowed the deeper self to sort out the difference between the illusion of the phenomenal world and the authentic vision of reality. On the ethical level it allowed individual moral conscience to take a critical stand against the collectivity. And it made possible a link between the moral and the spiritual aspects of the self, so that a path could be charted through virtues toward the ultimate goal of the spiritual quest.

One of the most distinctive forms of spirituality that became available in the Axial Period was monasticism. Although it had roots in the earlier Hindu tradition, it emerged in a clearly defined way in Buddhism and Jainism at the peak of the Axial Period and later developed in Christianity. Monasticism did not exist among primal peoples because their consciousness could not sustain it. Primal consciousness did not contain the distinct center of individuality necessary to produce the monk as a religious type. For the monks and nuns themselves take a radical stand as marginal persons, separating themselves from family and community, stripping themselves of material goods by practicing poverty and withdrawing from the fertility cycles by celibacy—as wandering beggars or as members of monastic communities who share their sense of radicalness.

Although Axial consciousness opened many possibilities, it tended to close off others and to produce some negative results. The release of spiritual energy thrust the Axial person in the direction of the spirit and away from the earth, away from the life cycles and the harmony with nature which the primal peoples experienced and which they made the basis of their spirituality. In some traditions this emergence of spiritual energy caused a radical split between the phenomenal world and true reality, between matter and spirit, between earth and heaven. Although in a number of traditions this separation was not central, nevertheless the emergence of Axial consciousness, with its strong sense of subjectivity, made that separation not only possible, but a risk and a threat. From the time of the Axial Period, the spiritual path tended to lead away from the earth and towards the heavenly realms above.

THE SECOND AXIAL PERIOD

If we shift our gaze from the first millennium B.C.E. to the eve of the twenty-first century, we can discern another transformation of consciousness. It is so profound and far-reaching that I call it the Second Axial Period. Like the first it is happening simultaneously around the earth, and like the first it will shape the horizon of consciousness for future centuries. Not surprisingly, too, it will have great significance for world religions, which were constituted in the First Axial Period. However, the new form of consciousness is different from that of the First Axial Period. Then it was individual consciousness, now it is global consciousness.

In order to understand better the forces at work in the Second Axial Period, I would like to draw from the thought of the paleontologist Pierre Teilhard de Chardin.[3] In the light of his research in evolution, he charted the development of consciousness from its roots in the geosphere and biosphere and into the future. In a process which he calls "planetization," he observed that a shift in the forces of evolution had occurred over the past hundred years. This shift is from divergence to convergence. When human beings first appeared on this planet, they clustered together in family and tribal units, forming their own group identity and separating themselves from other tribes. In this way humans diverged, creating separate nations and a rich variety of cultures. However, the spherical shape of the earth prevented unlimited divergence. With the increase in population and the rapid development of communication, groups could no longer remain apart. After dominating the process for millennia, the forces of divergence have been superceded by those of convergence. This shift to convergence is drawing the various cultures into a single planetized community. Although we have been conditioned by thousands of years of divergence, we now have no other course open to us but to cooperate creatively with the forces of convergence as these are drawing us toward global consciousness.[4]

According to Teilhard this new global consciousness will not level all differences among peoples; rather it will generate what he calls creative unions in which diversity is not erased but intensified. His understanding of creative unions is based on his general theory of evolution and the dynamic which he observes throughout the universe. From the geosphere to the biosphere to the realm of consciousness, a single process is at work, which he articulates as the law of "complexity-consciousness" and "union differentiates." "In any domain," he says, "whether it be the cells of a body, the members of a society or the elements of a spiritual synthesis—*union differentiates*."[5] From subatomic particles to global consciousness, individual elements unite in what Teilhard calls center to center unions. By touching each other at the creative core of their being, they release new energy which leads to more complex units. Greater complexity leads to greater interiority which, in turn, leads to more creative unions. Throughout the process, the individual elements do not lose their identity, but rather deepen and fulfill it through union. "Following the confluent orbits of their center," he says, "the grains of consciousness do not tend to lose their outlines and blend, but, on the contrary, to accentuate the depth and incommunicability of their *egos*. The more 'other' they become in conjunction, the more they find themselves as 'self'."[6] At this point of history, because of the shift from divergence to convergence, the forces of planetization are bringing about an unprecedented complexification of consciousness through the convergence of cultures and religions.

In the light of Teilhard's thought, then, we can better understand the meeting of religions on the eve of the twenty-first century. The world religions are the product of the First Axial Period and the forces of divergence. Although in the first millennium B.C.E, there was a common transformation of consciousness, it occurred in diverse geographical regions within already differentiated cultures. In each case the religion was shaped by this differentation in its origin, and developed along differentiated lines. This produced a remarkable richness of spiritual wisdom, of spiritual energies and of religious-cultural forms to express, preserve and transmit this heritage. Now that the forces of divergence have shifted to convergence, the religions must meet each other in center to center unions, discovering what is most authentic in each other, releasing creative energy toward a more complexified form of religious consciousness.

Such a creative encounter has been called the "dialogic dialogue" to distinguish it from the dialectic dialogue in which one tries to refute the claims of the other.[7] This dialogic dialogue has three phases: (1) The partners meet each other in an atmosphere of mutual understanding, ready to alter misconceptions about each other and eager to appreciate the values of the other. (2) The partners are mutually enriched, by passing over into the consciousness of the other so that each can experience the other's values from within the other's perspective. This can be enormously enriching, for often the partners discover in another tradition values which are submerged or only inchoate in their own. It is important at this point to respect the autonomy of the other tradition: in Teilhard's terms, to achieve union in which differences are valued as a basis of creativity. (3) If such a creative union is achieved, then the religions will have moved into the complexified form of consciousness that will be characteristic of the twenty-first century. This will be complexified global consciousness, not a mere universal, undifferentiated, abstract consciousness. It will be global through the global convergence of cultures and religions and complexified by the dynamics of dialogic dialogue.

This global consciousness, complexified through the meeting of cultures and religions, is only one characteristic of the Second Axial Period. The consciousness of this period is global in another sense: namely, in rediscovering its roots in the earth. At the very moment when the various cultures and religions are meeting each other and creating a new global community, our life on the planet is being threatened. The very tools which we have used to bring about this convergence—industrialization and technology—are undercutting the biological support system that sustains life on our planet. The future of consciousness, or even life on the earth, is shrouded in a cloud of uncertainty by the pollution of our environment, the depletion of natural resources, the unjust distribution of wealth, the stockpiling of nuclear weapons. Unless the human community reverses these destructive forces, we may not see the twenty-first century. The human race as a whole—all the diverse cultures and the religions—must face these problems squarely. In this Second Axial Period we must rediscover the dimensions of consciousness of the spirituality of the primal peoples of the pre-Axial Period. As we saw, this consciousness was collective and cosmic, rooted in the earth and the life cycles. We must rapidly appropriate that form of consciousness or perish from the earth. However, I am not suggesting a romantic attempt to live in the past, rather that the evolution of consciousness proceeds by way of recapitulation. Having developed self-reflective, analytic, critical consciousness in the First Axial Period, we must now, while retaining these values, reappropriate and integrate into that consciousness the collective and cosmic dimensions of the pre-Axial consciousness. We must recapture the unity of tribal consciousness by seeing humanity as a single tribe. And we must see this single tribe related organically to the total cosmos. This means that the consciousness of the twenty-first century will be global from two perspectives: (1) from a horizontal perspective, cultures and religions are meeting each other on the surface of the globe, entering into creative encounters that will produce a complexified collective consciousness; (2) from a vertical perspective, they must plunge their roots deep into the earth in order to provide a stable and secure base for future development. This new global consciousness must be organically ecological, supported by structures that will insure justice and peace. In the Second Axial Period this twofold global consciousness is not only a creative possibility to enhance the twenty-first century; it is an absolute necessity if we are to survive.

THE TASK OF RELIGIONS

What does this mean for religions on the eve of the twenty-first century? It means that they have a double task: to enter creatively into the dialogue of religions and to channel their energies into solving the common human problems that threaten our future on the earth. It means that they must strip away negative and limiting attitudes towards other religions. They must avoid both a narrow fundamentalism and a bland universalism. They must be true to their spiritual heritage, for this is the source of their power and their gift to the world. They must make every effort to ground themselves in their own traditions and at the same time to open themselves to other traditions. In concert with the other religions they should commit themselves to creating the new complexified global consciousness we have been exploring.

But to meet, even creatively, on the spiritual level is not enough. They must channel their spiritual resources toward the solution of global problems. For the most part, this calls for a transformation of the religions. Having been formed in the First Axial Period, the religions bear the mark of Axial consciousness: in turning toward the spiritual ascent away from the material. The religions must rediscover the material dimensions of existence and their spiritual significance. In this they can learn from the secular: that justice and peace are human values that must be cherished and pragmatically cultivated. But they must not adopt an exclusively secular attitude, for their unique contribution is to tap their reservoirs of spiritual energy and channel this into developing secular enterprises that are genuinely human.

Already the religions are awakening to this challenge of the Second Axial Period. We see this in the widespread concern of religions for disarmament, peace, ecology, and a just social, political, and economic order. As the religions face these common human problems, it is crucial, not merely to achieve a general consensus, but to tap the distinctive resources of each tradition. For example, what can Hinduism, as a religious tradition, contribute to disarmament? Buddhism to the resolving of the ecological crisis? The religions of the world contain not only a common spiritual wisdom, but distinctive resources which must be identified and utilized if we are to survive.

Within the different religions, movements have developed to tap their particular spiritual resources for the solution of human problems. In so doing these religions cannot merely draw from their resources as these existed in the First Axial Period, but must transform them in the light of the Second Axial Period. Since the last century, for example, Hinduism has been transforming its classical tradition in order to meet contemporary human needs. We see this in the work of the Ramakrishna Mission, the great political movement led by Gandhi, in the social and political thought of Aurobindo. In each case we see not a mere abstract application of ethical norms, no matter how enlightened, but rather a recovery of spiritual energies of the classical tradition which are then channeled into the secular realm in order to bring about a transformation. We see a similar trend in Christianity in the liberation theology that has developed in the Third World. In certain respects controversial, this movement has directed itself toward radical praxis, drawing from the Jewish Exodus and the death and resurrection of Christ as sources of spiritual energy to effect the liberation of the poor from social, economic, and political oppression. On the ecological issue, the most eloquent voice has been raised by primal people, whose pre-Axial consciousness uniquely qualified them to discern the basis of a harmonious relation between the human community and the earth. In the light of their traditional wisdom, the American Indians and other primal peoples have issued a prophetic warning against the destruction of our environment and have shared as a model for others their positive religious attitudes toward nature.

As a single human community we must tap the wisdom of all the great religious teachers of the First Axial Period: the cosmic harmony of Lao-tze and the virtuous life of Confucius; the compassion of the Buddha and the non-violence of Mahavira; the overcoming of illusion in the Upanishads and Socrates' search for the Good; the moral passion of the Jewish prophets and Zoroaster's struggle against evil; the universal love of Jesus and Muhammed's prophetic witness to God's justice and mercy. These moral and spiritual resources—the great legacy of the First Axial Period—must be transposed and rechannelled into the global consciousness of the Second Axial Period. If we perform that task successfully, then in the twenty-first century we will be able from the astronaut's perspective to look back upon the earth again. We will see peace, justice, and well-being securely established on a global scale and energized by the spiritual resources of the religions. The human community will have passed over its second great divide in history. Then with firm realism, the blue globe shining in the darkness of the universe will symbolize the peace, justice, and well-being that has been achieved in the global consciousness that will envelop the earth.

THE CHRIST OF THE 21ST CENTURY

In this context how can we view the Christ of the twenty-first century? At the outset it would be wise to make some preliminary methodological observations. In keeping with the emergence of global consciousness, we did not view history from a particular culture, for example, from Western culture, as is often done, and more specifically from the scientific, technological optic of the modern West. Rather we have viewed history from a global perspective, focusing on two major events that most of the human community has shared. Secondly we have not begun with a theology of history, whether Christian, Hindu, or Islamic. Rather we have sketched the historical process from outside, as it were, from our astronaut's position in outer space. However Christianity, and all of the other religions, have the task of exploring this outer phenomenon from within their own theologies of history.

Throughout this book we will be looking at the phenomenon of the Second Axial Period both from inside and outside. We will be exploring the mystery of Christ from within the Christian tradition and from within the Christian theology of history. At the same time we will be attempting to glimpse new dimensions of the mystery of Christ and the Christian theology of history as these unfold within the enlarged horizons of global consciousness. We will be asking: What is the significance of Christ in relation to world religions? In relation to ecology, to global peace and justice? We must remember, however, that these questions cannot be answered solely within the horizons of the First Axial consciousness of Christianity. They must be reformulated within the global consciousness of the Second Axial Period. It is for this reason that we did not begin with a classical or contemporary Christian theological perspective. In this we have followed Karl Jaspers. At the very beginning of his book on the Axial Period, he stated explicitly that he chose not to seek the axis of history in Christ or in Western culture, but in a larger process of history.[8] Of course, from a Christian theological perspective, one could identify his move as a shift from Christ to the Holy Spirit, provided the working of the Spirit be not confined to a narrow understanding of salvation history.

I would like to note here that this method has its antecedents in the classical Christian theological tradition. For example, in the prologue of his treatise on the redemption entitled *Why God Became Man*, Anselm of Canterbury bracketed out any preliminary consideration of Christ and examined the phenomenon of guilt in the human situation as a point of departure for his speculation. Then at a strategic later stage in the progress of his thought, he brought Christ into view. To describe his initial move, he used the strong Latin phrase *remoto Christo* (Christ having been removed).[9] In a similar way we have bracketed out or removed the mystery of Christ at the outset in order to reintroduce it in the enlarged horizon of the Second Axial Period. Having done that in the beginning, we now have another task immediately before us: namely, to retrieve the fulness of the mystery of Christ from the history of the Christian tradition—theologically and spiritually—so that we can participate in the further unfolding of this mystery in the twenty-first century.

II

Dwarfs, Giants, and Astronauts

After having bracketed out the mystery of Christ temporarily at the outset, we now begin the process of retrieving the mystery of Christ as this has been revealed and received through the centuries of First Axial consciousness. As I will develop in various stages throughout this book, I believe that for the human community creatively to make the transition into the global consciousness of the Second Axial Period, the various religious traditions should be in full possession of the spiritual resources from their past. In fact, this is more crucial than at any previous time in their history.

What I am proposing for the Christian tradition may seem novel—even naïve—in the light of the past four hundred years of its history. Since the rise of modern science, Christianity has been struggling to maintain its spiritual heritage along with its theological world view in the face of pressure from the mind-set of modernity. This mind-set was ushered in with the development of science and technology in the West, especially with the empirical method of scientific research. From the perspective of this mind-set, religious, spiritual, and metaphysical perceptions and values were ignored or reduced to an empirical substrate. It is not uncritical to see this development as only one possible trajectory of the First Axial Period, which emerged only in the West, and not as a final and normative stage to which all religious traditions should be made to submit. In fact, there is much evidence that this mind-set has been broken open by the developments of twentieth century science itself as well as the rediscovery of spirituality in the West over the last decades.

What I am suggesting here is not a version of what has been called post-modernity. This latter trend, while breaking with the scientific search for knowledge, does not move in the direction of spiritual depth but in an endless exploration of the formal elements of texts. I am proposing here a third position, which moves in the direction of retrieving spiritual depth not only for the values contained there but as a catalyst for producing the transformation into the global consciousness of the Second Axial Period. It is in this context that I will explore the retrieval of the riches of tradition in general in this chapter—both in terms of Christianity and other religions—and in the case of specific Christian doctrines in the next, with an emphasis on the mystery of Christ.

DWARFS AND GIANTS

To deal adequately with the retrieval of tradition is a challenging task at any time. But it is all the more challenging to do so in the shadow of modernity and post-modernity as well as in the process of transformation into global consciousness. Yet I am consoled by the fact that tradition itself can come to my aid since it is a storehouse of resources, containing the accumulated wisdom of the great minds of the past—a wisdom that has been handed down to aid us in our inadequacy. This sense of tradition was summed up in the Western Middle Ages in the famous observation of Bernard of Chartres: that we are dwarfs, but we stand on the shoulders of giants.[1] Bernard's statement is consoling in that it assures us of powerful assistance from the past. But it can also function as a mythic image opening to us tradition as an archetype.

By this I mean that tradition can be seen as an archetype, or primordial, dynamic structure of consciousness which establishes our roots in history, which links us to the great minds of our past, and which opens a channel for their wisdom to flow into our lives. Seen in this way, the archetype of tradition does not have content itself but is the dynamism through which the content of past wisdom can be retrieved. The significance of Bernard's image as archetypal can be seen if we invert his formula: We are giants, but we stand on the shoulders of dwarfs. Not only does this minimize the wisdom of the past and render us guilty of hubris, but it undercuts tradition as an archetype; it closes the door upon the flow of wisdom from the past. For tradition to function as an archetype, it must be evoked and cultivated by an attitude of reverence and respect; it must be received with humility and gratitude.

Granted its benefits, tradition—like all archetypes—has a dark side. It can be heavy and oppressive, a dead weight, a lifeless corpse, a prison of the human spirit. Even at its best, when it is alive and nourishing, it can present obstacles to innovation and stifle creativity. It is here that interpretation must enter to transform the dark side of tradition. Interpretation must retrieve the past and bring it to life in the present, but it must be critical and discriminating. It must be critical in recovering the past with accuracy, but it must also be discriminating in bringing the past into our lives; for not all of the past is worthy to live in the present. In addition to these demands, it must be sensitive to the direction of the future. It must have a tenacious and accurate memory of the past, a sense of vitality in the present, and a creative impulse towards the future.

JEAN LECLERCQ AND GLOBAL MUTATION

In treating such a challenging topic, I will follow the suggestion of Bernard of Chartres. Aware of my dwarf-like stature, I will stand on the shoulders of a giant—a great historian who has done perhaps more than anyone else to interpret the religious traditions of the Middle Ages—Jean Leclercq, the chief editor of the critical text of Bernard of Clairvaux, author of *The Love of Learning and the Desire for God*, along with more than twenty other books and more than eight hundred scholarly articles. Through his research he has retrieved a major portion of the medieval tradition—the monastic theology which preceded the scholastic theology of the universities, which had been forgotten by modern historians, and which lay buried by the massive scholarship on medieval philosophy during the era of the Neo-Scholastic revival. Like an archeologist at an excavation, he has unearthed monastic theology as a dimension of the medieval monastic tradition.

In 1976, when I was the director of the Graduate Program in Spirituality at Fordham University, I invited Jean Leclercq to give a lecture entitled: "The Role of History and Tradition in Contemporary Spirituality."[2] When I met him at the airport, he told me that his talk would be more abstract than I might have anticipated. As I listened to his lecture that evening, I realized why he had said that; for he was presenting his own theory of the nature of history and tradition—a theory that had grown out of more than forty years of dedicated scholarly work. He defined tradition as the past alive in the present, and history as the hermeneutics of tradition. In describing tradition as the past alive in the present, he was highlighting the positive side of the archetype I described above. From this perspective, historical research, as interpretation, helps us retrieve the past as a vital force in the present. It is not a cataloging of dead events recorded on the graves of a previous age, nor the assembling of lifeless exhibits in a museum. Rather it reaches into the past and taps its energy for the present and the future. As memory and interpretation of the past, history makes available the vitality of tradition.

So far Leclercq's shoulders have supported me with the concepts of tradition and interpretation. But what of the second part of the theme of this chapter: in a global context? On this Leclercq had something challenging to say, something similar to my notion of the Second Axial Period. For he claimed that we are in a radically new period in history that calls for a new stance toward tradition and interpretation. According to Leclercq history may proceed by way of an organic unfolding or by way of a mutation—a quantum leap in which a new context is produced by a break with the past and a leap into the future. In the case of organic unfolding, each generation passes on its values to the next. Of course, this is not necessarily a smooth process, but involves changes, new discoveries, revolutions, rejections of elements of the past. Granted these fluctuations, the changes in a continuous tradition are not so radical as those of a mutation.

As examples of mutations, Leclercq cited the barbarian invasion of Europe and the Westernization of Japan. These he characterized as regional since they affected only a limited area of the earth and a limited number of the earth's population. In contrast, he claimed that between the end of World War II and the 1960's a mutation occurred on a global scale. Science, technology, communication, and other forces, which had been building up for centuries, finally reached a point that produced a global matrix for culture. This worldwide mutation has brought about the convergence of cultural traditions and the encounter of world religions. This mutation is global not only in its extent but in its very content; for it is producing a global consciousness: a consciousness that is open to traditions other than our own and, in fact, to the traditions of the entire human community.

How does this mutation affect tradition and interpretation? What effect will this have on the archetype of tradition? On the religious level, we are now encountering many traditions: the Hindu, Buddhist, Islamic, and others. What is the task of interpretation in relation to these traditions—and in relation to our own Western tradition in the light of this mutation? At this point, Bernard of Chartres can no longer come to our aid since this global mutation is unique in history; there are no giants who have faced this situation before and on whose shoulders we can stand. And yet there is much that we can learn from the past and from those giants who emerged at the time of regional mutations.

Keeping in mind the global mutation described by Leclercq, I will examine, first, the issues of interpretation within our Western tradition, taking as my example the sixty volume series published by Paulist Press: The Classics of Western Spirituality. Secondly,

I will explore the role of interpretation of traditions in a global context, as seen in the twenty-five volume series being published by the Crossroad Publishing Company: World Spirituality: An Encyclopedic History of the Religious Quest. Thirdly, I will give two examples that I believe should be retrieved to further the creative transformation of the Second Axial Period.

THE CLASSICS OF WESTERN SPIRITUALITY

Before moving into the global context, I will examine the interpretation of tradition within Western culture through The Classics of Western Spirituality. This series provides a remarkable example of an attempt to recover a forgotten tradition. In its own way it is comparable to Leclercq's retrieve of monastic theology within the Middle Ages. For many reasons during the first part of this century, the great spirituality traditions of Western culture had slipped into forgetfulness. It is true that they were alive on the level of religious practice and devotion, in large communities and in specific religious orders, but they did not enter substantially into our general collective memory, nor ironically into theology or the academic study of religion. The academic community and its educational programs did not manifest an awareness of the great spiritual writers and their classical works in any way comparable to the discipline of philosophy, with its familiarity with Plato, Aristotle, Aquinas, Descartes, and Hegel; or English literature, with Chaucer, Shakespeare, and Milton. In other words, in the case of spirituality the past was not alive in the present. We spiritual dwarfs of the twentieth century did not have giants on whose shoulders we could stand. The archetype of tradition in our psyche was not functioning in relation to spirituality in a comprehensive way.

Then came the 1960's with its consciousness explosion, its critique of the scientific mind-set, its turn to Eastern ways of the spirit. By the seventies many Westerners had discovered the spiritual quest— not from their own traditions, but in psychotherapy, in the human potential movement, in yoga, or Zen. Simultaneously, in the academic world the history of religions was making available data from the Orient and from archaic cultures. In this ferment many felt the need to discover their own spiritual roots: as Westerners, as Jews, as Christians. They found themselves asking many questions: Does Judaism or Christianity have a spiritual wisdom? Techniques of meditation? Spiritual practices and disciplines? If so, where can they be found? Not likely in theology, it seemed, which for decades and even centuries had been expending much of its energy to reconcile traditional belief with the scientific worldview. The present need sprang from a deeper level of the person—not from his or her adjustment to scientific culture, but from the depths within, from the spiritual center that had been awakened in a new way. It was clear that an entire tradition had to be recovered, that an archetype had to be evoked, that giants had to be awakened, that their shoulders had to be brought to the support of our searching, stumbling feet.

It was at this point in the mid-seventies that the idea of The Classics of Western Spirituality was conceived by Richard Payne, then Associate Editor of Paulist Press. Clearly discerning the need to retrieve the Western spiritual tradition, he realized the necessity of having classical spiritual writings available in readable English translations based on the finest critical scholarship. Following the general lines of the Great Books of the Western World, he designed a sixty-volume series of the spiritual classics of Judaism, Christianity, Islam, and the American Indians. In this he was taking the term "Western" in a combined historical and geographical sense, including those traditions that trace their origins from Judaism, along with the primal traditions of North and South America. He chose— rightly, I believe—a closed series of sixty volumes, rather than an open-ended series with an unspecified number of volumes. This made the selection of volumes difficult, it is true; but it assured that the authors chosen were among the tallest giants with the broadest shoulders. Because of its success and the richness of resources, the series has been extended with supplemental volumes.

Extensive market research confirmed that there was a large group of potential readers in church ministry, in the academic community, and in the increasing number of spiritual seekers. With the support and direction of Father Kevin Lynch, President of Paulist Press, the series was launched. The first volume, *Julian of Norwich: Showings* was published in 1978,[3] and since then over seventy-five volumes have appeared. Among the Christian authors are Origen, Gregory of Nyssa, Bonaventure, Meister Eckhart, Catherine of Siena, Teresa of Avila, Jacob Boehme, Johann Arnt, John and Charles Wesley. Response to the series—both critical and popular—has been overwhelmingly positive.

It would be interesting to analyze The Classics of Western Spirituality as a case study in tradition and interpretation. In a literate society writings are among the most powerful means of transmitting tradition. It follows, then, that the interpretation of these spiritual classics is a major means of retrieving the tradition. Under the term "interpretation" I wish to include not only the intellectual representation of the past, but the more comprehensive process of remembering, understanding, and evaluating the past. In this I am explicit drawing from Augustine's analysis of the mind, or *mens*, as including memory, understanding, and will.[4] In this process, the editors of The Classics of Western Spirituality first remembered the past by searching out the critical texts if these had been edited. In the case of the *Showings* of Julian of Norwich, Edmund Colledge and James Walsh had been working for a number of years to establish the critical text, which appeared in print not long after the volume in the Classics.[5] Thus their modern English translation reaped the benefit of their long research in the historical immediacy of the critical text. Once the critical text of a work has been retrieved by memory and meaningfully translated, the interpretation process continues. Each volume in the Classics contains an introduction which situates the spiritual writer and the work in its historical setting, analyzes the major spiritual themes, and evaluates the work's contribution from a critical perspective. Each work, then, is retrieved from the past for the present by this complex process of interpretation, which includes memory, understanding and evaluation. Through this hermeneutical process, in terms of Leclercq's formula, the past is brought to life in the present.

Has the interpretive process at work in The Classics of Western Spirituality actually retrieved the spirituality tradition? Has the spiritual wisdom of the past, in Leclercq's phrase, become alive in the present? In its initial phase, in the academic community, I would say yes. The volumes are being used widely in courses, not only in religion programs, but in literature, history, and other disciplines. Certain courses are now possible for the first time because of this series. The spirituality tradition is being taken more seriously by various disciplines within religious studies: theology, history, psychology of religion, biblical studies. Individuals are reading the classics for spiritual nourishment. Efforts have been made to bring them into workshops, study groups, prayer groups, and other community settings. Since the effect of the series will undoubtedly be cumulative, its ultimate success in retrieving the tradition—on the academic and religious levels—will have to be judged in the future.

WORLD SPIRITUALITY

We have seen an example of the retrieve of a tradition through the interpretative process within Western culture. This fits the category of the continuous transmission of tradition described by Leclercq. But what of his other category: that of mutation, and specifically the global mutation he believes has occurred at the present time? I would like to address this from the standpoint of a second publishing project, the twenty-five volume series World Spirituality: An Encyclopedic History of the Religious Quest which is in progress now.

When Richard Payne developed the idea of The Classics of Western Spirituality, he conceived it as part of a threefold project. The Classics of Western Spirituality would be complemented by a similar sixty-volume series: The Classics of Eastern Spirituality, including English translations of the classics of Hinduism, Buddhism, Taoism, Confucianism, Jainism, Sikism, Zoroastrianism, and the primal traditions of Africa, Asia, and Oceania. A third project consisted of a history of world spirituality, a series of volumes containing essays by contemporary scholars covering the entire history of the human spiritual quest from prehistoric times, through the great traditions, into the present and future. When Richard Payne moved from Paulist Press to the Crossroad Publishing Company, he brought with him the plans for the history of world spirituality, which he developed into a twenty-five volume series entitled World Spirituality: An Encyclopedic History of the Religious Quest. For the most part the volumes are organized according to major traditions, e.g., two volumes on Hindu spirituality, two on Buddhist spirituality. Each volume is about five hundred pages in length, containing some twenty articles on aspects of the tradition's spirituality written by specialists in the field. There are also photos and illustrations. Each volume has an editor who plans its content and commissions articles. The general policy has been to choose editors and contributors both culturally and spiritually from the traditions. This means that Hindus are writing on Hinduism, Buddhists on Buddhism. There is a network of some five hundred scholars around the world writing articles for this project. Nine of the twenty-five volumes have appeared so far.

This series is a microcosm reflecting the global mutation described by Jean Leclercq. Each tradition is attempting to retrieve the wisdom of its past by the complex process of interpretation I described above. What is unique about the series is that it is global in scope. It is a concrete attempt to deal with the problem of traditions and interpretation in a global context, not merely by retrieving the traditions in their historical continuity, but by contributing to the encounter of traditions at the present time. The fundamental problems are different from those of the mere transmission of a tradition. What happens when spiritual traditions encounter each other? Volume 23 deals with this issue, with articles on the regional encounters in the past between the various traditions: e.g., Buddhism with Taoism and Confucianism in China. Volume 24, however, deals with the global encounter in the mutational context of the present and future. What happens when the traditions meet in this context? I will attempt to explore this complex problem, in the light of my position as General Editor, where I have had a privileged vantage point to observe the tensions and creative energies as these emerge. What I will say will be my own observations and may or may not be shared by our editors and contributors.

The fundamental issue, as I see it, is that traditions are meeting which have not only diverse content but diverse historical conditioning. The archetype of tradition within individual and collective consciousness has a different historical memory among Hindus, Christians, Buddhists, and Muslims. This is, I believe, the primordial fact we are facing; we must deal with this fact personally, collectively, and academically. Is it possible for me to share another's tradition? Can I share another's memory? Another's understanding? What of my evaluation of another's tradition? Is it to be judged according to the criteria of my own? Of the other? Of some norms that are emerging in our global context? I do not have answers to these questions, but I can venture some observations.

First, I tend to take a positive view: that we can assimilate the heritage of other traditions. Thomas Berry has said that for the first time in history each person can become heir to the spiritual heritage of humankind.[6] Prior to the present period, this has not been possible since geographic, historical, and cultural barriers have kept us apart. How will we receive this inheritance? Certainly not by sharing the different historical conditioning. Not by the memory of traditions, but by the convergence of tradition. In this convergence we must do two things: evoke a sense of belonging to the whole human race and cultivate an empathetic consciousness towards other traditions. Our first task is to associate our own sense of tradition with the traditions of the human community as a whole. This means to link our archetype of tradition not only with our own history but with that of the human race, as somehow sharing a common tradition, even though this has been historically diversified. This means to globalize our archetype of tradition; by so doing, we will enhance our openness to other traditions and render our interpretation of them more effective.

The second task is to cultivate an empathetic consciousness toward the other traditions. In John Dunne's words, we must "pass over and come back;" or in Raimundo Panikkar's terms, we must develop "dialogic dialogue," which is open to the values of other traditions, in contrast to "dialectical dialogue," which seeks to argue against the others.[7] I claim that on the theoretical level we must develop a "shamanistic epistemology" and on the practical level we must activate our "shamanistic faculty." By this I mean that like the shaman who in spirit leaves his body, goes to distant places, and returns enriched with new knowledge, so we have the capacity to leave the horizons of our own consciousness and enter into the consciousness of another tradition, returning to our own with a new awareness of the values of the other. In relation to the process of interpretation described above, "passing over" substitutes for memory. In effect, we "pass over" into the other's memory and share his or her tradition in that way. Then we can activate our understanding and evaluation, thus bringing to completion the process of interpreting tradition.

I would like to point out how important the memory of tradition has been in the design of World Spirituality: An Encyclopedic History of the Religious Quest. In principle, we have commissioned Hindus to write on their own spirituality, Buddhists to write on theirs. This means that the volumes will have the power of the collective archetype of traditions as these are evoked by their editors and contributors. Of course, it is not easy for an individual or group to come to a reflective, self-critical consciousness of their own tradition.

At this point I would like to make a suggestion which has grown out of this work and also my participation in a seminar organized by Peter Berger which produced the book *The Other Side of God: A Polarity in World Religions.*[8] I believe that the time is ripe for fruitful work to be done in the academic community by combining the model of the history of religions with that of ecumenical dialogue. By that I mean to develop collaborative research projects by scholars who share the living tradition on which they work. For example, I have attempted to develop research projects on Mysticism: Hindu and Christian, by having Hindu scholars work on Hindu mystics and Christian scholars on Christian mystics. They can strive to use a common methodology and to study together the evidence from both traditions. The history of religions in the West has relied heavily on texts and histories written by Westerners, without always tapping the living traditions studied. On the other hand, ecumenical dialogue has proceeded by testimony of traditional faith, without always bringing to bear the controls of critical academic scholarship. It may well be that such collaborative research projects would be the most effective means of helping us bridge the gap that exists between diverse traditions in this period of global mutation.

The present situation would be complex enough if all we had to deal with were the diverse religious traditions. But the problem is compounded by the impact of the secular. At the same time that the spiritual traditions are meeting in a mutually supportive atmosphere, each of them is struggling with the secularization of culture.

Western religion has been dealing with this for centuries, but it is now a Buddhist problem, a Hindu problem, a problem for all the spiritual traditions. Each will encounter the secular out of its own traditional resources. But there is emerging a consciousness that the problems evoked by the secular are common human problems: nuclear destruction, the pollution of our environment, widespread injustice and poverty.

The encounter of the traditions with the secular brings us to a further point: How do we interpret traditions when they themselves are being transformed? The very secular developments in culture that produced a global environment have not left the religious traditions unaffected. In fact, both the secular and religious trends in culture are caught up in a larger transformation which is having its effect on both: namely, Leclercq's mutation and my Second Axial Period. It follows, then, that the religions cannot merely draw from their past wisdom—merely retrieve their traditions by sophisticated interpretation—since these traditions reflect the distinctive horizons of First Axial Period consciousness. Does this undercut what I said about the need to recover traditions? Not at all! On the contrary, I believe that the Second Axial Period calls for the full richness of the traditions that were born and developed in the First Axial Period. These traditions must be recovered. But it calls for more; it calls for a sensitivity to the pre-Axial forms of consciousness, to the challenges of the present, and to possibilities of the future. In brief, it calls for the creative interpretation of tradition. That is a creativity that draws from the past, present, and future. This creative interpretation must retain the wisdom of the past, it is true, and build upon it; but it must also transform the past to open to wider and deeper horizons. Each of the traditions, in its own way through creative interpretation, must enter into the dimensions of the global consciousness of the Second Axial Period. They must discover the point of intersection between the cosmic, the human, and the transcendent. They must develop an integral view of life in a global context. Most of all, they must bring the spiritual resources of their distinct heritages to bear on the creative solution of common human problems.

RETRIEVING METAPHYSICS

At this point I would like to single out two areas of tradition whose retrieval is especially crucial for the Second Axial Period: metaphysics, which emerged in the First Axial Period; and the symbolic imagination, which flourished in the Pre-Axial Period.

Although metaphysics is one of the characteristics of First Axial consciousness, in the West in the last two hundred years, it has been eclipsed by a paradigm shift in epistemology towards empiricism and subjectivism.[9] As a result the entire realm of metaphysics has been discredited. There is urgent need to re-examine critically— both philosophically and historically—the widespread normative acceptance of this paradigm shift. After Kant both the scientific and the academic communities accepted this shift as a given assumption. There does not even exist a major intellectual forum where this examination can take place. I would recommend that the dialogue of world religions provide such a forum. Hinduism, for example, did not experience the same forces from the development of empirical science that led to the adoption of the paradigm in the West. Hence Hinduism, and other traditions as well, can offer an alternative perspective—free of the pressures of Western history—that can provide an open forum for critical investigation of the philosophical validity of such a shift.

Without such a re-examination, the full retrieval of tradition cannot take place on a global level. I have participated in interreligious dialogues around the world where Western scholars of religion have seriously held back the exploration of other traditions because of their own unexpressed Neo-Kantian assumptions, which so controlled their thinking unconsciously that they could not even acknowledge the metaphysical heritage of Hinduism, Zoroastrianism, and Islam. This is a special problem at the present time with the increasing academic interest in spirituality and mysticism. As products of the First Axial Period, the spiritualities of the world religions are permeated with metaphysics, especially the spiritual paths of *gnosis* or knowledge, with their accompanying mysticisms. To examine this issue philosophically would require much more space, even another book. All I can do here is to call attention to it as a serious problem in the retrieval of tradition in a global context.

There is another problem connected with metaphysics, which originates from Western religions themselves, specifically from the way in which metaphysics has been related to the sacred scriptures of Judaism and Christianity. In these books of revelation, explicit metaphysics is not contained but has been drawn into the Jewish and Christian traditions from the extrinsic source of Greek philosophy, which also provided the major resource of metaphysics for Islam. The relation of Greek metaphysics to Judaism and Christianity can be viewed from a number of perspectives. One can stand within each of these religions, as a Jewish or Christian theologian, judging the compatibility or incompatibility of Greek metaphysics with historical revelation. Or one may take the stand of a twentieth-century historian of Western culture, looking on these three traditions in interaction in the geographical area of the Mediterranean. It is possible, however, to perceive them from another perspective within a larger context: namely, from a global perspective. By this I mean viewing them in the geographical context of the earth as a whole—not only in relation among themselves but also in relation to other religions of the world: for example, Hinduism, Buddhism, Taoism, and Confucianism. The issues that arise, such as the relation of Greek metaphysics to the sacred texts of Judaism and Christianity, can better be analyzed and evaluated in the light of similar issues in the Orient.

Greek metaphysics has had a checkered history in Judaism and Christianity. Hellenistic thought began to permeate the Jewish world from the third century B.C.E., especially in the Wisdom literature. Yet explicit Greek philosophical thought did not find its way into the sacred texts of Judaism. The same can be said of the New Testament, which presents the early Church's experience of the Christ event without explicitly philosophizing. Yet in the early century of this era, Philo of Alexandria interpreted the Jewish scripture in the light of Platonism; and Christian thinkers, like Clement of Alexandria and his disciple Origen, drew from Greek philosophy in developing Christian theology. In the Greek and Latin Fathers, Hellenistic philosophy was assimilated but not without a certain critique and distance. In the medieval West, Greek philosophy— especially Aristotelianism—was the foundation for scholasticism. Yet scholastic theology was developed on the basis of a clear distinction between faith and reason, between theology and philosophy, between the sacred text and metaphysics. In a similar vein Maimonides used philosophical reason to interpret the Jewish tradition.

The Reformers added a new chapter to the Christian story when they returned to Scripture as the sole basis of Christian theology. The tension between metaphysics and theology has continued into the present in the thought of those philosophers who were heirs of the Greek thinkers: Descartes, Hegel, Heidegger. At the present time there are those who claim that Greek metaphysics is alien to Judaism and Christianity, that the importation of Greek philosophy into these traditions was a distortion, and that they should return to the pristine authenticity of their sacred texts, which are devoid of the corrupting influence of metaphysics.

I will argue a more integral position, claiming that there is a compatibility between Greek metaphysics and the sacred texts of both Judaism and Christianity. However, I will not attempt an internal analysis, which has been done at great length by Jewish and Christian theologians through the centuries. Rather I will highlight a harmony by viewing the issue from a global perspective, in the context of the First and Second Axial Periods.

Grounded in the new self-consciousness of the First Axial Period, metaphysics was born; for the Axial individual could become aware of the objective structures of being and explore their universal laws. Jaspers describes this emergence as follows: "For the first time *philosophers* appeared. Human beings dared to rely on themselves as individuals. . . . Man proved capable of contrasting himself with the entire universe. He discovered within himself the origin from which to raise himself above his own self and the world." This enabled him to mount to Being itself: "*In speculative thought* he lifts himself up towards Being itself, which is apprehended without duality in the disappearance of subject and object, in the coincidence of opposites." The Axial individual comes to self-consciousness within Being. "That which is experienced in the loftiest flights of the spirit as a coming-to-oneself with Being, or as a *unio mystica*, as becoming one with the Godhead, or as becoming a tool for the will of God, is expressed in an ambiguous and easily misunderstood form in objectifying speculative thought."[10]

The emergence of First Axial consciousness was not an unmixed blessing. In the burst of creative energy, the Axial individual came face to face with the dark side of his new consciousness. Gifted now with self-reflective, analytic awareness, he found himself alienated from nature and his community—severed from the deep web of relationships that sustained primal consciousness. Through his metaphysical speculation he felt the exhilaration of the discovery of being, but he also suffered the anxiety of non-being. In the midst of new possibilities, he tragically discovered his radical limitations.

METAPHYSICS AND SACRED TEXTS

What does Jaspers' theory of the Axial Period offer for an understanding of the relation of Greek metaphysics to Judaism and Christianity? It provides a global framework for examining the issues. The sacred texts of Judaism and Christianity contain a number of elements of Axial consciousness: especially the moral awareness expounded by the prophets. Metaphysics, however, comes from the Greeks. It is not found in the Jewish Bible or the Christian New Testament. Of course, there are implicit metaphysical dimensions in the sacred texts of both Judaism and Christianity; but it was left to the later Jewish and Christian theologians to integrate Greek metaphysics into the teachings of the sacred texts.

It is this dichotomy that caused tension through the centuries. If metaphysics were eliminated from Judaism and Christianity, these traditions would lack an essential element of Axial consciousness, which for over two millennia has been the dominant form of consciousness in both the West and the East. Since the Jewish and Christian sacred texts do not provide this essential element, it has been imported from the Greeks, a non-sacral or secular source. Hence it had to be validated, for example, by the theory, propounded by certain early Christian theologians, that Socrates and Plato were inspired by God in their philosophical thought. In this vein sacred history was extended to encompass Greek metaphysics. At the present time, in view of the meeting of world religions in a global context, there is reason to extend the meaning of sacred history to encompass world religions as well. Or to transpose this into our present context, the meaning of sacred history can be extended to encompass all the essential dimensions of Axial consciousness as this has developed in the diverse traditions of the world's religions.

The tension over metaphysics and sacred texts in the West can be clarified by comparing it to the case of Hinduism. When we examine the texts of the Upanishads, which were produced in the Axial Period, we find a very different picture from that of the Bible or the New Testament. Metaphysics is prominently in the Hindu texts—not merely implicitly or peripherally, but explicitly and centrally. The fundamental teaching of the Upanishads is that of the *atman*, the deeper self, and its relation to Brahman. The Indian texts read more like Plato's dialogues than the Bible or the New Testament. It is true that the key texts of the Upanishads became the basis for the subsequent development of diverse schools of Vedanta, with different metaphysical positions. However, this was not the result of importing an alien or secular philosophy to interpret the texts; rather the metaphysics unfolded in its diversity out of the texts themselves. In this sense, the Hindu sacred texts represent a more integral form of Axial consciousness than do the Jewish or Christian. This can be illustrated by the following citation from the *Chāndogya* Upanishad in which Uddālaka is instructing his son Svetaketu:

> "In the beginning, my dear, this [universe] was Being only—one only—without a second. True, some say that in the beginning this [universe] was Not-Being only,—without a second, and that from Not-Being Being was born."
>
> "But, my dear, whence could this be?' said he. 'How could Being be born from Not-Being? No, it was Being alone that was this [universe] in the beginning—one only, without a second.'"[11]

This text is explicitly metaphysical, employing the language of Being and Non-Being, and opening an extended discussion of the problem of the one and the many. We have here a classic example of the metaphysical dimension of Axial consciousness in the very sacred texts of Hinduism. In this discussion, although it takes place in India, Parmenides and Plato would feel at home, but not the writers of the Jewish or Christian Scripture.

The text proceeds to describe how the many emerged out of the oneness of Being and will return to Being. "My dearest child," the father says, "all these creatures [here] have Being as their root, Being as their resting-place (āyatana), Being as their foundation."[12] In the discussion the father repeats as a refrain the quintessential formulation of the Hindu Axial consciousness of the Real: "This finest essence—the whole universe has it as its Self: That is the Real: That is the Self: That *you* are, Svetaketu!"[13] This text has been the scriptural basis for diverse philosophical interpretations of the Vedanta tradition, for example, by Śankara and Rāmānuja. Yet the interpretations do not bring metaphysics to the text; rather the philosophical interpretations flow out of the metaphysics which is already present in the very heart of the text.

When we turn to Christianity, we see a different configuration, which can be illustrated by the case of Augustine. Unlike Śankara, he cannot go to a sacred text which contains explicit metaphysical content and from that develop his own specific philosophical interpretation. Rather in Augustine two strands converged: the Jewish-Christian scriptures and the metaphysics of Neoplatonism. He looked upon them as flowing from two different sources, but as eminently compatible. In his *Confessions* he tells how there had been brought to his notice "some books written by the Platonists, which had been translated from Greek to Latin." He then proceeds to describe how he found in them what he had read in the prologue of the Gospel according to John. This text of John is the classic point of convergence between Greek metaphysics and Christian scripture; for, perhaps more than any other New Testament text, it contains the raw material of metaphysics and historically may have been shaped by Greek influence.

> In these books I found it stated, not of course in the same words but to precisely the same effect and with a number of different sorts of reasons, that: 'In the beginning was the Word, and the Word was with God and the Word was God; the Same was in the beginning with God: all things were made by Him, and without Him was nothing made.' (John 1:1–3)[14]

Although he found the eternal Word of the Trinity in the books of the Platonists, he did not find there the incarnate Word. As he says,

"I did not find then that 'the Word was made flesh and dwelt among us' " (John 1:14).[15]

By linking the Neoplatonic *Nous* with the *Logos* of the Christian Trinity, Augustine was able to draw into the Christian tradition the heritage of Greek metaphysics: for example, the role of the Platonic forms in the Christian doctrine of creation and the reflection of the divine Eternity, Truth, and Goodness in the soul.

Much scholarship has been devoted to the study of the meaning of *Logos* in the prologue of the Gospel of John. Is it to be read metaphysically as Augustine did in the light of Platonism? Or is it to be read more in keeping with its traditional Jewish roots? Was Augustine justified in seeing explicit metaphysical content in a text which may not have had a metaphysical intent? However we interpret this particular text, the larger issue still stands: Is Greek metaphysics compatible with Jewish-Christian revelation? Was the importation of Greek metaphysics into Christianity an example of syncretism in a pejorative sense? Or was it a form of syncretism that was authentic and organic? I would affirm the latter, especially in light of a comparison with Hinduism in the context of the First Axial Period. This is even more so the case, I believe, in the light of the emergence of global consciousness at the present time in the Second Axial Period.

What does this mean for the topic of this chapter? I believe that the issues of Greek metaphysics in Judaism and Christianity must be viewed from the global perspective of the two Axial Periods. In a certain sense, these two Periods provide a single global perspective; for it may well be that only in the Second Axial Period can we become cognizant of the First Axial Period. If we are undergoing a Second Axial transformation of consciousness, it is crucial that the historical and theological issues be seen from this perspective. In order to foster this examination, we must develop models that are compatible with the dynamics of the Second Axial Period. Such a model, I believe, is found in the series World Spirituality: An Encyclopedic History of the Religious Quest. Its broad, global structure provides a comprehensive model for exploring the historical and theological issues of the relation of Greek metaphysics to Judaism and Christianity in the light of the First and Second Axial Periods.

In the process of exploring these issues, Christian theologians will have to transpose into a global context their conventional categories of salvation history, of faith and reason, of metaphysics and the sacred text. In the light of the two Axial Periods, they will have to develop a larger understanding of sacred history encompassing in some way the entire human community as it has experienced significant transformation of consciousness. Within this framework theologians can work out specific differentiations of the categories of metaphysics and sacred texts and of the distinctive authority of historical revelation. But these would be developed not merely within the horizons of one tradition, or of Western culture, but within the more comprehensive and inclusive horizons of both the First and the Second Axial Period.

THE SYMBOLIC IMAGINATION

In retrieving tradition the West must rediscover the rich realm of symbols as part of its spiritual heritage. Symbolic thinking was characteristic of the consciousness of the primal peoples of the Pre-Axial Period. They lived in a rich world of myth and ritual to whose meaning they had immediate access. However, the transformation of consciousness of the First Axial Period left this realm largely buried in the depths of the psyche. Abstract thinking and metaphysics itself disengaged consciousness from the symbolic imagination and moved it in the direction of the theoretical and the transcendent. Yet myth and symbol remained in the scriptures of the world's religions, in art, and literature. In the twentieth century the West has rediscovered the power of symbols through psychotherapy's probing of dreams. Mythic and religious symbols have been explored extensively in our time, for example by Mircea Eliade, C.G. Jung, and Joseph Campbell.

In the previous chapter I characterized the vertical dimension of the spirituality of the Second Axial Period as plunging into matter, as rediscovering the spiritual significance of matter. It is precisely in symbols and in the exercise of our symbolic imagination that this significance is manifest. For in a most remarkable way we are gifted with a faculty that thinks symbolically—by bringing to consciousness images of material objects that are fecund with spiritual meaning and which divinize spirit itself. One of the major retrievals of tradition in the Second Axial Period will be the reappropriation of our symbolic imagination and the rediscovery of the realm of religious symbols.

I would like to explore as an example of this retrieval the symbolic interpretation of Sacred Scripture in Christianity as this was formulated in the Middle Ages according to the fourfold sense of Scripture. Taking their point of departure from the literal meaning, medieval theologians proceeded to interpret a text on three other levels: the moral (or tropological), the allegorical, and the anagogic. The three latter senses were called spiritual, mystical, or allegorical in a generic sense of allegory. I will refer to these three spiritual senses as symbolic.

MEDIEVAL EXEGESIS

Throughout the Middle Ages the symbolic interpretation was a dominant approach to Christian Scripture. Found in Scripture itself, in both the Old and New Testaments, it was developed during the patristic period in the East and the West. In the early centuries the senses of Scripture were not yet divided into the fourfold pattern which was to become standard in the later Middle Ages. For example, Origen used a threefold division: "For just as man," he writes, "consists of body, soul and spirit, so in the same way does the Scripture, which has been prepared by God to be given for man's salvation."[16] Hence, according to Origen, there are three senses of Scripture: the somatic, psychic, and pneumatic, that is, the literal, the moral, and the spiritual. Gregory the Great is regarded as the principal initiator of the medieval division into four senses. In a homily on Ezekiel, he compared the words of Scripture to a square stone, which can stand on each of four sides because there are no rough spots on any side.[17] While retaining the literal and moral sense of Origen, later medieval theologians distinguished his spiritual sense into the allegorical and the anagogic. This division is summed up in the celebrated distich of Augustine of Dacia, O.P. (d. 1282):

> Littera gesta docet, quid credis allegoria,
> Quid agis moralis, quo tendis anagogia.[18]

It would be wise to give in full here the classical source in Dante on the meaning of the four senses of Scripture. Writing to Can Grande della Scala, Dante claims that his *Commedia* should be read according to the allegory of the theologians:

For the clarity of what will be said, it is to be understood that the meaning of this work is not simple, but rather it is polysemous, that is, having many meanings. For the first meaning is that which one derives from the letter, another is that which one derives from the things signified by the letter. The first is called 'literal' and the second 'allegorical,' or 'mystical.' So that this method of exposition may be clearer, one may consider it in these lines: 'When Israel went out of Egypt, the house of Jacob from people of strange language, Judah was his sanctuary and Israel his dominion.'[19] If we look only at the letter, this signifies that the children of Israel went out of Egypt in the time of Moses; if we look at the allegory, it signifies our redemption through Christ; if we look at the moral sense, it signifies the turning of the soul from the sorrow and

misery of sin to a state of grace; if we look at the anagogical sense, it
signifies the passage of the blessed soul from the slavery of this corrup-
tion to the freedom of eternal glory.[20]

This position of Dante was shared by the theologians of the
scholastic period of the Middle Ages. For example, Thomas Aquinas
describes the four senses of Scripture as follows:

> Therefore that first signification whereby words signify things belongs
> to the first sense, the historical or literal. That signification whereby
> things signified by words have themselves also a signification is called
> the spiritual sense, which is based on the literal, and presupposes it.
> Now this spiritual sense has a threefold division . . . so far as the things
> of the Old Law signify the things of the New Law, there is the allegorical
> sense; so far as the things done in Christ, or so far as the things which
> signify Christ, are signs of what we ought to do, there is the moral
> sense. But so far as they signify what relates to eternal glory, there is
> the anagogical sense.[21]

In the same vein Bonaventure writes in his prologue to the *Breviloquium*: "Many Scriptural passages have, besides the direct sense,
three other significations: the allegorical, the moral, and the anagogical." He goes on to describe the specific meaning of each of
these senses: "Allegory consists in this: that one thing signifies
another thing which is in the realm of faith; moral teaching, or
tropology, in this: that from something done, we learn another
thing that we must do; anagogy, or lifting up, in this: that we are
given to know what to desire, that is, the eternal happiness of the
elect."[22]

Medieval exegetes interpreted a number of central symbols on
four levels. For example, in addition to the Exodus as treated in
Dante, Jerusalem was interpreted literally as the city of David; morally as the soul adorned with virtue; allegorically, as the Church on
earth redeemed by Christ; anagogically, as the heavenly Jerusalem,
or the souls of the saved enjoying the beatific vision. In a similar
fashion the text in Genesis, "Let there be light," describing God's
creation of light was interpreted literally as referring to corporeal
light; morally, to the illumination of the soul by virtue; allegorically,
to the illumination of the Church by Christ; anagogically to the
illumination of the blessed in heaven by the beatific vision. Not all
such symbols were interpreted on four levels. At times a literal
sense would yield chiefly a moral meaning, as for example, in the
interpretation of the Mercy Seat in the tabernacle by Richard of St.
Victor as a symbol of the contemplative self.[23] This same symbol
was interpreted allegorically in Bonaventure as a symbol of Christ
in his *The Soul's Journey Into God*.[24]

THE FOUR LEVELS OF THE PSYCHE

We turn now from medieval exegesis to contemporary research into altered states of consciousness. Drawing data from recent scientific research into altered states of consciousness, I will point out a correlation between the four levels of the psyche discovered in this research and the four senses of Scripture. From this correlation, I will make a fundamental claim: the symbolic method of interpreting Scripture is not arbitrary, but is based on the very structure of the psyche. In actual fact, it is a method designed to allow a text to reveal its meaning on each of the four levels of the psyche. From this basic claim, a number of further claims will be derived: In the light of the correlation, a comprehensive hermeneutic can be determined with greater precision than was available to medieval theologians. For the rules of this hermeneutic can be ascertained from the structure and dynamics of each of the levels of the psyche. Once brought to light, this hermeneutic context can clarify the various types of symbolism used in the interpretation of Scripture. As we shall see, the levels of the psyche correspond to the themes of nature, human, and God. The three symbolic senses of Scripture (the allegorical, moral, and anagogic), correspond to the three levels of the psyche whose very structure and dynamics follow a symbolic pattern. This reveals that symbolic thinking is not alien or peripheral to the psyche, but constitutive of its most profound dimensions. Thus in the light of contemporary psychological research, the themes of nature, the human, and God can be seen to be rooted in the structure and dynamics of the psyche itself.

I will base myself chiefly on the research of Robert Masters and Jean Houston as reported in their book *The Varieties of Psychedelic Experience.*[25] Although the cases studied in this book involved psychedelic drugs, the same patterns of consciousness were revealed by their later research which was performed without the use of drugs. Similar patterns have emerged in the work of other researchers, for example, in the extensive work of Stanislav Grof.[26]

The research of Masters and Houston has revealed that the psyche has four levels, which are described as follows: (1) the sensorium, or the level of heightened sense experience; (2) the ontogenetic, or recollective analytic level, where the subject recalls his or her personal history. This level corresponds to Freudian psychoanalysis; (3) the phylogenetic or symbolic level, corresponding to the collective unconscious of Jung. Here the subject relives the great myths and rituals of humankind; (4) The level of integral consciousness, or the *mysterium.* This is the level of deep mystical consciousness, which is similar to that described by the mystics of the world.[27] These levels are markedly different, with their own horizons, structure, logic, and dynamics. Although there is a certain interpenetration of each in the others, they remain sufficiently distinct; yet one leads to the other.

After taking a dosage of a psychedelic drug, the subject usually experienced first heightened sensation. For example, having been handed an orange by the guide, a subject contemplated it for several minutes and said: "Magnificent . . . I never really saw color before . . . It's brighter than a thousand suns . . . (Feels the whole surface of the orange with palms and fingertips) But this is a pulsing thing . . . a living pulsing thing . . . And all these years I've just taken it for granted."[28]

After some time on the sensory level, the subject usually moved to the second level, that is the ontogenic or recollective analytic. For example, a subject experienced his deep emotions at the time of the death of his grandmother when he was not quite four years old. "Suddenly," he said, "I felt as if some obstacle were coming up to me—something large, dark, and vague, but very powerful—as if it were knocking on the walls of consciousness. . . . It's Granny's death! I must examine Granny's death!" The subject then felt a surge of guilt that he had experienced years before over his grandmother's death, but which he had repressed. In the course of the session he was able to free himself from the burden of this unconscious guilt.[29]

Because of the importance of the third level, we will give at length the case of a subject who relived the rites of Dionysus:

> The guide initiated the ritual process by suggesting to the subject that he was attending the rites of Dionysus and was carrying a thyrsus in his hand. When he asked for some details the subject was told only that the thyrsus was a staff wreathed with ivy and vine leaves, terminating at the top in a pine cone, and was carried by the priests and attendants of Dionysus, a god of the ancient Greeks. To this S nodded, sat back in his chair with eyes closed, and then remained silent for several minutes. Then he began to stamp the floor, as if obeying some strange internal rhythm. He next proceeded to describe a phantasmagoria consisting of snakes and ivy, streaming hair, dappled fawn skins, and dances going faster and faster to the shrill high notes of the flute and accelerating drums. The frenzy mounted and culminated in the tearing apart of living animals.
>
> The scene changed and S found himself in a large amphitheater witnessing some figures performing a rite or play. This changed into a scene of white-robed figures moving in the night towards an open cavern. In spite of her intention not to give further clues, the guide found herself asking the subject at this point: 'Are you at Eleusis?' S seemed to nod 'yes,' whereupon the guide suggested that he go into the great hall and witness the mystery. He responded: 'I can't. It is

forbidden . . . I must confess. . . . I must confess . . . ' (The candidate at Eleusis was rejected if he came with sinful hands to seek enlightenment. He must confess, make reparation, and be absolved. Then he received his instruction and then finally had his experience of enlightenment and was allowed to witness the mystery. How it happened that this subject was aware of the stages of the mystery seemed itself to be a mystery.) S then began to go through the motions of kneading and washing his hands and appeared to be in deep conversation with someone. Later, he told the guide that he had seemed to be standing before a priestly figure and had made a confession. The guide now urged the subject to go into the hall and witness the drama. This he did, and described seeing a 'story' performed about a mother who looks the world over for her lost daughter and finally finds her in the world of the underground (the Demeter-Kore story which, in all likelihood, was performed at Eleusis).

This sequence dissolved and the subject spoke of seeing a kaleidoscopic pattern of many rites of the death and resurrection of a god who appeared to be bound up in some way with the processes of nature. S described several of the rites he was viewing, and from his descriptions the guide was able to recognize remarkable similarities to rites of Osiris, Attis, and Adonis. S was uncertain as to whether these rites occurred in a rapid succession or all at the same time. The rites disappeared and were replaced by the celebration of the Roman Catholic Mass. Seeking to restore the original setting, the guide again suggested the image of the thyrsus. S imaged the thyrsus, but almost immediately it 'turned into' a man on a tree (the Christ archetype). The guide then said: 'You are the thyrsus,' to which S responded: 'I am the thyrsus. . . . I am the thyrsus. . . . I have labored in the vineyard of the world, have suffered, have died, and have been reborn for your sake and shall be exalted forevermore.'[30]

Another remarkable experience is recorded by Grof in an LSD session of a clergyman:

. . . I began to experience the passion of our Lord Jesus Christ. I was Christ, but I was also everyone as Christ and all men died as we made our way in the dirgelike procession toward Golgotha. At this time in my experience there was no longer any confusion; the visions were perfectly clear. The pain was intense, and the sorrow was just, just agonizing. It was at this point that a blood tear from the face of God began to flow. I did not see the face of God, but his tear began to flow, and it began to flow out over the world as God himself participated in the death of all men and in the suffering of all men. The sorrow of this moment is still so intense that it is difficult for me to speak of it. We moved toward Golgotha, and there in agony greater than any I have ever experienced, I was crucified with Christ and all men on the cross. I was Christ, and I was crucified, and I died.

This was followed by a resurrection experience: "When all men died on the cross, there began the most heavenly music I have ever heard in my entire life; it was incredibly beautiful. It was the voice of angels singing, and we began slowly to rise."[31]

Although a relatively large number of subjects reached the third level, only a small proportion attained the fourth: the level of integral consciousness or the *mysterium*. Those who did reported experiences similar to those of the acknowledged mystics of the world's religions. For example, one subject reported:

> . . . I, who seemed to have no identity at all, yet experienced myself as *filled with God*, and then as (whatever this may mean) *passing through God* and into a Oneness wherein it seemed God, Being, and a mysterious unnameable One constituted together what I can only designate the ALL. What 'I' experienced as this ALL so far transcends my powers of description that to speak, as I must, of an ineffably rapturous Sweetness is an approximation not less feeble than if I were to describe a candle and so hope to capture with my words all of the blazing glory of the sun.[32]

CORRELATION WITH SENSES OF SCRIPTURE

We will now explore the correlation between the four levels of the psyche and the four senses of Scripture. The sensorium corresponds to the literal sense, since the latter deals with the meaning of a text in its concrete, particular facticity, similar to our sense data. The second level, the ontogenetic or recollective analytic, corresponds to the moral sense, since this level of the psyche involves consciousness of the individual subject in his personal history, his affectivity, and personal commitments. The third level, the phylogenetic or symbolic, corresponds to the allegorical sense, for this level of the psyche links early historical ritual material with Christ. The fourth level, the *mysterium* or the realm of integral consciousness, corresponds to the anagogical sense, for the latter deals with the ultimate union of the soul with God.

It would be of special interest to explore the allegorical sense in the light of the data drawn from the phylogenetic level of the psyche. The case from Houston and Masters which I presented above gives a striking example of the material from this level. It is highly symbolic, consisting of clusters of archetypal symbols and primitive rituals. Most strikingly, these rituals emerge in a temporal sequence which culminates, in the case cited, in the image of Christ and the Mass. The very fabric and dynamic of this level reveals the logic of the process of allegorizing Scripture. Christian theologians drew events and symbols from the Old Testament and saw them as reaching their culmination in Christ. From one point of view this could be seen as an arbitrary procedure; but from the standpoint of the dynamics of the third level of the psyche, the logic is completely coherent. It is not by chance, then, that the early Christian community incorporated the Old Testament into their prayer, liturgy, and belief precisely by allegorizing, that is, by seeing this data symbolically reaching a climax in Christ. In fact, in the light of the phylogenetic level of the psyche, it is possible to extend the procedure back beyond the Old Testament and into the entire context of primitive religious ritual and symbol. As in the case cited, the many transformation rituals from the Greek world can be seen as reaching their climax in the person of Christ and in the continuing transformation ritual of the Mass.

In conclusion, I would like to suggest that the most appropriate image of the interpretation of tradition in this mutational Second Axial Period is not that of dwarfs standing on the shoulders of giants—although this image has its place within the separate traditions. A more appropriate image, I believe, is the one I developed in the previous chapter: the image of the earth as it was seen by the astronauts when they first moved into outer space. Looking back, they saw the beautiful blue globe shining against the black background of space. Although they were far distant, they felt their rootedness there in the earth. From this distant point of view, they could see the earth as a whole and feel that they belonged to the earth as a whole. This image of the earth, then, seen from outer space can symbolize the horizontal and vertical dimensions of global consciousness that I described above. It can also be the symbol of the archetype of the common tradition that underlies all diverse traditions; and it can be the symbol of a spirituality that integrates the cosmic, the human, and the transcendent. As I mentioned above, it is not by chance that the emergence of global consciousness has coincided with the first time that humans have had a concrete sense experience of the earth as a single sphere; for this type of sense experience is the quarry of archetypal symbols that flourished in Pre-Axial spirituality and are a vital force for Second Axial consciousness. Furthermore, the great distance required for the astronauts to obtain such a view can symbolize the First Axial perspective and the distance that is required for our interpretation of the many traditions that have flourished on this planet as these are coming into view in the Second Axial Period. Instead of dwarfs on the shoulders of giants, then, we have been transformed into astronauts in outer space—overwhelmed, it is true, by the size of the universe and the task it enjoins, but simultaneously supported by the clarity of vision it affords and stimulated to take up the challenging task of the creative interpretation of traditions in a global context.

III

Retrieving Tradition
Through Models and Spirituality

What is the task of Christian theology on the eve of the twenty-first century? Is it to follow its strategy of the past four hundred years? To react against and to adjust to the rise of scientific-technological culture? If we are in a Second Axial Period that is enlarging the horizons of traditional religious consciousness, as this had been constituted in the First Axial Period, then our theological task is multi-dimensional. A major thrust of this task is to establish Christian identity by retrieving its tradition in depth—its belief and its spirituality, its doctrine of the Trinity, Christ, and the Spirit and its classical spiritual wisdom—and at the same time relate to other religions and to the enormous cultural changes that are accelerating at a rapid pace.

We are undergoing a cultural change so radical that it affects not only our religious symbols, but every facet of our life. Our social institutions and mores are altering; even the structure of our experience is being transformed by mass media and the electronic environment. We must get our bearings and situate ourselves anew in the on-going process. Like teenagers at adolescence, we are suffering an identity crisis; we must discover who we are and find our place in the universe. But unlike teenagers, we are not moving from childhood to adulthood. The present crisis is not so much an adolescent passage from dependency to responsibility, although certainly we have a new and frightening responsibility for our destiny. The present crisis is more a rebirth into a new world. From a world of limited experience, which could be described as one or two dimensional, we are born into a multi-dimensional environment. We are no longer merely religious or secular, but multi-dimensional persons in a multi-dimensional global environment.

MULTI-DIMENSIONAL PERSONS

In our new environment, we are open to a variety of experiences that have not been available before. To our bewilderment and enrichment, space and time are being compressed; different types of human experience throughout the world are converging; and new possibilities are opening on the horizon. To encompass the fulness of our new experience, we must enlarge our consciousness. The secular theology that drew traditional religious persons into the modern world must expand to encompass the richness of religious experience. For persons of the future must be in command of their psychic potential. They must be scientific and technological, mystical and mythopoeic, intensely individual and autonomous, and at the same time deeply related to all humans and the cosmos. They must be persons of the past and of the future so that they can live the present in all its complexity. The era of specialization of experience has passed. Those levels of the psyche that moderns had previously stifled to develop science, industrialization, and technology must be opened once again. We can no longer be fractional beings, with only a portion of our powers activated. It is only with the full resources of our psychic life that we can move into the future.

As we move into our future, we are moving more and more into our past. Although there is a reaction against history as a mass of static data or a set of stereotyped norms of behavior, history as experience is more present to us than ever before. Each age tends to view the past in its own setting and to dress it in its own fashions. Chaucer's Greek warriors in *The Knight's Tale* wore chain mail and fought jousts like the knights of medieval England. In our time, however, we have been alerted to the uniqueness of past experience. Archaeology, anthropology, and historical research, museums and libraries, television and computers have made past experience present in its most concrete and tangible details. We are learning more and more ways of recreating the concrete environment of past civilizations so that children need not have their experience limited to those of a given time or historical epoch. Thus from their earliest years children are oriented to a diversified style of life by moving in and out of radically different experiential environments.

Just as we are not limited to the experiences of a single historical epoch, so we are not limited to the experiences of a single culture. In the past children would grow up within the envelope of their own culture, learn the traditions of their tribe or nation, and relate to those beyond the border as foreigners or enemies. This is no longer possible. Air travel, movies, and television have brought about a convergence of cultures. Western children do not grow to maturity merely by absorbing their European past. The electronic environment brings them sights and sounds from Africa and India. Much of this is superficial, it is true, but it can open the way for a deeper penetration into other cultures. This convergence of cultures will have an enormous effect on our religious experience, for we will have to learn to live in a complex religious environment.

That we have already begun to open to the varieties of religious experience is indicated by the development of the ecumenical movement and the dialogue of world religions. In the meeting of world religions the missionary of the future will not be attempting conversion, in the classical sense, but convergence. What form this convergence will take is difficult to predict because we are not fully in the environment that will provide its matrix. But this much seems to be clear: as persons of the future we will have to find new ways to enlarge our religious experience in order to be responsive to the religious experience of others, not merely to the simple variety within our own tradition, but to the radically different religious experiences of those from other great traditions.

What is the role of theologians at this time? They can help us move into the future. As learned in their own religious tradition, theologians can bring its resources and wisdom to self-consciousness. As sensitive to the religious experience of different traditions, they can discover ways of relating positively across cultural barriers. As responsive to the times, they can join with others in a common openness to the future. In the recent past the theologian's task was marked off by the forms of secular culture that had emerged in Western civilization. Since religious belief had become divorced from developments in secular culture, theologians submitted their beliefs to radical criticism and demythologizing in order to bring them in line with the limits of secular experience so that religion would be meaningful to modern persons. But the very technology that led to the need for demythologizing has produced an environment in which multi-leveled experience is possible. Instead of engaging in demythologizing and radical criticism, theologians will be called upon to bring to light the richness of their tradition. Having long been alienated from the mystical, cosmic, and mythic levels of consciousness, contemporary persons must now open themselves to the depth and power of these levels and integrate these resources into their full conscious life. It is in this process of rediscovery, reintegration, and expansion that theologians can make a special contribution.

THE THEOLOGICAL TASK

Theologians, then, must know the forms of religious experience of their own tradition, and must know the concepts and symbols in which they are expressed. They must have a method that will bring these forms into self-consciousness with precision and clarity, that will be rooted in the historical process, and that will be open to the experiences of other religious traditions. In the sixties two methodological approaches emerged that gave theologians access to the riches of their tradition and opened their horizons to other traditions. Drawing from the natural sciences, theologians adapted what has been called the "models method." As it had in the sciences, this method allowed theologians to look at complex reality from many different perspectives. It is this openness to variety that is the chief value of the method, especially at the present when our horizons are expanding. During the same period, there occurred in the West a reawakening of spirituality, stimulated by spiritual teachers form the East. Through spirituality Westerners recovered the depth dimension of religious experience. In the seventies Christians and Jews began searching for their spiritual roots in their past in a major attempt to assimilate their spiritual wisdom with its accompanying spiritual experience. Thus spirituality provided a major methodological tool for the retrieval of the religious experience that undergirds theology.

Since the sixties, I have used these two methods in an attempt to retrieve tradition in a global context. In 1969 an article of mine appeared in the journal *Continuum* under the title "Models and the Future of Theology."[1] In this I formulated my attempt to adapt the models method to theology, extending it to include the varieties of religious experience, thus linking it to the experiential dimension of spirituality. My work in spirituality began in translating classical spiritual texts of the Christian tradition and moved into editing series of Western and world spirituality. In the following sections I will examine both the models method and the spirituality approach to the retrieval of tradition.

Aware of the complexity of their subject matter, the natural sciences use various models to express the various aspects of the material world.[2] For example, light manifests aspects of a wave and of particles. The data is so complex that scientists must use two models—that of a wave and that of particles—for understanding the phenomenon of light. The fact that these models are opposite and irreducible one to the other does not deter scientists because they can employ them as complementary models. The social sciences and psychology have adopted the concept of model and have used it in studying human behavior. For example, the social scientist may use the computer as a model, seeing human beings as data-processing mechanisms and studying their social interactions as information input, processing, and feed-back. At times the model may be used in a picturing or suggestive manner, or it may be elevated to a more theoretical and mathematical level where it will provide a conceptual and mathematical matrix to give form and coherence to a variety of data.

Inspired by the use of models in science, theologians attempted to apply the model method to theology.[3] They looked upon theological language and symbols as models that reveal something about God just as scientific models reveal something about the physical universe. According to Ian Ramsey, for example, both theology and science are concerned in their own way with the disclosure of a mystery.[4] Because of the vastness, complexity, and depth of the physical universe and the limits of the human mind, it is appropriate for scientists to use models. In that way they can obtain some knowledge, but only a part of the whole. The same can be said for theological concepts and symbols. Theology is concerned with the ultimate level of religious mystery, which is even more inaccessible than the mystery of the physical universe. Hence our religious language and symbols can be looked upon as models because, even more than the concepts of science, they only approximate the object they are reflecting. As Ramsey has said:

> . . . the number of models is legion—strong tower, king, father, shepherd . . . waves, particles, elastic strings. . . . Many are logically disparate at that; nor is there any finite bound either to verification and empirical fit. It is in these ways and for these reasons that we may say that theorizing by models is the understanding of a mystery whose depths are never sounded by man's plumb-lines, however long and however diverse these lines may be, however far developed. It is in these ways that both science and theology provide us with different and characteristically different understanding of a mysterious universe.[5]

To use the concept of model in theology, then, breaks the illusion that we are actually encompassing the infinite within our finite structures of language. It prevents concepts and symbols from becoming idols and opens theology to variety and development just as the model method has done for science. Perhaps the most effective use of the models method in theology has been by Avery Dulles in *Models of the Church* and *Models of Revelation*.[6]

Yet Theologians may copy the sciences too closely. They may take the scientific method as a normative model, or they may so shape their use of the method that they emphasize those aspects of theological models that most correspond to scientific models. In so doing, theologians may not take into account the experiential-cognitive element at the core of religion, which has various levels of depth and various modes of perceiving the spiritual structures of reality. The religious experience has a depth and penetration that has no correlation in our experience of the physical universe. Religious experience touches the innermost part of the person; it may be felt as coming from outside: as revelation, grace, or divine illumination; or it may appear as the discovery of the hidden depths of one's soul, the finding of the true self, the touching of the ground of the soul, or an overwhelming encounter with divine reality. It may be experienced through symbols or language, or it may not. It has a creative power that expands one's vision and opens new ways of seeing the world.

To be comprehensive, then, a theological method must take religious experience seriously and deal adequately with its varieties both in the past and in the future. As a step in this direction, I proposed extending the model method into the area of religious experience in my 1969 article.[7] This involved building a two-level approach to the model method. One level would deal with religious experience and search out what I termed "experiential models." By this I meant the structures or forms of religious experience and the structures and forms of spiritual and divine reality. The second level of the method would deal with the expression of religious experience in words, concepts and symbols: for example, Biblical imagery, Christian creeds, and theological systems. This is the level of what I termed "expressive models," the term "expressive" suggesting the formulation of the experience and the term "model" the varieties of expression. These two levels—experiential models and expressive models—formed the basic structure of a method to be employed extensively over the history of theology with an orientation towards the future.

It is important to note that I hold an epistemology in religious knowledge that differs from the reigning epistemology used in scientific research. Hence my use of the term "model" in religious knowledge has to be adjusted accordingly. As I will spell out in Chapter Five, I hold that religious experience—especially mystical experience—can attain an immediate knowledge of God; I also hold that certain symbols are so related to the object of religious experiences that there can be an interpenetration of expressive and experiential models. Because of the problem of the term "experiential model" being taken in a purely subjective way, I later tended to use in certain cases the term "spiritual archetype," by which I mean a spiritual structure of reality perceived by the psyche, especially by the unconscious.

To extend the model method into the realm of religious experience has the value of opening theologians to the varieties of religious experience—or in my terms, the varieties of experiential models. This variety stems from two sources: the vastness of the divine reality from which the experience emanates; and the complexity of human beings and of the human situation in which the revelation is made. For example, Rudolf Otto has described the numinous as having opposite qualities, for it is both *tremendum* and *fascinans*.[8] Thus the manifestation of the divine as *tremendum* would produce a different experiential model from that resulting from its manifestation as *fascinans*. On the other hand, the variety may come from the human side. For example, one may experience redemption as liberation from personal sin and guilt or as the restoration of the image of God within oneself. These would be different experiential models. Further, one may experience the presence of God in places set apart as holy, such as churches or shrines throughout the natural world. In all of these cases we would be dealing with different experiential models.

A great deal of research has been done in the area I refer to as that of experiential models. Theologians can draw from the pioneering work of William James, *The Varieties of Religious Experience*,[9] the basic analysis of the numinous by Rudolf Otto in *The Idea of the Holy*,[10] the studies in primal religion by Mircea Eliade,[11] the studies in religious psychology by C.G. Jung,[12] and the empirical studies in the phenomenology of states of consciousness by Masters and Houston and by Stanislav Grof.[13]

From the mid-sixties, I increasingly drew from the research of Masters and Houston in order to bring to light the experiential models or spiritual archetypes, although I did not present this in my 1969 models article. Beginning in 1965, I had the privilege of working with them on their research for some ten years and found their exploration of the four levels of the psyche the most profound and comprehensive framework for developing a typology of religious experience. Although I cannot present the material extensively here, I would like to recall what I dealt with in the final section of the previous chapter when treating the fourfold sense of Scripture. There I described how their research revealed four major levels of consciousness in the human psyche: (1) the sensorium, or level of sense experience; (2) the ontogenetic level, where one recalls events from one's earlier life, especially events charged with negative and positive feelings; (3) the phylogenetic level, where one experiences the great mythic and ritual structures and dynamics of the collective human race; (4) the mysterium, where one experiences the divine or absolute reality. Although the second, or ontogenetic, level deals largely with subjective feeling reactions to events, the others focus more on the perceived objectivity that is revealed in the level, with a progression in intensity from the sensorium, to the phylogenetic, to the mysterium. Both the intensity of energy felt and the objectivity of the reality perceived increases as one moves along this spectrum of consciousness.

I believe that each level of consciousness has its own distinctive epistemology. I believe, for example, that the psyche has capacities for grasping the mysterium that are intuitive, and that function according to the connaturality of faith, and that can be had with brilliant luminosity in the ecstatic mystical experience. This is why I believe that the religious experiences of the great mystics have a privileged place in bringing to light the cognitive content, the form, dynamism, and affectivity that are part of the experience of the mysterium. In the light of this, one can readily see the limitations and distortions that follow from using an exclusively empirical epistemology to examine the wide range of religious experience. Such an approach would either exclude all the other levels or reduce them to the first. In a similar way, I believe that each level of the psyche has symbols which function in a way distinctive and characteristic of that level.

ANSELM'S REDEMPTION MODEL

It is important to know the experiential model that stands behind a particular expressive model. This is made difficult by the complexity of expressive models and the fact that much religious language is drawn from non-religious areas of experience. Human beings have expressed their religious experience in words, concepts, and symbols derived from the social and economic structures in particular cultures. For example, Christians have spoken of their liberation from evil as a redemption, a buying back. One way to determine what this language means is to study its origin in history, through etymology and cultural linguistics, in order to see what area of social custom it is reflecting. This task is not made easier as theology progresses, for these expressive models often become more complex. For example, in medieval theology Anselm developed an elaborate theory of the redemption based on the concept of satisfaction. Not only did he use intricate rational argumentation, but drew from feudal customs and perhaps from Roman and Germanic legal practices.[14] In studying Anselm's satisfaction theory, theologians would have to explore the legal and sociological models at work in his thought. But this would not be enough. Theologians would not reach the heart of the matter until they uncovered the religious experiential model behind the expressive models. They would have to be on guard to avoid a type of reductionism, in which symbols are simply reduced to cultural models.

In Anselm's case the very legal model acts as an expressive model for a much deeper religious experiential model. Rudolf Otto has pointed out that Anselm had a consciousness of the mystery of sin on the level of depth religious experience.[15] In the history of religion, the mystery of evil has been reflected in a variety of experiential models. The specific experiential model in Anselm's case was the overpowering burden of guilt. At its center was a grasp of the infinite dimension of evil which causes the burden of guilt to weigh down on human beings with such force that they are unable to remove it and need the Infinite itself to lift the burden.[16] It is this depth religious experience that Anselm conveys by sketching the outlines of the feudal lord to whom satisfaction is due because of his offended honor. This image and Anselm's exploration of the infinite dimension of evil and the inexorable logic of guilt coalesce to form an elaborate expressive model. Once the underlying experiential model has been isolated and explored, the theologian can chart the correlations between the experience and its expressive model. It is here that various theories of language and predication can be brought to bear on a concept or symbol to determine the specific use of language that the author is employing. For example, Aristotelian analogy, Platonic participation, Otto's theory of schematization, or Ramsey's concept of disclosure models.[17]

One of the constant dangers in theology is to remain on the level of expressive models and to fail to take into account experiential models. In the case of Anselm's highly complex expressive model—and of Western medieval theology in general—this would lead to a science of verbalizations and conceptualization. A theology that would neglect the entire experiential level and concentrate solely on expressive models would lack vitality and depth. It would be lifeless and abstract. This was the danger with the catechetical method and the scholasticism of the theological manuals. Throughout the history of theology, there has been a constant return to the experiential models. When the expressive models become too elaborate or disengaged from experience or convey the wrong level of experience, theology has attempted to return to its roots, as it did at the Reformation and in the thinking that led up to and surrounded Vatican II. The return to experiential models is usually brought about by a return to the early Christian experience as expressed in Scripture.

COSMOLOGICAL MODELS

Not only do expressive models reflect and express religious experience, but they shape it as well. This is especially true of cosmological
models. Since primitive times, cosmological models have been
bound up with religious experience and belief. In Western civilization from the time of the Copernican revolution and the rise of
modern science, cosmological models have been at the storm center
of religious controversy.[18] Since they are so basic, a shift in cosmological models can radically affect the entire structure of one's belief.
The change from the Ptolemaic to the Copernican universe affected
the Christian's self-image and challenged cherished religious ideas.
From the time of the Renaissance and into the nineteenth century,
debate raged over the status of the cosmology of Genesis in relation
to that of science. With the aid of Biblical scholarship, theologians
began to see cosmological models as expressive models in which
human beings formulated their religious experience. Thus theologians could accept an evolution in cosmological models which did
not undermine the significance of the Genesis narrative. For they
could see in the Genesis cosmology the expressive model of a
religious experience that transcends the primitive cosmology.

Not only do expressive models evolve, but experiential models
evolve as well. At the present time we are entering a change on the
experiential level that is as radical as the Copernican revolution was
on the level of expressive models. Human beings are severing their
ties with earth and moving into outer space. For the first time they
are actually experiencing the Copernican universe and not merely
understanding it intellectually with the aid of an abstract model of
the solar system. The more that the earth-bound community shares
in the space travels of the astronauts, the more their experience of
space will take on new dimensions. Because of the close tie between
cosmological models and religious models, this new experience of
space will open new varieties of religious experience and give new
meaning to cosmological symbols. If the experience of the desert
sun can evoke the model of the Sky-God and if the experience of
the fertile land can evoke the experiential model of the Earth-mother
goddess, then our new experiences in outer space could evoke other
experiential religious models of the divine and add new dimensions
to our old models.[19] The classical religious symbols of up and
down—programmed into the human body by the force of gravity—
can lose their experiential references in a state of weightlessness.
Light and darkness, sky and earth, sun and stars, distance and speed
will be experienced differently in outer space. As human beings
view the earth from outer space, they may grasp more profoundly

the meaning of their traditional earth symbolism. And the new elemental experiences of the vastness of space may awaken experiences akin to the experiences that stand behind cosmological models of primal peoples. The person of the future, then, as earth-dweller and space-traveller, will learn to live in a complex cosmology: with multiple experiences of space and an enlarged spatial symbolism. Theologians, having learned from the theological debates of the past over changing cosmology, can be sensitive to the expressive nature of cosmological models and so help others open to the religious significance of their new experiences in space.

Closely associated with cosmological models is the experiential model of the cosmic sense. This is the experience of being related to the entire cosmos, whether the cosmos is looked upon as the physical universe, the historical process, or the entire human community. This sense of being related to the whole has long been submerged in Western culture. Yet many signs indicate that it is emerging again, having been evoked by science, space travel, the communications network around the earth, and a rising sense of solidarity felt throughout the world, especially among the younger generation. The cosmic sense is emerging, not as a romantic escape to nature or a loss of individuality in the collectivity, but on a deeper level and as the matrix of the experience of the future. This has great significance for theologians. From primitive times the cosmic sense has been bound up with religious experience, especially religious experience on the sensorium and phylogenetic levels of the psyche. It played an important role in the Bible and in the theology of the Greek Fathers and of the medieval West. The doctrines of Christology, redemption, and the sacraments, for example, have not only an individual level, but a cosmic level as well. Since it is often this cosmic level that is expressed in religious symbols and concepts, many of the traditional expressive models can be understood only when situated within the experience of the cosmic sense. In the light of the re-emerging cosmic sense, then, theologians can better understand a major level of their past tradition and with this historical awareness, can be more sensitive to the religious dimension of the cosmic sense in our time.

Perhaps the most striking example of the cosmic sense in contemporary theology is in the thought of Teilhard de Chardin. His profound cosmic sense converged with his scientific knowledge and Christian faith to produce an evolutionary vision and a cosmic theology.[20] Aware of the presence of Christ in matter, Teilhard saw Christ as the Omega of evolution—the dynamic force operating throughout the cosmos drawing the universe to its fulfillment. With the cosmic sense as a matrix and the cosmic Christ as a focus,

Teilhard gave a cosmic interpretation to other doctrines, such as the Incarnation, redemption and the Eucharist.[21] Although Teilhard's vision has unique features, in its cosmic dimension—especially in its cosmic Christology—it is not unlike the Christologies found in the New Testament, in the Greek Fathers, and in the medieval Franciscans.[22] All of these Christologies are built on the experiential model of the cosmic sense. If they are not rooted in the cosmic sense, they seem to be highly abstract models rather than deeply experiential.

The emergence of cosmic Christology in our times challenges theologians to re-examine the Christological models of their tradition. The Christian experience of Christ has generated a variety of models. Throughout the history of Western theology, there has been an increasing emphasis on the historical Christ and redemption from evil as contrasted with the cosmic Christ and the completion of the universe. In the Middle Ages devotion to the humanity of Christ intensified the West's concern for the concrete and the particular. Hence it was the historical Christ in the concrete circumstances of his earthly life who became the moral model for the individual Christian.[23] Satisfaction theories of the redemption, such as Anselm's, gave expression to the West's sense of the burden of guilt. At the time of the Reformation, these trends became the matrix in the Christology of redemption in which Christ, through his death on the cross, has brought personal salvation to the individual Christian and liberation from the burden of sin.[24] Elements of this classical Western model could be seen in existential theology.[25] If the cosmic sense is emerging as a widespread cultural experience, then theologians have the task of examining both the individual and cosmic models of Christology and of charting their interrelation. This is especially needed if theologians are to approach the future with the fulness of their tradition's resources.

MODELS OF THE TRINITY

At the present, when human beings are experiencing themselves more and more in a process, theologians are called upon to examine those theological models in their tradition that express an experience of process. Of paramount importance here is the doctrine of the Trinity. At first glance, to propose the Trinity as a theological model of process might appear paradoxical since Trinitarian theology has developed in a highly abstract and mathematical fashion. By the late Middle Ages in the West, Trinitarian theology had become a type of super-geometry in which the processions, relations, and persons were analyzed with refined logical precision. Underlying this schol-astic overlay was a basic trinitarian model which has been traced to Augustine. In arguing against the Arians in the *De Trinitate*, Augus-tine had conceived of the single divine nature first and then con-sidered it constituted by the three persons.[26] This model combined with scholastic logic to produce a Trinitarian theology in which the divine nature was conceived as a type of static substrate and the persons abstract relations. As Karl Rahner has pointed out,[27] empha-sis on this model led to the separation in the Middle Ages of the treatise on the One God from the Treatise on the Trinity and caused the doctrine of the Trinity to be disengaged from other doctrines, such as Christology and grace. Thus for many the Trinity seems remote from human experience, salvation history, and a sense of process or development.

The Augustine model, however, with its abstract superstructure, has not been the only model in the history of Trinitarian theology. A more ancient model takes its point of departure not from the divine nature common to all three persons, but from God the Father, the unengendered origin in the Godhead and the source of the Trinitarian procession. God the Father is both the source of the divine unity and the origin of the dynamic inner life of the Trinity. Thus at the very core of the model is built the element of self-communication and creative process. This model underlies the Nicene Creed and the main current in the Trinitarian theology of the Greek Fathers; it shaped an important tradition in Western medieval theology and has a continuing history into modern times, when it has emerged in the theology of Barth, Tillich, and Rahner.[28] This model is more closely associated with the Biblical experience of revelation, a dynamic concept of creation, and a sense of process in history. The expressive models of this tradition did not develop into the intricate logical superstructure that emerged out of the Augustinian approach, but remained more deeply rooted in the symbolic imagination. Such images as the generation of the Son and the expression of the Word evoke a sense of energy and creativity. Behind these expressive models is an experience of the divinity as dynamic, self-communicating, infinitely fecund, and infinitely creative within its own inner life, which has been experienced ecstati-cally by mystics on the mysterium level and intuited by contempla-tives. It is this inner creativity that bursts out in the creation of the world, in revelation, and salvation history.[29] This type of experiential model of the divinity, then, has a sympathetic resonance with the contemporary experience of process and development in history.

At first glance, this dynamic model of the Trinity—which can be called the Greek model because of its centrality in Greek theology—seems the antithesis of the Augustinian model. There is no doubt that the expressive models of the Augustinian approach tend to create a static, remote, and irrelevant impression of the Trinity. Both the logical superstructure and its conceptual base add to this impression. Yet there is reason to think that this static quality is caused chiefly by the abstract nature of the expressive models. For one can glimpse behind these expressive models an experience of the divinity that is dynamic, but dynamic in a way that is different from the Greek experiential model and complementary to it. The Augustinian model focuses on the unity of the divine nature and the distinction of the person. This points to a dynamic coincidence of opposites within the divine life: at the core of the divine mystery there are reconciled unity and multiplicity, oneness and distinction, community and individuality, the absolute ground and dynamic relations. In the mystery of the inner life of God, unity does not absorb distinction but intensifies it.[30]

If we follow Paul Henry's analysis of Augustine's language in Book V of the *De Trinitate*,[31] we move behind the static structures into the Augustinian experiential model, in which union and difference interpentrate and intensify each other. Thus Henry can propose the Augustinian model of the Trinity—as further developed by Thomas Aquinas—as the ideal of human interpersonal relationships; for the more one gives oneself to another in creative union with the other, the more one becomes oneself.[32] Thus the Augustinian Trinitarian model becomes the archetypal ideal for the process of growth in human persons as they attempt to achieve their full identity by self-transcending love for other persons. This process of personal growth Teilhard de Chardin formulates in a cosmic law: union differentiates, which he sees operating throughout the universe from elementary particles to human persons.[33] It is precisely the movement towards more centered unions, in which individuality is not absorbed by the union but rather intensified, that is the driving force in evolution. Paradoxically, then, it is the Augustinian experiential model—stripped of its static abstractions—that is an underlying process model in the evolutionary vision of Teilhard de Chardin. While an analysis of Teilhard's thought points in this direction, scattered texts in his writing referring to the Trinity suggest that this model was operating in his thought, at least at times, as a conscious trinitarian model.[34]

On the experiential level, then, the Greek and the Augustinian Trinitarian models are both models of process. Once we have penetrated beyond the expressive to the experiential level, we can ask how the Greek and the Augustinian models are related. It is most appropriate to see them as complementary models. The wave-particle complementarity in the models of physics has its resonance here in the Christian experiences of Trinitarian revelation.[35] The mystery of the Trinity is too profound and complex to be grasped in a single experiential model. The Greek and the Augustinian models emerge out of a single historical revelation, it is true, and each reflects a dynamic aspect of the Trinitarian life. Although each pre-supposes the other, they cannot be reduced one to the other; for each manifests something unique about the mystery. The Greek is the model of emanation, with all things ultimately flowing from the Father. The Augustinian is the model of the goal of the cosmic process, in which there is a constant Trinitization of the elements into more complex unities that intensify the uniqueness of each element. Although these two models are among the most basic in Christian history, they are not the only Trinitarian models. The history of Christian theology and experience has been enormously rich in the variety and complexity of Trinitarian models.[36] Perhaps as contemporary experience becomes more process-oriented and more complex, we will discover new models—both experiential and expressive—that will reveal new aspects of the mystery of the Trinity.

INTERRELIGIOUS ENCOUNTER

The very process carrying us into this future is drawing the religions of the world towards an encounter that is unique in human history. At the present time the theologians have a threefold task: to make available the richness of their own tradition; to become aware of those elements in their tradition that will make them sensitive to the heritage of other world religions; and to bring to expression those experiential models that will be characteristic of the shared consciousness of the Second Axial Period. They will have to pene-trate beneath the layers of expressive models to contact the under-lying religious experience and spiritual archetypes. They may find little similarity between the religions of the East and West in the area of language, concept, economic, sociological, and cosmological models; for they have developed largely independently of each other and in diverse cultural settings. Yet by going to the level of depth experience, they may be able to establish points of contact across cultural lines. For example, Christians may be able to detect an experiential similarity between their own image-of-God tradition and the Hindu atman-Brahman tradition, which discovers at the ground of one's soul ultimate reality or Brahman.[37] On the experien-tial level the Christian and the Hindu traditions both appear as the inward way, in which their followers turn in upon themselves and by penetrating through their inner world reach the base of their subjectivity, where they discover the Infinite, or God, or Brahman.[38]

To arrive at the experiential level of the inward way, Christian theologians may have to rediscover an experiential model of their own tradition. In Christianity, the image-of-God expressive model has both an objective and a subjective meaning. Viewed as objects, human persons are the images of God because they have intelligence and therefore resemble the supremely intelligent divine nature. From the standpoint of their own subjectivity, they are images of God because in the depths of their subjectivity, they can discover the presence of God. By turning within themselves, they can move through the various layers of their personality until they discover God at the ground of their being.[39] This is a movement from the depths of the ontogenetic level of consciousness to the mysterium. To point out the similarities between the Christian experiential model and the Hindu model is not to gloss over complexities and differences. For example, the Christians' experiential model of the inward way is bound up with their experience of salvation history and redemption through Christ. Sensitive to both similarities and differences on the experiential level, theologians can explore new ways to relate to other religions and to enlarge their own experiential horizons.

Through the above examples I have attempted to illustrate various aspects of my adaptation of the model method. The instances have been proposed as illustrations and not as definitive positions. It has been impossible to amass all the evidence on a particular point, and in some cases much research has yet to be done. Some examples are open to different or more complex interpretations. In this form, they can indicate the general lines of an approach which can be summarized as follows: (1) Distinguish between expressive and experiential models. (2) Begin with an expressive model at a given point in history and explore all levels of language, concept and symbol and all the cosmological, social, legal, economic forces in culture that have entered into the formation of the expressive model. (3) Bring to light the experiential model that the expressive model is formulating. This presupposes an awareness of the varieties of religious experience and the levels of consciousness, as well as an attempt to view these varieties in a systematic fashion. (4) Explore the multiple relations between expressive models and experiential models: in past history, in relation to contemporary culture and in reference to the future, not only in one's own tradition but in the context of world religions.

Such a method can aid theologians in their task of assisting contemporary persons to move into their future. Inspired by the model method in the sciences, it can open theology to the varieties of experience that are emerging on the horizon of an expanding and converging world. At the same time that it opens theology to variety, it calls for an extensive use of analytic precision and critical evaluation. Within this context, theologians can face squarely the complex issue of norms in theology. They can examine the question of the normative nature of religious experience and the pluralism of religious forms in the face of the claims of historical revelation and individual religious experience. They can view these normative issues in the complex context in which they are emerging in our times. Such a method would hopefully teach us not to trap ourselves in our models; we can break out of the limits of our own cultural forms and open ourselves to the richness and complexity that will be the heritage of the multi-dimensional human persons of the future.

SPIRITUALITY: A RESOURCE FOR THEOLOGY

In recent years we have witnessed a renaissance—or an explosion—of interest in spirituality. It followed upon the ferment of the sixties, with the invasion of America by spiritual teachers from the Orient and the journeying of Americans to the East to find spiritual meaning. Closely allied to psychology, the interest in spirituality was buoyed along by the development of existential, humanistic, and transpersonal psychology. For many psychoanalysis led to the discovery of interiority, which launched them on a spiritual quest, with a search for a spiritual path and a spiritual discipline. Many found their path in the New Age Consciousness movement, with its centers and programs throughout the country.

In the Christian community by the end of the sixties, the pendulum had swung from the flight into the world to a rediscovery of contemplation. After Vatican II had thrust Catholics into the world and had effected radical changes in external forms of religious life, many felt the need to ground themselves interiorly by rediscovering their own spiritual tradition, assimilating the findings of psychology and opening to the wisdom of the East.

Among the earliest signs of the reawakening of spirituality for Christians were houses of prayer that mushroomed in the late sixties. Unlike retreat houses, these were experimental monastic-type communities—with religious and lay members, spending long periods of time cultivating the practice of prayer. The retreat movement itself was renewed by the return to the original Ignatian formula of the directed retreat, with emphasis on individual discernment and spiritual direction. The most dramatic development in Catholic spirituality was the charismatic movement, encompassing large numbers and flourishing in diverse groups throughout the country.

As interest in spirituality spread, there sprang up throughout the country workshops, institutes, and programs in prayer, spiritual direction and contemporary spirituality. Academic programs began to appear on the campuses of universities, offering an M.A. and, in some instances, a Ph.D. in spirituality. Meanwhile academic programs in spirituality flourished in the Roman Universities: for example, the Gregorian and the Angelicum. In publishing, spirituality supplanted theology as the best seller in the religious field. Books on spirituality abound. Witness the two major multi-volume series: The Classics of Western Spirituality and World Spirituality: An Encyclopedic History of the Religious Quest.

During this period monastic spirituality flourished. At a time when vocations were dwindling, certain contemplative monasteries were drawing more candidates than they could handle. Monastic spirituality overflowed into the larger community. For example, stimulated by transcendental meditation, Cistercian monks developed the method of centering prayer based on the *Cloud of Unknowing* and the Jesus prayer. This method of prayer, which is rooted in the classical monastic tradition, is now being taught in numerous workshops and centers throughout the country. Christian monks and nuns have been bridging the gap between East and West. Following in the path of Thomas Merton, they have reached out towards the East. The international Benedictine monastic organization A.I.M. has focused its energies on dialogue with Hindu and Buddhist spiritualities. In the emerging dialogue of world religions, Christian monasticism has been at the forefront and will very likely continue to be, since it provides a natural bridge into Eastern spirituality.

But spirituality has not remained within the monastery. The post-Vatican II period has witnessed the emergence of a spirituality of action that is concerned with every aspect of life in the world. A major formulator of such a this-worldly spirituality was the scientist Teilhard de Chardin. More recently, liberation theology, dedicated as it is to radical orthopraxis, has created a new style of active spirituality. That spirituality is not banished from the political arena or the marketplace is verified by the fact that two of the leading spiritual personalities of our time have been secular leaders holding the office of Secretary-General of the United Nations: Dag Hammarskjold and U-Thant.

What are the characteristics of this renaissance of spirituality?

Taken as a whole, it cultivates both contemplation and action, attempting in certain instances to establish the link between the two. It is concerned with both modern culture and ancient tradition. It attempts to assimilate the findings of psychology and the social sciences while rediscovering the classical wisdom of the past. At the same time that it attempts to integrate its own resources—present and past—it reaches out toward the spiritualities of the East and towards a future which is evolving in the direction of global consciousness. It is here that the present renaissance may have its greatest significance, for it is precisely in the area of spirituality that the convergence of religions is being most strongly felt and systematically cultivated.

SPIRITUALITY AND THEOLOGY

What does this renaissance mean for theology? If theology grows out of the life of the Christian community, then contemporary theology should reflect developments in spirituality and be enriched by spirituality. In a basic way, spirituality is experiential; it is bound up with praxis, specifically orthopraxis. As such, it should provide material for theological reflection. At the same time, spirituality should be enriched and guided by theology. In this book I am viewing spirituality as experience with all the complexity described above, and theology as the reflection on experience. Spirituality should be situated within the experience of faith, as a significant dimension of the total faith-experience. For it involves our experience of growth in the life of the Spirit, that is, growth in the life of faith towards that goal of union with the Triune God that faith points out for us. Since growth is the central experience, the journey has been a primary symbol in spiritual literature, which has charted the stages of the journey, the role of the spiritual guide, and the praxis which leads to the goal. Out of this literature has grown a separate division of theology, which in the Middle Ages was called *theologia mystica* and more recently in Catholic seminary training by the title: ascetical and mystical theology. In this sense, spirituality is a branch of theology like moral theology. However, I am not focusing on this meaning of the term spirituality, but rather on the more basic experiential meaning which includes praxis; and I am taking theology to mean primarily dogmatic-systematic theology, although indirectly I am including the other branches of theology, viewed as reflection on the total experience of faith.

Seen in this way, can contemporary spirituality be a resource for theology? Can spirituality help theology move into the Second Axial

Period? My answer is an emphatic yes, but I must make certain qualifications. First, if we prescind from liberation theology, spirituality has not as yet had a significant influence on theology. Although there are many academic programs of spirituality on campuses, they have not produced a proportioned impact on theology. Can contemporary spirituality have such an impact? There is reason to doubt that it can. The trends are diverse and diffuse; they often lack depth; where they are strong, they lack direct channels into theology. The greatest task for contemporary spirituality is to acquire depth and maturity by grounding itself in its spiritual roots, by appropriating the wisdom of its classical heritage. Its second task is to relate itself to contemporary culture—to psychology, sociology and the praxis of the secular world—assimilating with discernment the resources offered by secular wisdom. Thirdly, it must open itself creatively to the East, drawing upon this ancient wisdom and viewing itself as a partner in the spiritual quest of humankind. If it can achieve this threefold task, it can be a major vehicle in developing a new systematic theology of the Second Axial Period, which, while being firmly rooted in its own historical identity, will take into account the total experience of humankind: Eastern as well as Western, secular as well as sacred.

If spirituality is to influence theology today, we must break down the barriers that have kept them apart. To do this we must understand the history that has shaped their relationship—at times in intimacy, at times in isolation, at times in antagonism. The ferment today in spirituality has it counterparts in the past. In the early thirteenth century, poverty movements gave birth to the new mendicant orders, which deeply influenced the rise of university theology. In the fourteenth century, spiritual movements abounded, specially in the Rhineland and the low Countries. These, however, had little influence on university theology since the latter had developed in a direction far removed from the spiritual experience at the base of patristic and early medieval theology. The tension between spirituality and academic theology was felt at the very founding of the universities in Western culture. What began as a tension soon became a split and eventually an abyss. By the later Middle Ages, the abstract speculation of the schools had drifted far from its experiential moorings. To this day, it is doubtful if this split has been healed. Throughout the centuries, we have been reenacting the stages of the drama of the antagonism between academic theology and spiritual experience. The tension as first was produced by Aristotelian philosophy, then nominalism, in the nineteenth and twentieth centuries by Biblical criticism, scientific historical studies, and more recently, by the social sciences.

In the light of this perennial tension, I will examine three periods in the past where harmony existed between spirituality and theology. From each period I will draw a specific example of how spirituality served as a resource for Christology. In subsequent chapters I will explore these examples in greater detail. In the present context, I am highlighting the significance of spirituality for theological method, especially in the area of Christology, for Christology is an area of controversy today. Spirituality has much to say to this controversy, for it can call attention to the experiential base of theology, which has been largely overlooked; secondly, it can draw enormous riches from the past which have unfortunately been ignored. Throughout the history of Christianity great spiritual writers have deeply experienced the mystery of Christ and have channelled this experience into their theology. By seeing spirituality as a resource for theology, we can appropriate this richness for our needs today. I am presenting these three case studies, then, not as museum pieces from a dead past, but as dynamic, living resources for the present: as examples of the historical retrieval of tradition in Leclercq's sense. By drawing upon the spiritual resources of our past, we can deepen our theology in the present, enabling ourselves to enter more creatively into the emerging global spirituality of the Second Axial Period.

I will begin with the early patristic period, in which Christian theology remained closely linked with spirituality. Influenced by Greek culture, Christian spirituality took the form of a *gnosis*, a way of knowledge and wisdom. Into this spiritual quest it incorporated the emerging philosophy of Neoplatonism. Drawing also from Biblical sources, it blended these elements to produce Christian theology in the East and the West. Thus at an early stage a link was forged between spiritual experience, philosophy, theology, and mysticism which persisted through the Pseudo-Dionysius and into the Rhineland mystics. In Augustine, we find the classic example of this integration in the patristic period of the West. In the context of Augustine's Neoplatonic spirituality, I will explore his experience of Christ as the interior Teacher of Wisdom.

The second period under examination will be the early Middle ages in the West, characterized by what Jean Leclercq has identified as monastic theology.[40] This is a spiritually based, experiential theology, deeply rooted in the monastic lifestyle of liturgy, *lectio divina*, contemplation and the symbolic interpretation of Scripture. Monastic theology contrasts sharply with the scholastic theology developed in the medieval universities in the thirteenth century. This monastic theology reached its climax in the Cistercian movement of the twelfth century, especially in the experiential theology of

Bernard of Clairvaux. For my case study of Christology, I will draw from Bernard's experience of Christ as interior Lover, which he explored through a symbolic interpretation of the Song of Songs.

The third period to be explored will be the thirteenth century, when devotion to the humanity of Christ emerged in the West in the Franciscan movement. This devotion to Christ's humanity had an enormous impact on the latter Middle Ages and subsequent history. It led to *The Imitation of Christ* and to *The Spiritual Exercises* of Ignatius of Loyola. In its early phase this Christ-centered spirituality was closely linked to theology, which it significantly influenced. For my case study, I will draw from Bonaventure's Franciscan devotion to the humanity of Christ, which led to a transformation of his Trinitarian theological perspective into one of the most Christocentric visions in the history of theology.

NEOPLATONIC SPIRITUALITY

It is a commonplace that Christian theology was born out of a meeting of the Judaic-Christian experience with Greek philosophy. What is not so widely acknowledged is that at the beginning of Christianity, Greek philosophy itself was taking the form of a spiritual journey, a quest for spiritual wisdom. As Louis Bouyer states, "When Christianity was born, the Greek philosophies were turning into religious philosophies. They tended to go on, as by an irresistible transition, from the search for truth to the search for salvation; or, to put it another way, the 'truth' that they were seeking at this period was precisely 'salvation.'"[41] This search for knowledge and wisdom was developed by Clement of Alexandria and his pupil Origen as a Christian *gnosis*. In the Greek spirit, it was a search for truth, for *logos* which opened up to the infinite, incomprehensible divine Logos. In his *17th Homily on Numbers*, Origen states:

> For those who labor at Wisdom and gnosis, as there is no end to their efforts—for where will be the limit of the Wisdom of God?—the more we approach it, the more depths we discover; the more we examine it, the more we understand its ineffable and incomprehensible character; for the Wisdom of God is incomprehensible and inestimable.[42]

Outside of the Christian community, the philosophical journey was being shaped by Plotinus into a mystical ascent. This Neoplatonic philosophy-spirituality flowed into Christianity, becoming the common matrix of both Christian theology and the Christian spiritual journey. This fact is crucial for developing a typology of Christian spirituality and mysticism. Running through the history of Christianity is a highly speculative spirituality, which cannot adequately be separated from speculative mysticism. A speculative mystical ascent is found, for example, in Origen, Gregory of Nyssa, and the Pseudo-Dionysius; in Augustine, Bonaventure, and the Rhineland mystics. In fact, there is reason to claim that the most characteristic form of Christian mysticism is speculative. Such a claim undercuts the widespread assumption that spirituality deals exclusively with affectivity or devotion, or is concerned merely with growth processes, devoid of any intellectual content. On the contrary, intellectual reflection is precisely the praxis of this form of spirituality. The ascent is through speculation (*speculatio*, in the Latin term).[43] The journey is a journey of the soul, it is true, but the path is through intellect.

What is the experience at the base of this spirituality? It is the experience of the intellectual perception of truth, which is sought through the praxis of intellectual contemplation. Such a praxis does not consist of merely abstracting universal concepts or exercising technical reason. On the contrary, it plunges much deeper into the intellectual realm through a mystical intuition of *logos*, which experiences truth as light, as ultimate reality itself shining in the mind. This intellectual *praxis* of metaphysical and epistemological contemplation has its counterpart in Oriental spirituality: for example, in *jnana* yoga, and the spiritual path of Hindu vedanta, especially the non-dualism of Śankara.

In this praxis, spirituality and systematic theology coincide; for they share the common path of intellectual contemplation. In this praxis also, experience and reflection coincide, making spirituality a resource for theology and theology a resource for spirituality. A graphic example of this spiritual praxis can be found in Augustine's journey into his soul, where he found the light of Christ as Truth shining in his mind.

AUGUSTINE'S EXPERIENCE: CHRIST WITHIN

At the beginning of his conversion, Augustine turned his gaze within his soul, as he describes in Book VII of *The Confessions*:[44] "I was admonished by all this to return to my own self, and, with you to guide me, I entered into the innermost part of myself, and I was able to do this because you were my helper." His inner journey was inspired, he tells us, by his reading the books of the Platonists.[45] Within his soul Augustine perceived an unchangeable light: "I entered and I saw with my soul's eye (such as it was) an unchange-

able light shining above this eye of my soul and above my mind."
He identifies this light with God:

> It was higher than I, because it made me, and I was lower because I was
> made by it. He who knows truth knows that light, and he who knows
> that light knows eternity. Love knows it. O eternal truth and true love
> and beloved eternity! You are my God; to you I sigh by day and by
> night.[46]

Not only was Augustine's perception intellectual, but the praxis
by which he arrived at it was also intellectual. Again in *The Confessions*, he probed his mind and asked himself, "what criterion I
had to make a correct judgment of changing things and to say: 'this
is as it should be, this is not.'"[47] When he considered how he
came to make these judgments, he again "discovered that above my
changing mind was the unchangeable and true eternity of truth."
He then went by stages, as he said, from sensation to the soul and
to intellect, until finally "in the flash of a trembling glance, my mind
arrived at that which Is." By means of a similar praxis he and his
mother together made an intellectual ascent in the mystical experience they shared at Ostia shortly before her death:

> Then, with our affections burning still more strongly toward the Self-
> same, we raised ourselves higher and step by step passed over all material
> things, even the heaven itself from which sun and moon and stars
> shine down upon the earth. And still we went upward, meditating and
> speaking and looking with wonder beyond our souls to reach that region
> of never failing plenty where *Thou feedest Israel* forever with the food of
> truth and where life is that Wisdom by whom all things are made. . . .
> And as we talked, yearning toward this Wisdom, we did, with the
> whole strength of our heart impulse, just lightly come into touch with
> her, and we sighed and we left bound there *the first fruits of the Spirit.*[48]

Augustine identifies the unchangeable light of Truth specifically
with Christ as Logos. His treatise *On the Teacher* is oriented to
showing that Christ is the Teacher within: *Christus intus docet* (Christ
teaches within).[49] As the Word of the Father in the Trinity, the Son
is the total expression of Truth. As the light of Truth shining in the
minds of all human persons, Christ is the Teacher, through whose
illumination we know whatever we know. By following the light
of this Truth, the guidance of this Teacher, we grow in Wisdom,
for he himself is the fulness of divine Wisdom. For Augustine, then,
the spiritual journey is a path into the human mind, using the mind
itself as the vehicle of the journey; but instead of remaining in the
finite dimensions of the mind, the journey leads to that point where
God is more intimate to him than he is to himself. The unchangeable
light of Truth interpenetrates his changing mind; Christ as Logos

resides within the very structures of his consciousness, teaching him Truth and guiding him in Wisdom, even when he is not aware of Christ's presence. This experience of Christ in the mind is integrally spiritual, philosophical, theological, and mystical. Here in the depths of the mind spirituality and theology coincide. Between the experience and thought there is no gap, no separation; for the experience is of the divine Thought, who is the personal expression of the Father.

MONASTIC THEOLOGY

We turn now from the patristic period to the period of monastic theology. As with Clement of Alexandria, Origen, and Augustine, spirituality and theology interpenetrated in this monastic period. However, the tone of monastic theology was less speculative than that nourished directly by Neoplatonic philosophy. Jean Leclercq has identified the theology of this period as "monastic" to distinguish it from the later scholastic theology. It developed in the West in the Benedictine monasteries of the early Middle Ages and reached a high point in the Cistercian milieu of the twelfth century, especially in the work of Bernard of Clairvaux.[50] According to Leclercq, monastic theology appears more and more to be a prolongation of patristic theology.[51] It developed its distinctive form from the spirituality pursued in the monastic environment. As Leclercq says, "In the cloister, theology is studied in relation to monastic experience, a life of faith led in the monastery where religious thought and spiritual life, the pursuit of truth and the quest for perfection must go hand in hand and permeate each other."[52]

The fundamental characteristic of monastic theology is that it is based on experience, specifically the experience of spirituality. "A certain experience of the realities of faith," Leclercq writes, "a certain 'lived faith,' is at one and the same time the condition for the result of monastic theology."[53] This experience is cultivated within the monastic environment and through the praxis of the monastic lifestyle. According to Leclercq, "monastic speculation is the outgrowth of the practice of monastic life, the living of the spiritual life which is the meditation of Holy Scripture."[54] As part of its contemplative praxis, monastic theology draws from Scripture, not for proof texts or for scientific exegesis, but to discover its spiritual meaning, which can be tapped for spiritual growth. The specific techniques of this praxis are meditative reading called *lectio divina* and the symbolic interpretation of Scripture on the three levels of spiritual meaning: the allegorical, the moral, and the anagogic. In characterizing monastic theology, Leclercq states: "Everything comes back finally to a problem of spirituality; what is important is the way in which the work of salvation becomes one's possession of his or her interior life."[55]

This rich orientation towards spiritual experience stands in sharp contrast to the attitude of scholastic theology towards experience. Scholastic theology, according to Leclercq, "puts experience aside. It can subsequently hark back to experience, observe that it agrees with its own reasonings, and that it can even receive nourishment from them; but its reflection is not rooted in experience and is not necessarily directed towards it."[56]

Reflection on spiritual experience issues in monastic theology. The type of knowledge the monk was seeking did not differ from that sought in the practice of Greek *gnosis* which we explored in our previous section. Leclercq observes:

> On the whole, the monastic approach to theology, the kind of religious understanding the monks are trying to attain, might better be described by reviving the word *gnosis*—on condition naturally that no heterodox nuance be given it. The Christian *gnosis*, the 'true *gnosis*' in its original fundamental and orthodox meaning, is that kind of higher knowledge which is the complement, the fruition of faith and which reaches completion in prayer and contemplation.[57]

BERNARD: CHRIST AS INTERIOR LOVER

In Bernard of Clairvaux, monastic theology achieved its most eloquent expression. In his *Sermons on the Song of Songs*, he drew together the main themes of monastic theology, presenting a comprehensive treatise on spiritual growth by means of the symbolic interpretation of Scripture. His focus was on experience, affectivity, and Christ as the Bridegroom of the soul, the interior Lover who at the height of the spiritual ascent embraces the soul with "the kiss of the mouth."[58]

In his *Sermons on the Song of Songs*, Bernard takes his point of departure from the opening verse: "let him kiss me with the kiss of the mouth."[59] In monastic fashion he tells his monks who form his audience: "Today the text we are to study is the book of our own experience."[60] But he reads the book of his experience in the light of the book of Scripture, which he interprets symbolically in order to evoke and deepen his experience. In the classical tradition of Origen's commentary, he interprets the bride as the soul and the bridegroom as Christ. He explains his approach in an eloquent passage:

"Let him kiss me with the kiss of his mouth," she said. Now who is this "she"? The bride. But why bride? Because she is the soul thirsting for God. In order to clarify for you the characteristics of the bride, I shall deal briefly with the diverse affective relationships between persons. Fear motivates a slave's attitude to his master, gain that of a wage-earner to his employer, the learner is attentive to his teacher, the son is respectful to his father. But the one who asks for a kiss, she is a lover. Among all our natural endowments love holds first place, especially when it is directed to God, who is the source whence it comes. No sweeter names can be found to embody that sweet interflow of affections between the Word and the soul, than bridegroom and bride.[61]

Bernard leads the soul through three kisses: the kiss of the feet, the kiss of the hands, and the kiss of the mouth. These kisses symbolize the three stages of the spiritual life; purgative, illuminative, and unitive. For the kiss of the feet symbolizes conversion, repentance, and humility; the kiss of the hands, growth in virtue; the kiss of the mouth, mystical union with Christ the Beloved. This final stage Bernard describes from his own experience:

I confess to you I have many times received the visits of the Word. I could not perceive the exact moment of his arrival. He did not enter by the senses, but whence did he come? Perhaps he did not enter at all, for he who enters comes from without. But I found him closer to me than I to myself. How can I perceive his presence within me? It is full of life and efficacy, and no sooner has he entered than my sluggish soul is awakened. He moves and warms and wounds my heart, hard and stony and sick though it may be. It is solely by the movement of my heart that I understand that he is there, and I realize the power of his action when I see my evil tendencies disappear and my carnal affections quieted. . . . Once he leaves, everything falls back into slumber, all grows cold like a boiling pot of oil withdrawn from the fire.[62]

What does this mean for theology, specifically for Christology? It means the Christ is in the depths of the soul, at the roots of our subjectivity, and the very center of our person. This is not primarily the incarnate Christ, but Christ as Logos, who penetrates our being with his presence and at times manifests himself in his power and love. Augustine finds Christ as Truth in the structure of the mind; Bernard finds Christ as love in the dynamics of our affectivity. With Augustine through the praxis of *gnosis*, we can reach this ground and be united to it as Truth and Wisdom. With Bernard through the praxis of love, we can reach this ground and be embraced by it in a union that is best described as a mystical marriage.

Both contemporary spirituality and contemporary theology can be enriched by Augustine and Bernard. For example, contemporary spirituality has been deeply influenced by depth psychology, from which it has drawn many resources. Yet depth psychology has set limits beyond which it will not pass; except for C.G. Jung, psychology has not explored the presence of the Christ archetype in the soul. Contemporary spirituality has been reticent; it has failed to take the lead and plunge boldly into the depths of interiority where Augustine and Bernard have discovered Christ. Perhaps it has held back because theology has not offered guidance. How many centuries have passed since theologians have seriously studied the mystery of Christ as interior Teacher and as interior Lover. If Christianity is to have a significant encounter with Oriental traditions, which for millennia have exercised varieties of a sophisticated praxis of interiority, it cannot ignore its own heritage which sees Christ at the very center of interiority.

DEVOTION TO THE HUMANITY OF CHRIST

In the history of Christianity one of the most significant developments was the emergence of devotion to the humanity of Christ during the High Middle Ages. Rooted in the West's sensitivity to the particular, the historical, and the human, this devotion developed comparatively late in the history of Christianity. In the first millennium, Christ as Logos, as Pantocrator, and Risen Savior dominated art, spirituality, and theology. Through the centuries in Western Europe, devotion to Christ's humanity germinated slowly. It was nourished by pilgrimages, by shrines housing relics, by the religious motivation of the crusades: to recapture the Holy Places where Jesus was born, walked the roads, preached, suffered, and died. Relics of Jesus's historical existence were brought triumphantly to Europe: the true cross, the crown of thorns.

In the twelfth century within the monastic ethos, the focus of spirituality began to center on the human Christ, as can be seen in the *Meditations* attributed to Anselm and in Bernard of Clairvaux's cultivation of "the carnal love of Christ." However, it was Francis of Assisi who brought this devotion to its full flowering in the thirteenth century. Inspired to imitate Christ as fully as possible, Francis embraced what he discerned to be the Gospel lifestyle of radical poverty. With tenderness and charm, he awakened devotion to the infant Jesus by creating a crib at midnight Mass at Greccio in 1223. Devotion to Christ's passion received its most dramatic expression when in 1224, two years before his death, Francis received the gift of the stigmata, the first recorded case in history.

The praxis of this devotion consisted of meditating on the historical events of Christ's life in such a way that one imagined the scene, entering into it as an actor in the drama. Out of this would come consciousness of Christ's virtues to be imitated in one's own life. Examples of this meditation can be found in Bonaventure's *The Tree of Life*, and the *Meditations on the Life of Christ*, formerly attributed to Bonaventure. Influenced by this tradition through the latter work, Ignatius of Loyola imparted to the praxis an organized method and detailed techniques. This praxis of meditation overflowed to a praxis of action: for example, the choice of the religious life, radical poverty, apostolic work. In such cases the ultimate motivation was always the imitation of Christ, especially compassion for the suffering Savior.

The relation of this devotion to theology is complex. It arose at the very time that scholastic theology developed in the universities. The split between spiritual experience and academic theology was, in fact, widened by its emergence. The human emotions of tenderness and compassion, cultivated by the devotion, were even farther removed from the abstractions of the universities than was the mystical affectivity of monastic spirituality. There was, however, an exception in the early Franciscan school. Although based at the University of Paris, the early Franciscan theologians—Alexander of Hales and Bonaventure—were nourished by the twelfth-century monastic theology of the Victorines and Bernard of Clairvaux. In the case of Bonaventure, Franciscan devotion to the humanity of Christ was assimilated into his academic theology, issuing in a comprehensive Christocentric vision. In the next generation, this Franciscan devotion reached a high level of theological formulation in Duns Scotus's affirmation of the primacy of the incarnate Christ in creation.

BONAVENTURE: CHRIST THE CENTER

It is interesting to trace the evolution of Christocentricity in Bonaventure's theology. His first period, at the University of Paris, is marked by a blending of monastic theology and the scholastic method. Strongly influenced by Augustine and the twelfth-century monastic theology of the Victorines, he developed a comprehensive theological system based on a dynamic notion of the Trinity and Platonic exemplarism. There is little emphasis on the humanity of Christ in shaping this vision. However, in his second period, when he composed his spiritual works, Francis and the devotion to the humanity have a central role, although he does not integrate this systematically into his theology. The turning point of his life came

when he went to the mountain of La Verna in 1259. While meditating on the vision which Francis had seen thirty-six years before
when he received the stigmata in that very place, he grasped its
symbolic meaning. This was a vision of a six-winged Seraph in the
form of the Crucified. The image of Christ crucified penetrated
Bonaventure's spirituality. He saw it as the gateway into the spiritual
journey. In the prologue of his treatise *The Soul's Journey into God*,
he writes: "There is no other path but through the burning love of
the Crucified. . . . This love so absorbed the soul of Francis that his
spirit shone through his flesh when for two years before his death
he carried in his body the sacred stigmata of the passion."[63] Shortly
after writing this, he composed his series of meditations on the life
of Christ entitled *The Tree of Life*, where meditation on the humanity
of Christ, with emphasis on the passion, is the gateway into growth
in the life of virtue. During the same period, he composed his
biography of Francis in which he presented his patron as a most
intimate imitator of Christ, precisely through his humanity.

In the third period, when he was engaged in controversies over
Averroism at the University of Paris, the humanity of Christ transformed the structure of his theological system. Christ now becomes
central; in fact, he uses the notion of Christ the center (*Christus
medium*) as the architectonic paradigm for his final theological *summa*:
The Collations on the Hexaëmeron. In the first of these lectures, which
serves as an overture for a series of more than twenty lectures, he
develops the theme: Christ the Center of All the Sciences (*Christus
medium omnium scientiarum*). Christ is the metaphysical center, the
physical center, the mathematical center, the logical center, the ethical center, the political center, the theological center. As center of
these sciences, he is the center of the total reality studied by these
sciences.

Christ is the metaphysical center in his eternal generation. Bonaventure refers to him as the central or middle person in the Trinity
(*persona media*). Through exemplarism, we all come forth from this
center, reflect this center, and return to this center. Therefore, Bonaventure observes, each one of us should say:

> Lord, I have gone forth from you, who are supreme; I come to you,
> who are supreme, and through you, who are supreme. This is the
> metaphysical center that leads us back, and this is our whole metaphysics:
> emanation, exemplarity, and consummation; that is, to be illumined by
> spiritual rays and to be led back to the supreme height. Thus you will
> be a true metaphysician.[64]

Christ is the physical center in his incarnation, since as a human
person he is the microcosm of the physical world, embodying in

himself the realms of the inorganic, vegetable, animal, and rational. He is the mathematical center in his crucifixion. Just as the mathematician measures extremes, Christ measured the extremes of humility and suffering to bring about our redemption. "How great is the divine wisdom," Bonaventure states, "which worked out our salvation through the ashes of humility. For when the center of a circle is lost, it can be found only by two lines intersecting at right angles."[65]

Christ is the logical center in his resurrection. He is the middle term of a cosmic syllogism, linking the divine and the human. Bonaventure envisions a debate between Christ and Satan on the model of a scholastic disputation. Satan has deceived Adam with his deceptive logic, promising life and giving death. Christ subsumes the minor premise of Satan's syllogism, transforming its destructive logic into a creative conclusion. Out of his death on the cross, he brings forth the conclusion of his resurrection.

Christ is the ethical center in his ascension, since he leads us with him back to heaven through a life of virtue. He is the political or juridical center in his final judgment, for then he will establish the order of justice in the universe. Finally he is the theological center in the beatific vision, for he is the middle person in the Trinity, who draws us back to union with the Father.

Around the notion of Christ the center, Bonaventure has constructed an entire theological vision, which he proceeds to examine in detail throughout the subsequent lectures. He has produced one of the most thorough-going Christocentric systems in the history of Christian theology. But what is more significant for our purposes is the fact that this system was shaped by his devotion to the humanity of Christ. A spiritual-mystical devotion to Christ's humanity has led him to see the entire universe in Christocentric terms. Into this vision he integrates explicitly Augustine's experience of Christ the interior Teacher and Bernard's experience of Christ the interior Lover. For Bonaventure the humanity of Christ is not separated from Christ the Logos or the cosmic Christ.

This is a crucial point for contemporary spirituality and contemporary theology, which have focused heavily on the humanity of Christ. But both have a tendency to see the humanity in isolation from the other aspects of the mystery of Christ. Unlike the case of the interior Christ, there has been in Teilhard de Chardin a contemporary spokesman for a cosmic Christocentricity not unlike that of Bonaventure. However, in Teilhard's case, it is precisely the historical Jesus, in his humanity, that is not adequately treated in his theological vision. On this point, both contemporary spirituality and contemporary theology can learn from the early Franciscan movement, where devotion to the humanity of Christ was the very path into the fulness of the mystery of Christ.

CHALLENGE TO SPIRITUALITY AND THEOLOGY

In the light of these three examples, we can now return to the question: Can spirituality—as experience and praxis—provide resources from theology? Contemporary spirituality and theology can learn from those periods in the past when creative energy flowed harmoniously between the two. The three areas of spiritual experience which we have studied—drawn from Augustine, Bernard, and Bonaventure—provide resources, it is true, but first they present challenges. They challenge contemporary spirituality to deepen itself, by rooting itself more firmly in its classical heritage, thus appropriating to itself more abundantly the riches of the Christian experience. They challenge contemporary theology to examine its presuppositions so that it can more readily open itself to spiritual experience as a resource for its own enterprises. More specifically, they challenge contemporary Christology to become more experiential: to break out of the narrow confines of its current horizons and open itself to the breadth and the length, the height and the depth of the Christian experience of the mystery of Christ. This is all the more urgent now as Christianity faces the power of the Hindu and Buddhist experiences.

If contemporary spirituality and theology can respond to these challenges, then spirituality indeed can be a resource for theology and lead to the emergence of new meaning in theology. What that meaning will be is yet to be manifested. Yet the lines are already clear; it will be global, encompassing world religions, subsuming into itself all the multi-dimensional aspects of the secular world and the human. Theology cannot respond to the overwhelming tasks of the Second Axial Period without the creative energies that surge from spirituality.

IV

Panikkar: The Systematic Theology
of the Future

In the last chapter we traveled back into the past, using history to tap the spiritual resources for the future. In this chapter we will project ourselves into the future, into the Second Axial Period, in order to get a glimpse of the systematic theology of the future. At this point, we can see only certain lines of development, identify directions, extend our horizons. Perhaps the best way to proceed is to examine, as a case study, the thought of a person who has already made the leap into the future and who has begun to create a systematic theology for the complexified, global consciousness of the Second Axial Period. There is sound methodological reason for proceeding in this way; for if we are in a mutational moment, as Leclercq discerns, within a larger shift in the forces of convergence towards planetization, then it would be wise to search out those who have already made the "quantum leap" into the future. There is reason to claim that in a mutational world there is no present—only a gap or an abyss where the present would be if we were in a continuous evolutionary phase. Some are lost irrevocably in the past; others—a few extraordinary personalities—already live in the future. The rest fluctuate between the past and the future, not knowing where they are. Among those who have made the transition, some become the mediators of the future for the others who can make the passage. These spiritual mutants may return from the future to draw others from the past across the abyss of the present and into the world of the future. I suggest that Raimundo Panikkar is such a spiritual mutant, one in whom the global mutation has already occurred and in whom the new forms of consciousness have been concretized. What are the characteristics of such mutational persons? First of all, they are cross-cultural, for in them the great cultural traditions—formerly distinct through their diverse historical origin and development—now converge, making these mutants heirs, for the first time in history, to the spiritual heritage of

humankind. As such, they become multi-dimensional, for they com-
bine the polarities of the East and the West, outer and inner consciousness, science and mysticism, mythic and rational thinking,
pragmatic involvement in the world and spiritual detachment.[1]

MULTI-DIMENSIONAL PERSON

Panikkar clearly fits such a description. His thought presents a complex challenge. It has remarkable depth; his sentences are like
entrances to the shaft of a mine, drawing the reader to treasures
below. Dynamic with playfulness and power, full of bubbling joy
and cascading energy, it covers a breathtaking range—encompassing
many disciplines, the entire globe, and the sweep of history. By
birth he is cross-cultural, being the son of an Indian, Hindu father
and a Spanish, Roman Catholic mother; and he has attempted to
assimilate the fulness of these traditions into his personality. In his
professional training and career he is a multi-dimensional man, for
he is a natural scientist and a spiritual teacher, a philosopher and a
man of prayer, a phenomenologist of religion and a theologian,
sensitive to mystical intuition and skilled in rational speculation.

He holds three doctorates: in science, philosophy, and theology.
In science he specialized in chemistry, studying at the University of
Barcelona and the University of Bonn, completing his Ph.D. at the
University of Madrid in 1958. His doctorate in philosophy is like-
wise from the University of Madrid, 1946; and his doctorate in
theology from the Lateran University, Rome, 1961, with a dissertation on the relation of Christianity to Hinduism.

In 1946 he was ordained a Roman Catholic priest and is presently
attached to the diocese of Varanasi, India. In 1955 he went to India
to search out his cultural roots and to study Indian philosophy and
religion. From 1967 to 1971 he was Visiting Professor of Comparative Religion at the Center for the Study of World Religions, Harvard University; and from 1971 until his retirement in 1987 he was
Professor of Comparative Philosophy and History of Religions in
the Department of Religious Studies of the University of California
at Santa Barbara. In addition to holding these positions, he has
taught and lectured in many universities throughout the world: in
Europe, Asia, North and South America. Since coming to the
United States in 1967, he has retained close ties with the East,
spending at least half of most years in India. Since his retirement
from teaching in 1987, he has resided in the village of Tavertet,
north of Barcelona. Although he has devoted his time chiefly to

writing, he has participated in many conferences and given many lectures around the world.

Panikkar has published some thirty books and over seven hundred articles. His work falls into three overlapping areas: the history of religions, theology, and hermeneutics. His achievement in these areas, he observes, is in large measure supported by his earlier work in metaphysics and science. In the history of religions, he has taken up the task of making available for cross-cultural understanding the philosophical and religious traditions of India. Some thirty-five years ago he conceived a monumental project to produce, through the collaboration of many specialists, a Handbook of Fundamental Terms of the Indian Tradition, containing over 1,000 entries of terms drawn from Indian philosophy and religion. Although under his guidance the contents of the work were determined, the contributions identified, and the methodology specified, he since made this material available for another project which is being published through the Indian government. However, his *The Vedic Experience*[2] can be seen in the context of this larger project since it brings to cross-cultural light a major stratum of Indian religious consciousness. In the field of theology, he has pioneered in interpreting Christian doctrines in an interreligious context. The first of his major publications in this vein was his doctoral thesis at the Lateran University: *The Unknown Christ of Hinduism*.[3] Another seminal book is *The Trinity and the Religious Experience of Man*.[4] Together they lay the groundwork for a comprehensive Christian systematic theology that not only takes into account other religions but is profoundly enriched by them. His theology is simultaneously experiential and speculative. It is rooted in religious experience, tapping the wellsprings of Christian spirituality at a point that can make contact with the depths of Eastern spirituality. This wealth of spiritual experience is then reflected upon with his rare gift for metaphysical speculation that draws from both the mainstream of Western European philosophy and the great philosophical traditions of the East.

The question of hermeneutics permeates the entire corpus of Panikkar's writings. Because of his cross-cultural experience, he has been acutely aware of the limits of Western thought. Although trained in contemporary European hermeneutics, he has constantly warned against applying uncritically Western principles of interpretation to the diverse religious experience of humankind. He has urged scholars to penetrate to the depth of religious experience—in its diversity—before beginning to interpret; and he has cautioned against a superficial 'translation' across cultural and experiential boundaries.

On the practical level, he has set guidelines for interreligious dialogue; on the theoretical level, he has attempted to develop a cross-cultural, interreligious hermeneutic. A major forum for the latter enterprise has been the prestigious Castelli conference on hermeneutics, at the University of Rome, which since 1961 has attracted the leading specialists in hermeneutics from European universities. A founding father of the conference, Panikkar has participated in almost all of the sessions. In that setting he has produced a series of papers which form a basis for his comprehensive cross-cultural hermeneutics. Two of his books on the subject are: *The Intrareligious Dialogue*[5] and *Myth, Faith and Hermeneutics.*[6]

One might be tempted to call Panikkar a Renaissance person because of the broad scope of his intellectual cultivation and professional competence. But this would be anachronistic since the Renaissance was a regional mutation within Western culture. The present mutation is global and calls for a new type of Renaissance person: a cross-cultural, multi-dimensional personality who has appropriated the complex forms of consciousness not only of his or her own civilization but of the world and who already lives comfortably within a mutational context that has not yet fully taken shape.

Having identified Panikkar as mutational person, I will concentrate on his contribution to Christian systematic theology. As a crowning honor to an illustrious career, he was invited to deliver the prestigious Gifford Lectures in 1989. He is presently completing the manuscript which will be published by Orbis Press under the title *The Rhythm of Being: The Dwelling of the Divine in the Contemporary World.*

SYSTEMATIC THEOLOGY AT THE CROSSROADS

Where does Christian systematic theology stand at the present moment and what is its future? In the twentieth century we have witnessed a rich flowering of the genre of systematic theology in the great syntheses of Karl Barth, Paul Tillich, and Karl Rahner.[7] Each case represented a conscious attempt to recapture a vital tradition of Christianity— the Calvinist, the Lutheran, and the Roman Catholic—and to make it alive in the present, chiefly through the existentialist perspectives of Kierkegaard and Heidegger. These three syntheses were impressive analytic and synthetic achievements— massive architectonic theologies of the past.

Other theologies have emerged in the twentieth century which reflect many aspects of classical systematic theology. Teilhard de Chardin developed an evolutionary cosmology which became the systematic matrix for a reinterpretation of Christian belief, chiefly through the doctrine of the cosmic Christ. Christian process theologians adopted the metaphysics of Alfred North Whitehead and employed it for the systematic exploration of the Christian message in process categories. Marxist and Hegelian thought merged with Biblical eschatology to produce the theology of hope. In the third world the theology of liberation emerged out of the experience of the oppressed.[8]

When we look at the present theological scene, we might conclude that classical systematic theology has no future. There would be no need or impetus to repeat the great enterprises of Barth, Tillich, and Rahner. Since the sixties the theological mood, especially in the United States, has become more pluralistic. Furthermore, the Marxist influence on Christian theology has turned its concerns towards action and away from the speculative impulse needed to construct a classical systematic theology.

Granted this situation within Christian theology, what has happened outside its horizons opens the door to an unprecedented development of systematic theology. I am referring to the global mutation I described above. For the first time in history, the great religions of the world are meeting each other within a global environment. Christian theology must take this fact into account and ask itself what it means. Already Christian theology has attempted to relate itself positively to other religions by developing a theology of salvation history which encompasses world religions. An example of this outreach can be seen in Heinz Schlette's *Towards a Theology of Religions*.[9] Such a thrust is needed at the present time, but it is limited in scope for two reasons: it restricts itself to merely one aspect of Christian theology, namely divine providence in salvation history; and it makes no attempt to enter into the unique religious experiences of other traditions and to relate these in their uniqueness to Christianity. Rather it remains exclusively within the Christian experience and deals with all non-Christian religious experience in a uniformly universal way.

AN UNPRECEDENTED CHALLENGE

Christian systematic theology has a much deeper need and faces a much more demanding challenge. The encounter of world religions calls for the forging of a Christian systematic theology that will encompass within its horizons the religious experience of humankind. This global religious experience must be related to all the central Christian doctrines—not merely to salvation history as Schlette has done. This means that the Christian doctrines of the

Trinity, of Christ, and of redemption must be explored in such a way that they will be open to, in relation with, and enriched by the religious experience of humankind. This must be done not in a mere universalist and objectivist way, by standing within the Christian worldview, looking out from a distance upon Hinduism, Buddhism, and the other traditions and dealing with them all under the universal concept "religions." Rather, Christian theologians must reach out and enter into the very subjectivity of the other traditions in their distinct variety, and must bring this into the structure of a systematic theology.

This is an unprecedented task. Never before in the history of Christianity has this challenge been raised. When Christian systematic theology was born in the second and third centuries, it emerged out of the Hebrew, Greek, and Roman religious cultural environment of the Mediterranean world. It took shape in the Greek East and in the Latin West with a common Greek philosophical base but with the distinct characteristics of Greek and Roman cultures. The genre of systematic theology grew in logical precision and architectonic structure with the development of scholasticism in the Western Middle Ages. Peter Lombard assembled his *sententiae* into an organized structure which became the basis for commentaries for more than two centuries. Concurrent with the commentaries there emerged the genre of the *summa theologiae*. Alexander Hales was a seminal figure in its development in the early thirteenth century leading the way to the classical *summa* of Thomas Aquinas.[10] The Reformation brought a new Biblical grounding for the genre, and subsequent waves of philosophy provided new resources for developing the internal content of the system: through rationalism, idealism, and into the existentialism of the twentieth century.

All through this process Christian systematic theology has remained engulfed within Western culture and its intellectual history. Neither in its formative period nor in its subsequent history did it have a fruitful encounter with Hinduism, Buddhism, Taoism, Confucianism, or for that matter, with Islam. The only major religion that Christianity has formally related itself to is Judaism, from which it emerged—and the history of this relationship has been marred by distortion and tragedy. One can find traces of Greek and Roman religion in Christian theology and only indirect and negative reactions to Islam. To this day Christian theology remains uninfluenced and unenriched by the majority of world religions. This is no longer possible. Our enormous store of information drawn from the history of religions, our global communication network, and the recent influence of Eastern spiritual teachers in the West are effectively breaking the envelope of isolation that has for centuries encased Christian systematic theology. When Christian consciousness opens to global consciousness, a new type of systematic theology can be born. This new theology calls for a new kind of theologian with a new type of consciousness—a multi-dimensional, cross-cultural consciousness characteristic of the mutation of the Second Axial Period.

CHRIST AND WORLD RELIGIONS

In the past, when Christian theologians sought to universalize their vision, they have done so by interpreting Christology in its broadest lines. They have moved from the historical Jesus to the eternal Logos, who is present throughout the universe and history. In this way they were able to encompass within the Christian vision the entire physical universe and the unfolding of human history in its cultural and even religious diversity. By viewing Christ as eternal Logos, Christians could see all things as emanating from him, as expressing him, and as leading towards him. This is the case in the cosmic hymns of the New Testament: in the Johannine prologue and in Colossians.[11] Here Christ is the pre-existing Logos through whom all things have been made and in whom all things hold together. In the second and third centuries, when Christian belief encountered Greek philosophy, it was again Logos Christology that was the universalizing element. Justin Martyr spoke of Christ as "the Logos, in whom every race of humans has participated." Justin claimed that "all who have lived according to the Logos are Christians, even though, like Socrates and Heraclitus among the Greeks, they were considered atheists."[12] Clement of Alexandria claimed that Pythagoras and Plato were illlumined by the light of the eternal Logos, who burst into the world in his brilliance in the incarnate Christ.[13] In the West Augustine saw Christ as the "interior teacher," illumining the minds of all whenever they attain certitude.[14] In the Middle Ages, Bonaventure saw Christ illumining all of culture, both secular and religious: as eternal Word incarnate in history, Christ was the center of all the sciences and the archetype of all the mechanical arts.[15] In the twentieth century the cosmic and universalizing functions of Logos Christology have appeared in a new way in the thought of Teilhard de Chardin. For the Jesuit scientist, Christ is the Omega of evolution, drawing the entire universe to its ultimate development, from the least particle of matter to the expanded consciousness of the world community.[16]

To universalize through Logos Christology has been fruitful for Western culture since in the Graeco-Roman-Christian West both religion and general culture are based on logos—as word and thought. Furthermore, Christianity could relate itself to Judaism and differentiate itself from Islam through its doctrine of Christ as Word of the Father since both Judaism and Islam are founded on God's word revealed to man. But Christianity faces a different situation when it confronts the great religions of the East in anything more than an imperialistic way. For these religions do not have the same grounding in logos as Western culture or Judaism and Islam. When Christians dialogue with Buddhists and Hindus, they are confronted with new questions that did not arise at the time of Christianity's emergence out of Judaism, or its encounter with the Greek world in the second and third centuries, with Islam in the Middle Ages, with the American Indians in the age of exploration or with secular Western culture at the present time. In confronting the East, Christians have to ask themselves certain radical questions. They have to examine whether Christology, even in its universalized form, is the most viable bridge between West and East.

The problem shows itself most acutely in two doctrines of Eastern religion which not only have no grounding in logos, but negate it in such a way that all contact with logos seems lost. One is the Buddhist doctrine of nirvana and the other the advaitic Hindu doctrine of the non-duality of the self and the Absolute.[17] Buddhists have nothing to say about ultimate reality; they have received no word from the Absolute, and they formulate no word about it. They remain silent. Even their most profound experience and ultimate goal they call by the name *nirvāna*, etymologically a blowing out, and by the name of *śunyāta*, meaning emptiness or void. This causes their Western friends no little confusion and frustration. Are Buddhists atheists? Nihilists? For Buddhists consider not only logos irrelevant, but even deceptive and harmful—a burden to be discarded. And in discarding it, they seem to affirm nothingness and to negate the Christian's most cherished religious values. In the case of advaitic Hindus, who deny all duality in relation to the Absolute, Christians are also confused and frustrated. For the Hindus seem to be undercutting the autonomy of the person, upon which so many of Christianity's religious values are built. Even in the height of the mystical union, the Christian remains a distinct *I* in dialogue with God as *Thou*; God's personal revelation in the Old Testament and its climax in the person of Christ intensify the Christian's individuality and promises him or her personal immortality. Hence Christians are dismayed when the advaitic Hindu says that Brahman is one's ultimate self. To Christians this looks like pantheism—an undifferentiated union which melts into nothingness that autonomous personality of which Christ is the exemplar.

The problem is intensified by the fact that these two doctrines are not mere isolated opinions, nor do they hold a subordinate position in the respective systems. On the contrary, they epitomize the chief thrust of the entire spirituality; for they describe the goal of the spiritual journey. Therefore, they present a basic challenge to Christians, since they call into question the very possibility of Christians entering into ecumenical dialogue with two of the major spirituality traditions of the world. These two doctrines—the one by negation and the other by absorption—seem so opposed to the Christian Logos spirituality that Christians may feel that there is no way to relate to them, hence that dialogue is impossible. Or they may feel that dialogue is possible only on their own terms. If they do not demand religious conversion, nevertheless they might expect that Buddhists and Hindus recast their thought in modes that approximate Christianity. Or Christians may search their own tradition for elements that have at least some resonance with their Buddhism and Hinduism. If they follow this path, Christians will have to go beyond the universalizing tendencies of the past, which have been confined to the sphere of logos. To move from the incarnate historical Christ to the universal Logos will not be sufficient to contact traditions that are not grounded in logos. If Christians, then, are to move out of the limits of even universalized Logos, they must move into the fulness of the doctrine of the Trinity.

This is the suggestion of Panikkar, who poses the Trinity as a framework for Christians to relate to other religions. He describes three aspects of the divinity and three corresponding forms of spirituality: 1) the silent, apophatic dimension, which he relates to the Father, since the Father expresses himself only through the Son and of himself has no word or expression; 2) the personalistic dimension, which Panikkar relates to the Son, since the Son is the personal mediator between God and man, through whom creation, redemption, and glorification flow; and 3) the immanent dimension, which he relates to the Spirit, since the Spirit is the union of the Father and the Son. According to Panikkar the apophatic spirituality of the Father is similar to the Buddhist experience of nirvana. The personalist spirituality of the Son has its roots in Yahweh's revelation to the Jews, and from the Christian perspective, its completion in the person of Christ. The immanent spirituality of the Spirit has its resonance in the advaitic Hindu doctrine of the non-duality of the self and the Absolute.[18]

From Panikkar's perspective, then, one could in a most general fashion designate Buddhism as the religion of the Father, since the Buddhist moves to the experience of apophatic silence by negating the way of the word, of thought, of logos. In the Buddhist silence the Christian can glimpse a reflection of the depths of the Father, seen by prescinding from the generation of the Word. On the other hand, Judaism, Islam, and Christianity are religions of the Word, since they claim to have received a personal revelation from the divinity in words, images, and concepts. The Jew and Muslim see ultimate reality expressed in the word of God; and the Christian in the person of Christ, who is the personal Word of the Father. The Word of God, then, is personal and intensifies personality since it differentiates at the same time it unites. In contrast, the advaitic Hindu seeks undifferentiated union with the Absolute; in this he or she reflects the spirituality of the Spirit since the Spirit's work is primarily that of union. It is true that in Christianity the spirituality of the Spirit never appears in its pure form as in advaitic Hinduism, just as the spirituality of the Father never appears as in the pure apophatism of Buddhism. In Christianity, the Father and Spirit are united through the Word. The Father's silence comes to expression in the generation of the Word; and the Spirit leads Christians to a differentiated and dialogic union with the Son, and through the Son to the Father. Hence for Christians, the Word colors and integrates the spirituality of the Father and the Spirit. Both in their experience and understanding, the Christian's spirituality of the Father and that of the Spirit are always mediated by the Word. Nevertheless, Christians can glimpse through the Word the spiritual attitudes of the Buddhist and the Hindu as reflecting dimensions of their own Trinitarian spirituality.

I can remember the first time I met Panikkar. It was in the fall of 1967 at Fordham University. My colleague Thomas Berry invited me to lunch with a friend of his from India, as he said, whom he wanted me to meet. At that time I had not yet heard of Panikkar, who had just come from India to teach at Harvard University. When we met on the campus, I was immediately struck by Panikkar's warmth and vitality. We went to a nearby restaurant off campus and, as we were settling down at the table, he explained to me in about ten minutes his approach to world religions through the Trinity, which I have just summarized above.

I was thrilled with his position, which I saw as a major breakthrough in both the theology of the Trinity and interreligious dialogue. Since I had recently written a dissertation on the doctrine of the Trinity, I marveled at his technical precision and at what I thought was the most original outreach of twentieth-century theology. What impressed me most of all was his methodology. He did not look at Buddhism and Hinduism from outside—from a Western cultural and Christian standpoint. Quite the contrary! He began by identifying the characteristic horizon of consciousness of

Western culture and religion as that of logos; then through empathy he entered into the depth religious experiences of other traditions. This echoed my own first contact with non-Western culture some ten years before—with two American Indian tribes: the Pottawato-mie in Kansas and Sioux in South Dakota. I realized at the time that I could not merely translate their experience into my categories or filter their experience through mine. Although the experiences that Panikkar explored in Buddhism and Hinduism were different from the experience of the American Indians, I nevertheless recognized the validity and even necessity of his methodological approach.

By using the Trinity to approach other religions, we may, in Panikkar's terms, "discover a meeting ground for the religions based on these different spiritual attitudes without doing violence to their fundamental intuitions."[19] This is where Panikkar's proposal has special merit, for it provides a model of dialogue allowing for a pluralism that retains individuality while at the same time affirming a most profound unity. Whereas the Christological approach has an imperialistic tendency to reduce other forms to its own pattern, the Trinitarian approach is open to variety. The Trinitarian model of pluralism is not a class model, in which all individuals have to be fitted together under a least common denominator; nor is it an atomistic model, in which all individuals remain eternally aloof; nor is it a unitary model, in which all individuals are absorbed into a single one. Rather it is a model of unity in diversity, of profound interpenetration and yet individual identity. Although the Trinity is a Christian term and Christians rightly claim a uniqueness for their Trinitarian spirituality and understanding of the doctrine, the Trinity has a twofold universality: (1) it reflects essential aspects of the religious experience itself and so is found as a pattern throughout the world religions and philosophies; and (2) it provides an over-arching pattern for seeing in relationship the fundamental spiritual attitudes of humankind as these have been differentiated and made thematic in the major religions of the world. Against this back-ground, Christians can situate their Logos Christology and can face the complex question of the relation of their incarnational Christol-ogy to world religions. With the Trinity as a model, Christians can see the great spiritual traditions as dimensions of each other. They can realize that they may not know their own mystery of the Trinity until they have opened themselves to and responded in depth to the Trinitarian dimensions of other traditions. They may see further with Panikkar that "the meeting of religions—the *kairos* of our time—finds its deepest inspiration and its most certain hope in the trinitarian possibilities of the cosmic religions, in the striving of each towards the synthesis of these spiritual attitudes."[20]

Not only does Panikkar's Trinitarian approach provide a model for pluralistic dialogue, but it situates the dialogue primarily in the realm of spirituality and not in that of dogmatic formulation or metaphysical speculation. From the Christian point of view, this is paradoxical since in more recent times the doctrine of the Trinity has tended to lose contact with its roots in the Christian's spiritual life. By calling the Trinity back to its experiential roots, Panikkar not only vitalizes the Christian doctrine but draws it into its most fruitful contact with other traditions. "We have chosen to view our theme," he says, "from the point of view of spirituality, for it is in the spirituality of a religion that we come to its very heart."[21] Not only is spirituality at the heart of a religion, but it is there—on the level of spiritual experience—that religions tend to converge. Thus Panikkar's approach has the advantage of going beyond the divisive tendencies of creeds and concepts to spiritual experience, where unity is more readily discovered. Yet at the same time, he acknowledges that there are different kinds of spiritualities and different kinds of spiritual experiences, although they may be related. Hence he does not fall into the error of merely distinguishing between words and concepts, on the one hand, and religious experience on the other—assuming that religious experience is all of a piece. On the contrary, the Trinitarian pattern, applied to religious experience, indicates precisely that there are differences that must not be reduced to a simple unity. The use of the Trinity has the further advantage of drawing the Christian's spiritual experience into self-awareness. The self-consciousness of the Trinitarian mystery—worked out by councils and theologians over the centuries—if rooted in a deep and vital spirituality, can heighten the spiritual awareness of Christians and thus make them more sensitive to their affinity with other traditions.

While Panikkar's approach provides a pluralistic model for dialogue grounded in spiritual experience, it raises certain questions. To some it may appear bold—breaking out of the usual framework of dealing either with the Trinity or with Eastern religions. To Christians, it may seem to lower their lofty and unique mystery of the Trinity to the level of universal religious experience. To the non-Christian, it may seem merely another form of Christian imperialism—more subtle than the Christological form, but nonetheless strong. Yet if we stand now at a unique moment in history, when the great religions of the world are converging, then new and bold modes of thought are called for. Christians must break out of their traditional categories and investigate new modes of experience. This is an age of exploration and discovery—of expansion, not consolidation. Our ventures into outer space have their counterpart in the depths of the human spirit. While we are breaking way from the earth into new areas of space, the convergence of religions is pressuring us to penetrate to new levels of our inner world and to explore its richness. To make this exploration, we must develop new structures of thought and relatedness; we must be ready to take new steps. Our venture calls for us to be both creative and critical — to propose ideas imaginatively, but also gropingly and tentatively. As we proceed, we will have to test our proposals in the multi-dimensional context that is emerging. In our new complex spiritual environment, we must learn to think in a multi-dimensional way: to test our ideas for the future against the present and the past and against the religious experience of all humankind.

ROOTS IN THE TRADITION

In this context we will examine Panikkar's proposal. Is it a radically new approach to the Trinity, or does his application of the doctrine to world religions have at least some antecedents in the Christian tradition? In the history of Trinitarian theology there have been two tendencies: (1) a restricting tendency which limits the action of the Trinity to the revelation in Christ and the sanctifying work of the Spirit in the Church;[22] and (2) a universalizing tendency which links the Trinity to the entire expanse of the universe, in its creation and history. Since Panikkar's proposal is clearly related to the universalizing strand of the tradition, we shall examine it in the light of three universalizing currents in the history of Trinitarian theology: the vestige doctrine of medieval Augustinianism; the Trinitarian doctrine of creation of the Greek Fathers; and the appropriation doctrine of the Western Fathers and scholastics. Each of these currents in its own way tends to universalize the Trinity beyond the limits of Christian revelation in its historical unfolding. If Panikkar's proposal is situated within each of these frameworks, it can be seen to harmonize with each and at the same time to draw each into a new level.

The vestige doctrine, taken in the broad sense of the term, refers to the reflection of the Trinity throughout the universe. It has roots in the cosmic Christology of the New Testament and the Trinitarian doctrine of creation of the Greek Fathers. But it flourished in the West, where its basis was laid by Augustine. While the Greeks had a general mystical awareness of the dynamic activity of the Trinity in the universe, the Western theologians, with a more empirical and concrete cast of mind, examined the specific structures of the created world; and by an analysis performed in the light of faith, they discovered reflections of the Trinity — in the physical world, in the human soul, in the community, in the Old Testament revelation, and in Greek philosophy. To add the phenomenon of world religions to this data, then, is to bring the vestige tradition to a new level, by drawing into a Trinitarian focus an area of human experience that is entering more and more into the life of the Christian at the present time.

Perhaps the most graphic expression of the vestige doctrine is found in medieval Augustinianism, where it was not only explored theologically and philosophically, but was developed into a form of meditation. Basing their position on the metaphysics of exemplarism, inherited from Platonism, theologians reasoned that if, as Christian revelation teaches, the first cause of all things is Trinitarian, then its Trinitarian stamp must have been left on the physical universe and on human beings. Christians, therefore, can contemplate the universe to become more aware of the Trinitarian reflections and thus enter more deeply into the mystery. Although the vestige tradition in the West has its classical source in Augustine,[23] it was fused in the thirteenth century with the Franciscan cosmic sense, which was aware of the divine presence both in the entire expanse of the universe and in each object, no matter how insignificant. Meditating on the universe, Christians could become aware not only of the presence of the divine nature, but in the light of revelation could discern the reflection of the Trinity; and since the Trinity was intimate to the structure of creation, it could be found reflected even in the tiniest particle of matter.

Thus Robert Grosseteste could meditate on the reflection of the Trinity in a speck of dust, such as one sees floating in a sunbeam.[24] Although the speck of dust is tiny, it is at least not nothing, and reflects the infinite power that brought it into being. Thus it reflects the Father; for in an ancient theological tradition power is associated with the Father, who is the source of the Trinitarian processions. Secondly, the speck of dust has shape and form, which can be studied in an infinite number of ways by mathematical sciences. This intelligible form reflects the infinite wisdom through which the dust was made by infinite power. Here the Son is reflected, for he is the Wisdom and Image of the Father, through whom all things have been made. Finally, the dust has been very useful for the mind since it has drawn it to this meditation; and it could be useful in a similar way for an infinite number of minds. Again, in an ancient theological tradition, goodness is associated with the Spirit since he is the fulness and completion of the Trinity and the Gift in whom all gifts are given. Thus from the power, wisdom, and goodness reflected in the speck of dust, Robert moves to the Father, Son, and

Spirit, through whom the universe has been made and whose vestige is found even in the least element.

From the speck of dust, we can turn our gaze to the universe as a whole and see there the reflection of the Trinity. This is what Bonaventure does in the first stage of his *Soul's Journey into God*, where he sees the physical universe as a vast mirror reflecting the Father, Son, and Holy Spirit. Bonaventure contemplates the whole sweep of creation from seven points of view: the origin, greatness, multitude, beauty, fulness, activity, and order of all things. From each angle of vision, he sees the universe manifesting the power, wisdom, and goodness of the Triune God.[25] Elsewhere Bonaventure sums up his view as follows: "The creation of the world is like a book in which the creative Trinity shines forth, is represented, and is read according to three levels of expression: by way of vestige, image, and likeness. . . . From these as up the steps of a ladder the human intellect has the power to climb by stages to the supreme principle which is God."[26]

Having contemplated the reflection of the Trinity in the material universe, Bonaventure turns in the next section of the *Soul's Journey* to the human person, who is more than a vestige which merely reflects the Trinity from its outside or objective structure. Since human persons reflect the Trinity in the depth of their interiority, Bonaventure gives them the technical term of images of the Trinity. From a general perspective, human persons are called images of God, since in the depths of their subjectivity, God shines as the light of truth. But from the point of view of the dynamism of the psyche, the human person is also an image of the Trinity. For the divine light shines in that dimension of the soul that Augustine calls memory—not the faculty of simple recall, but the ground of the soul that is open to the infinite, the unconscious depths of the psyche where God's brilliance filters into the soul. This memory-ground of the soul is dynamic; it is the primordial depth of creative psychic energy, out of whose fecundity emerges self-reflective understanding and the impulse of love. Thus the memory reflects the Father; self-conscious intelligence reflects the Son; and love, the Spirit. Bonaventure describes the Trinitarian image as follows:

> For from the memory comes forth the intelligence as its offspring, because we understand only when the likeness which is in the memory emerges at the crest of our understanding and this is the mental word. From the memory and the intelligence is breathed forth love, as the bond of both. These three—the generating mind, the word, and love—exist in the soul as memory, intelligence, and will, which are consubstantial, co-equal and contemporary, and interpenetrating.[27]

Thus Bonaventure can call the soul a mirror in which the Trinity is reflected. For through this mirror one glimpses "the Father, the Word, and Love, Three Persons co-eternal, co-equal and consubstantial, so that whatever is in any one is in the others, but one is not the other, but all three are one God."[28]

A century before Bonaventure, Richard of St. Victor developed another extension of the vestige doctrine by seeing the reflection of the Trinity in the human interpersonal community. This aspect of the Trinitarian reflections was touched briefly by Augustine, but not developed as a major theme. According to Richard the excellence of human self-transcending love has its fulness in the creative and dynamic love of the Trinitarian life. Richard's interpersonal approach to the Trinity was taken up by Alexander of Hales and was channeled by him into the thirteenth century.[29]

In scanning the vestige tradition, we can discern a logical progression from Grosseteste's speck of dust to Bonaventure's contemplation of the entire physical universe. From there we turn to the individual human person, whose soul in its religious depths is not only an image of God, but an image of the Trinity. From the individual soul we can move with Richard of St. Victor to the human interpersonal community. It is not a major step, then, to rise to the larger human community and to take into account its historical development to the point of its highest spiritual achievement. At this level it would not be surprising, then, to discover, as Panikkar does, a reflection of the Father, Son, and Spirit. To extend the vestige tradition into the sphere of religion and philosophy is not without precedent in Christian theology. From the early centuries, Christian theologians explored what they considered to be the foreshadowing of the Trinity in the Old Testament and the reflection of the Trinity in Greek philosophy. Although Christians saw the Trinity in many of the patterns of Greek thought, they discerned its chief reflection in the three hypostases of Neoplatonism: the One, the Nous, and the World Soul.[30] While Christians rejected the subordinationism of Neoplatonism, they recognized its similarity with their own belief and interpreted it as a reflection of their own doctrine of the Trinity. At the present time, if Christians are to expand their horizons beyond the Mediterranean world and relate Christianity to a larger spectrum of human experience than is found in Judaism and Greek philosophy, it would not be inappropriate to encompass within their doctrine humankind's religious experience as this has developed in its highest forms.

CREATION AND APPROPRIATION

A second universalizing current in Trinitarian theology is found in the Trinitarian doctrine of creation of the Greek Fathers. While the Western theologians meditated on the reflections of the Trinity throughout the structure of the universe, the Greeks tended to interpret all of their doctrines in Trinitarian terms. This applied not only to those doctrines related to the redemption and sanctification of the Christian, but also those that relate to the universe as a whole. As a result of the revelation of the Trinity through Christ, the Greeks were able to see creation as a Trinitarian act: from the Father, through the Son, and in the Spirit. The Greek tradition of Trinitarian creation is epitomized in the statement of Athanasius: "The Father himself through the Word and in the Spirit has made and has given all things".[31] Speaking of the creation of the angels, Basil writes: "In creation, consider the primordial cause of all things that are made, the Father; the operative cause, the Son; and the perfecting cause, the Spirit; so that the heavenly spirits subsist by the will of the Father, they come into being through the operation of the Son, and they are perfected by the presence of the Spirit."[32] In the same vein, Gregory of Nyssa writes:

> . . . the fountain of power is the Father, and the power of the Father is the Son, and the spirit of that power is the Holy Spirit; and Creation entirely, in all its visible and spiritual extent, is the finished work of that Divine power . . . we should be justified in calling all that Nature which came into existence by creation a movement of Will, an impulse of Design, a transmission of Power, beginning from the Father, advancing through the Son, and completed in the Holy Spirit.[33]

Since the Greeks saw creation as a Trinitarian act, they were able to be aware of the action of the persons of the Trinity in the universe and history. Thus Justin and Clement of Alexandria could see the Logos enlightening Socrates, Plato, and Pythagoras; and Gregory Nazianzen could see the Spirit as a power active throughout the world. Gregory speaks of the Spirit as "the Maker of all these, filling all with His Essence, containing all things, filling the world in His Essence, yet incapable of being comprehended in His power by the world."[34] Against the background of the Trinitarian action in creation, the Greeks saw the Trinitarian work of redemption and sanctification. As the Son was the archetype in whom all had been made, he is the redeemer in whom all is restored. As the Spirit was the vivifier, the giver of life to creation, so he is the giver of new life in baptism.

This, then, is the universalizing tendency of Greek Trinitarian theology. Once the Trinity has been revealed, theologians look upon the entire universe, history, and their theological doctrines in Trinitarian terms. The dynamic activity of the persons in the Trinitarian processions is extended into the act of creation and into the movement of the universe back to its source. If Panikkar's proposal is situated within this framework, it is possible to see the dynamic action of the Trinity not only in creation and Christian redemption and sanctification, but in the highest religious experience of humankind. Thus the impulse of the Greeks to see everything as coming into the dynamic action of the Trinity can be extended beyond their horizon to universal religious history. In this perspective, the Christian can see the action of the persons in their differentiated modes outside of Christian salvation history. And in this way the door is opened for Christians to interpret their doctrine of salvation in more universal terms by encompassing within the Trinitarian action the varied religions of the world.

A third universalizing current in Trinitarian theology is found in the doctrine of appropriations. Although the term and its logical refinements were developed in the late twelfth century, the tradition goes back to the origins of Western theology. A classical source is the *De Trinitate* of Hilary of Poitier in the fourth century,[35] but the foundations of the tradition were laid by Augustine. In his *De Trinitate*, Augustine distinguished sharply between the single divine nature and the three persons conceived as relations.[36] Attributes that pertained to the divine nature were possessed equally by all three persons. "Therefore," Augustine wrote, "the Father is omnipotent, the Son omnipotent, and the Holy Spirit omnipotent; yet there are not three omnipotents, but one omnipotent, 'from whom all things, through whom all things, in whom all things'" (Rom. 11:36).[37] Although essential attributes were possessed by all three persons, certain attributes were associated with individual persons because of a similarity between the attribute and the distinct property of the person based on the processions: e.g., power with the Father, because he is the source of the Trinitarian processions; wisdom with the Son, because he proceeds as the Word and Image of the Father; and goodness with the Spirit, because he is the fulness and completion of the Trinity and the Gift in whom all gifts are given. In the twelfth century, after Abelard's Trinitarian thought caused problems leading to a condemnation, theologians refined the logic of appropriations.[38] In the thirteenth century the following apropriations were widely accepted: (1) power to the Father, wisdom to the Son, goodness to the Spirit; (2) unity to the Father, truth to the Son, goodness to the Spirit; (3) unity to the Father, equality to the Son, harmony or connection to the Spirit; (4) eternity to the Father, form or beauty to the Son, fruition to the Spirit; (5) omnipotence to the Father, omniscience to the Son, will to the Spirit; and (6) efficient cause to the Father, exemplarity to the Son, finality to the Spirit.[39]

From the standpoint of universalizing the Trinity, the technique of appropriation has two major advantages: First, it allows theologians to discover the reflections of the Trinity throughout creation, as Robert Grosseteste did in the reflection of power, wisdom, and goodness in the speck of dust. Secondly, it allows the Christian to relate the Trinity to a non-Christian's doctrine of the divinity. For example, Bonaventure, speaking of the Greek philosophers, said that they could know the Trinity of appropriations (the power, wisdom, and goodness of the divinity, seen in dynamic relation) but not the Trinity of persons, since Christian faith is required for the latter.[40] By appropriating in this way essential divine attributes to the Trinity, the Christian can see many reflections of the Trinity in the beliefs of other religions concerning the divine nature. In an example from Hinduism: Both Śankara and Rāmānuja hold that the only terms that can be assigned to Brahman, the ultimate reality, are *sat*, *chit*, and *ananda* (being, consciousness, and bliss).[41] Note the similarity with the classic appropriations that Western theology makes to the Father, Son, and Spirit. Do Śankara and Rāmānuja intend by this something that approximates the Christian Trinity? This question would have to be explored with considerable knowledge and subtlety. But with the technique of appropriations, the Christian theologian could at least make the minimal affirmation that the Indian philosophers know the Trinity of appropriations if not that of the persons.

The appropriation tradition can throw light on aspects of Panikkar's proposal. He speaks of three conceptions of the Absolute, of three spiritual attitudes, and of three spiritualities developing from them; and he associates these with the Christian Trinity, relating them to the Father, Son, and Spirit. A Christian—especially a Western Christian accustomed to make a sharp distinction between the divine nature and the persons—may feel that Panikkar is confusing several levels that should be kept distinct. If, however, his proposal is situated within the framework of appropriations, it can take on a logic that would sustain the connections made by Panikkar. If, for example, a Hindu encounters the divine nature as unifying absolutely, the Christian could say, in a minimal sense at least, that the Hindu has contacted an essential aspect of the divine nature that by the technique of appropriations can be related to the Spirit. Thus the Christian can speak here of the spirituality of the Spirit. How much the distinctive personal action of the Spirit, in the Christian sense, would be present here would depend on the Christian's particular theory of appropriations.[42] While Panikkar's position can be brought into the logic of appropriations, it pushes the appropriations to a new level of universalization; for it goes far beyond the medieval contact with Greek philosophy. It does not linger on Trinitarian patterns in particular religions, but in a panoramic sweep discerns a Trinitarian pattern in the complex of world religions as a whole.

SILENCE OF THE FATHER

Thus we see that the universalizing thrust of Panikkar's position is not without roots in the history of Christian theology. But even if we concede this, a serious question remains. Has Panikkar been faithful to the Christian understanding of the Trinity? Most specifically, has he been correct in associating silence with the Father—and, to such an extent that the Father can be associated with the extreme apophatism of Buddhism?[43] Even in the universalizing traditions we studied, the Father is associated not with silence, but with power. This is true of Robert Grosseteste's speck of dust which reflects the Father as infinite power; it is true of the Greek Fathers' Trinitarian doctrine of creation, where the Father is the dynamic source of the processions and of the creation of the universe; it is true also of the appropriation tradition, where the chief essential attributes appropriated to the Father are power, omnipotence, and efficient causality. The question arises, then, whether there is within the Christian tradition a basis for the extreme apophatic silence that Panikkar associates with the Father.

The same question could arise over his associating absolute unification with the Spirit. Although it would be of interest to explore this point, we cannot venture upon it here. But it is not so pressing a problem as the silence of the Father. Unity is a traditional note of the Spirit although it is pushed beyond its Christian understanding in advaitic Hinduism. On the other hand, silence seems to be the opposite of the Christian understanding of the Father, whose very essence consists in his generating the Word.

We will examine, then, whether there is a basis in the Christian tradition for the silence of the Father. Surprisingly, we can find such a basis in one of the earliest witnesses to Christian belief: in a text of Ignatius of Antioch dating from the early part of the second century. In his letter to the Magnesians, Ignatius writes: ". . . there is one God, who has revealed himself through Jesus Christ his Son, who is his Word, proceeding from silence, who in every respect was pleasing to him who sent him."[44] Although Ignatius develops the theme of silence throughout his writings, this is the only text where the term "silence" (σιγή) is directly associated with God, and the precise meaning of the text is not clear.[45] Yet there is reason to interpret the text in such a way that silence refers to the Father and to see the text expressing a basic theme in Ignatius' thought: that the Father is related to the Son as Silence to Word.[46] In this perspective, the Son is seen as the Word that emerges out of the silence of the Father. The notion of the Father as silence, however, did not find its way into the creeds, nor did it enter explicitly into the formulations of classical Trinitarian theology. This was due, at least in part, to the Christians' hesitation to use the term "silence" after the Gnostics had adopted it as their own.[47]

Although Ignatius' text is an isolated witness, it contains a suggestion that we can apply by way of theological reasoning to classical Trinitarian theology. In this way, we can draw out from classical Trinitarian formulations the latent apophatic dimension that is expressed in the phrase "the silence of the Father." If Christianity is the religion of Logos, of the spoken Word of the Father, Christians know the Father only through his Word. If we could, so to speak, strip away this Word, we would find a depth of silence from which the Word springs. Thus from the standpoint of the Word spoken, the Father is power; but from the standpoint of himself, he is silence. By following this path, we can bring to light the apophatic aspect of the Father in the various traditions of Trinitarian theology. We will attempt this briefly in the vestige tradition—in Grosseteste's speck of dust and in the Greek Fathers' concept of the Father as the fountain of the divinity.

If we look at the speck of dust, we see its shape, its pattern, its form. This pattern suggested to Robert Grosseteste that it could be measured and studied mathematically in a variety of ways and hence that it could lead him to infinite wisdom, or the Son. If we turn our gaze back to the speck itself, we see that the form expresses what the speck of dust is; for it is through the form that it has existence and can be known by us. If we physically strip away the form, we destroy the speck of dust. But if we mentally penetrate beneath the form, we can contact what is expressed in the form— that silent depth of reality that emerges into being through the form, that expresses itself in the form and that makes itself known through the form. When we touch that which is being expressed in the form and then mentally strip away the form, what do we have? Silence.

Although such examples from the world of matter can reflect the silence of the Father, they reflect it from afar and dimly because of the ambiguity of being and non-being in the material world. However, when we turn to human beings, we can discern a clearer reflection of the Father as silence. Augustine considered human beings the images of God because they reflect God in the depths of their soul; and they are images of the Trinity because of the dynamic interrelation of their faculties of memory, understanding, and will.[48] As we indicated before, memory corresponds to the Father because it is the primordial depth of the psyche out of which emerges self-reflective understanding and the impulse to love. Seen from the angle of the emergence of understanding, memory is energy and power. But from the other side, memory is the primordial silent depth of the soul. In its depth, memory is without a spoken word, without consciousness—it is silence. As Gilson has pointed out, Augustine's concept of memory approximates that of the contemporary concept of the unconscious:

> . . . memory means much more than its modern psychological connotation designates, i.e. memory of the past. In St. Augustine it is applied to everything which is present to the soul (a presence which is evidenced by efficacious action) without being explicitly known or perceived. The only modern psychological terms equivalent to Augustinian *memoria* are 'unconscious' or 'subconscious' provided they too are expanded, as will be seen later, to include the metaphysical presence within the soul of a reality distinct from it and transcendent, such as God, in addition to the presence to the soul of its own unperceived states.[49]

Pushed to its depths, the Augustinian memory is not only the dark abyss of psychic energy out of which consciousness springs; but it is also the mystical ground of the soul, where the soul's roots plunge into the infinite. Titus Szabó describes it as follows: "The Augustinian memory is the faculty by which the soul is 'open' to the Infinite, like a vast and infinite sanctuary, where there is present the divine light, the supreme Truth, the light of the soul. The term memory denotes the inner depths of the soul, where the illuminating presence of God is a hidden fountain of the innate ideas of spiritual reality."[50] As the mystical ground of the soul, the Augustinian memory could serve as a meeting point between the Christian and both the Hindu spirituality of the Spirit and the Buddhist spirituality of the Father. For in the depths of the memory, the soul's reality is plunged into the Infinite; and the depths of the memory are shrouded in silence—beneath words, beneath concepts, beneath reflective consciousness. In the Augustinian memory, then, we touch that aspect of the spirituality of the Father that Panikkar describes by saying: "There exists in us a dimension—the deepest of all—that corresponds to this total apophatism."[51]

Corresponding to the apophatic dimension of the soul is a silent dimension of the divinity. But can this be associated with the Father?

At first glance it seems not, because the Father is viewed as dynamic power. We will examine this aspect of the Father in the theology of the Greek Fathers since there it finds its most forceful and thematic expression. Unlike the Latins, the Greeks did not distinguish between the divine nature and the three persons.[52] Rather they looked upon the Father as possessing the divine nature and as the dynamic source of the Trinitarian processions. Thus they developed a profoundly dynamic concept of God, based on the fecundity of the Father. They speak of the Father as the ἀρχή (principle) or the πηγή (spring, source, fountain). Thus he is called the principle of divinity: θεότητος ἀρχή.[53] Basil writes: "For the Father has perfect and complete being; he is the root and the font of the Son and the Holy Spirit."[54] With his characteristic vividness, the Pseudo-Dionysius writes: "The Father is the gushing-forth divinity; Jesus and the Holy Spirit are, so to speak, the divine offshoots of the creative divinity, and like blossoms and luminous superessential rays."[55] John Damascene writes: "I know that the Father is the superessential sun, the fountain of goodness, the abyss of substance, of thought, of wisdom, of power, of light, of divinity: by generation and by procession, the fountain of the good hidden within him."[56]

This tradition has its counterpart in the West, partially as a result of Greek influence. Tertullian calls the Father the root (*radix*), the spring (*fons*), and the sun (*sol*). Thus the Son comes forth from the Father as the offshoot from the root, the stream from the spring, and the ray from the sun.[57] In the creed of the Eleventh Council of Toledo, the Father is called the fountain and origin of the whole divinity (*fons et origo totius divinitatis*).[58] In the thirteenth century Bonaventure makes the dynamic notion of the Father the basis of his theological system. He describes the Father as *fontalis plenitudo* (fountain-fulness) and proposes a type of *coincidentia oppositorum* as a basic principle: the more primordial a thing is the more fecund it is. Since the Father is absolutely primordial, he is absolutely fecund.[59]

Although these theologians emphasize the Father's dynamic fecundity, they hint at the hidden recesses of the divinity, the silent depths from which this power springs. I believe that Bonaventure's principle of the *coincidentia oppositorum* can be applied in terms of speech-silence. Thus the expressiveness of the Father necessarily implies the silence out of which this expression emerges. This is obviously not intended in a temporal sense, since the generation of the Son is eternal, but in the sense of an aspect of the Father. It is interesting to note that in the history of theology the Father has been given two notes which do not coincide except as opposites: unbegottenness (*innascibilitas*) and paternity.[60] I believe that the silence of the Father is rooted in his aspect of unbegottenness.

This leads to a point which we can only touch here. It seems especially fruitful to explore the great apophatic traditions of Christian theology precisely under the aspect of the silence of the Father, along the lines suggested by Panikkar. By looking at the Father as the Greek Fathers did, as the fountain of the divinity, one can penetrate beyond his self-expression in the Word to the abyss of darkness and silence that the great mystics have experienced. As we will see later, this is a way of interpreting Meister Eckhart's desert of the Godhead.[61] Of central importance here would be the Pseudo-Dionysius, the great formulator of the apophatic way for the Christian East and West, whose vision is epitomized in the opening lines of his *Mystical Theology*:

> O Trinity, beyond essence and beyond divinity and beyond goodness, guide of Christians in divine wisdom, direct us towards mysticism's heights, beyond unknowing, beyond light, beyond limit, there where the unmixed and unfettered and unchangeable mysteries of theology in the dazzling dark of the welcoming silence lie hidden, in the intensity of their darkness all brilliance outshining, our intellects, blinded—overwhelming, with the intangible and with the invisible and with the illimitable.[62]

In emphasizing the silence of the Father, then, Panikkar draws into focus an element in Trinitarian theology that has been often submerged, but has been nonetheless there. Perhaps it is only by an encounter with Buddhism that this dimension can be brought clearly into the fore. In such an encounter, then, Christians need not feel threatened but enriched.

In our study of Panikkar's proposal, we have emphasized its roots in the Christian tradition and its originality in meeting a new situation. At this time in the encounter of religions there is need for a sense of one's own identity and to have at one's disposal the resources of the past, while at the same time being open to other spiritual traditions and to the future. Panikkar's proposal touches the nerve center of these needs; for it has the originality to challenge Christians—and Buddhists and Hindus—to examine their own traditions and to tap their resources, and it provides them with tools to develop a more fruitful encounter. At this time many are becoming increasingly aware that all spiritual traditions are dimensions of each other and that at this point in history individuals throughout the world are becoming heir to the spiritual heritage of humankind. For Christians this means that they cannot know the depths of their own mystery of the Trinity until they face seriously the spiritual experience of Buddhism and Hinduism. Perhaps future historians will designate the period from Nicaea to the twentieth century an early stage in the development of the doctrine of the Trinity, for a new phase is ushered in when the Logos perspective of Christianity opens to encompass the apophatism of Buddhism and the unifying spirituality of Hinduism.

PANIKKAR'S NEW SYSTEMATIC THEOLOGY

Having examined Panikkar's exploration of the Trinity in relation to world religions and having seen its roots in the tradition, we can return to the question of the systematic theology of the future. I believe that he has already begun to develop such a Christian systematic theology. He has already produced the fundamental building blocks of this systematic theology, but has not assembled them together and shaped them into the classical genre of systematic theology. We are fortunate to have available in Panikkar's work a sample of this new theology taking shape, since it is difficult to conceive in the abstract what the new theology of this mutational age will be like. Having identified and analyzed these foundational elements, we can explore how they might be constructed into the classical genre of systematic theology, and we can observe how this genre will be transformed in the process. To build the structure of a Christian systematic theology, I believe that two—and only two— doctrines are necessary and sufficient: the Trinity and Christology. For these two doctrines are distinctly Christian and contain within themselves, at least implicitly, all the other Christian doctrines. Theology must involve two dimensions or poles in its basic structure: namely, the God or transcendent pole, and the world. For Christians the doctrine of the Trinity is the expression of their God-pole, and from it are derived their understanding of God's action towards the world: in the origin of creation, revelation, Christology, redemption, grace, the church, and eschatology. In Christology there is contained not only the person of Christ, but the entire world-pole of the structure. Since Christ is human in space and time, there are implicitly present in Christ the doctrines of creation, human persons, and history. Because redemption is effected in Christ, in him are focused the doctrine of the fall, restoration, sanctification, and salvation. Since Panikkar has produced a doctrine of the Trinity which relates to world religions and is far advanced on a similar Christology, he has provided, at least implicitly, all the building blocks of a completely systematic theology. In addition, he has developed explicitly a number of the elements in the world-pole of the structure—for example, a doctrine of human persons and of history. Furthermore, he has explored the hermeneutical presuppositions of interreligious dialogue and has laid the ground-work of a fundamental theology which sees revelation and salvation in relation to world religions. Although he has not assembled these elements in the classical structure of a systematic theology, they are already on hand in various stages of development and available for such a constructive enterprise.

PANIKKAR'S CHRISTOLOGY

Since we have examined Panikkar's Trinitarian theology at length, we will now turn to his Christology. Although Christology has been a continuing concern of his, as is evidenced in his early work *The Unknown Christ of Hinduism*, in the Logos dimension of his Trinitarian theology and in his extended essay on the Supername, I believe that his Christology has not reached the mature crystalliz-ation of his Trinitarian theology. This is not surprising since Christ-ology is the critical area of any ecumenical theology. While the Trinity can be seen as an archetype of unity and diversity drawing together world religious experience without eliminating its auton-omy, Christ divides world religions; or if he draws them together, it is usually by transforming them into his likeness. In the works listed above, Panikkar has moved in the direction of the transcendent dimension of Christology, indicating that the mystery of Christ extends far beyond a narrow particularity.

The crucial problem of an ecumenical Christology is precisely its particularity. According to Christian belief, the Logos was incarnate in Jesus of Nazareth, an individual human being who lived in a specific place and time, who emerged out of a specific history and gave impetus to a specific historical movement. I believe that Panikkar should follow the same paradoxical strategy which he pursued in his Trinitarian theology—plunging into the very unique-ness of the Christian archetype, and discovering there, in its apparent opposition to world religions, the very breakthrough that opens to the depth of their own archetypes. Some years ago at the Castelli Conference in Rome, while Panikkar was giving a paper on Christ and secularization, I detected that he had done just that, although the position which I will now describe was very much submerged in the text and has not to this day been formulated by Panikkar in print.[63] Therefore, it is with some caution that I venture to give an exposition of it here.

Panikkar turned to the particularity of Jesus and interpreted this according to the mystical-symbol of the center and the microcosm. As particular human being, Christ can be seen as the microcosmic center through which all authentic religious experience is reflected, given an ontological ground to support its autonomy, and a point of focus for establishing interrelationship. This means that all the variety of religious experience — and we can include here cosmological and metaphysical systems and the vast panorama of human experience — can be grounded and related through this center without having to be related by crossing over from one tradition to the other, by way of translation. This liberates one from the impossible task of finding a universal language or conceptual system to establish a dialogue between radically different religions.

Since Christ includes the entire world-pole of theology, as we pointed out above, we possess implicitly in this mystery the remaining elements of a comprehensive systematic theology. But observe the ecumenical sweep; for through Christ as microcosmic center we can encompass, at least in some way, all the cosmological, anthropological, and historical systems that are part of the fabric of world religions. Much remains to be done in this area of Panikkar's Christology. I believe that it is the linchpin of his emerging systematic theology; for it will fill out the necessary second pole of his theology to complement his Trinitarian theology, providing the focal point for drawing into the genre of systematic theology the many areas he has already developed in anthropology — for example, his notion of cosmic theandrism. This latter notion is very rich and will play a major role in his emerging Christology. The term "cosmic theandrism" contained the three components — the cosmos, the human, and the transcendent — which Panikkar sees should be present in a holistic way in an authentic spirituality. Christ embodies these three elements in a pre-eminent way.

CHARACTERISTICS OF PANIKKAR'S THEOLOGY

What are the characteristics of Panikkar's theology? First of all, it is distinctly Christian. He is not attempting a least-common-denominator theology which would emphasize the common elements of world religions and allow the distinctly Christian archetypes to remain in the background. It is interesting to compare Panikkar's strategy with that of two thirteenth-century theologians who responded to the influx of Aristotelian thought into Christianity — an influx which is not unlike the present wave from the Orient. Thomas Aquinas responded by building his system out of common elements in the Aristotelian metaphysics and the Christian faith. Bonaventure took another tack: he rooted himself first within the Christian archetypes of the Trinity and Christology and proceeded to relate these to the new knowledge. Panikkar is following the Bonaventure strategy, which I believe is especially called for at this moment. Perhaps in the thirteenth century Aquinas made the right move in the light of the dynamics of Western culture; however, I believe that in the mutational environment of the twentieth century, with its radically pluralistic religious context, the distinct individuality of each tradition must be maintained and re-enforced. Only out of this radical individuality can there be a creative encounter of traditions.

Although Panikkar begins with the Christian archetypes, in opening these to world religions he may seem to some observers to so transform these archetypes that they cease to be Christian. This is not unlike the accusation brought against Thomas that he had reduced Christian faith to Aristotelian philosophy. This is a perennial risk of all outreaching Christian theology, especially in transitional periods—a risk that Panikkar has not hesitated to take boldly and imaginatively. It remains for the future of critical reflection to judge the success of his attempt.

A second characteristic of Panikkar's theology is that it is comprehensively ecumenical. Although rooted in the Christian archetypes, it plunges into the archetypes of other traditions and allows these to enrich and expand Christian experience and self-consciousness. For Panikkar world religions are not a mere appendage to theology—to be treated in a prologue to fundamental theology under revelation or in the dogmatic treatise on providence under the salvific will of God. Rather he allows world religions to enter into the very center of dogmatic theology—into the Trinity and Christology— and to permeate the entire structure of his theology. The result is a theology which reflects the cross-cultural, multidimensional, global consciousness of our mutational era.

A third characteristic of Panikkar's theology is that it is not triumphalistic or imperialistic. An attempt such as his requires a delicate balance. How maintain Christian identity and ecumenism without falling into the inherent problems of each? On the one hand, the ecumenical outreach might lead to loss of identity—to distortion and even absorptions into another tradition or into an undifferentiated mixture of the whole. On the other hand, it is difficult to retain Christian identity without adopting a triumphalistic and imperialistic self-image. The third world has rightly asked whether Christian ecumenism is not merely another form of its missionary imperialism. Since this complex issue cannot be explored adequately here, I can touch only a few cardinal points. The fact that Panikkar relates the Trinity and Christology to world religions does not mean that he intends to affirm a triumphalistic finality for Christianity.

Certainly, he does not wish to propose his as a universal theology of world religions to be adopted or even sympathized with by all non-Christians. In fact, he holds that such a universal theology of world religions is impossible. Rather he attempts to retain his Christian identity, while plunging into the experience of other religions and affirming their authenticity and autonomy. How to accomplish this in practice and at the same time to justify its theology is a demanding challenge. Panikkar himself has provided an admirable example in practice; and he has elaborated a complex hermeneutics of world religions which would allow one to maintain simultaneously the absolute claims of Christianity while respecting and affirming the absolute claims of other traditions.

A fourth characteristic of Panikkar's theology is that it takes its point of departure not from philosophy but from religious experience. Although his thought has a strong metaphysical dimension, he is not attempting to construct a theological synthesis by using principles derived from a specific metaphysics—as, for example, Thomas did with Aristotle's metaphysics, and twentieth-century process theologians have done with Whitehead's. Rather, he moves immediately into the depth of the religious experience of the various traditions and examines this experience from the standpoint of spirituality. In this he is again like Bonaventure and the early Franciscan theologians, who took their point of departure from the mainstream of Christian spirituality as this had been dramatically transformed by Francis of Assisi. Perhaps Panikkar has greatest affinity with the monastic theology that preceded medieval scholasticism. Although Panikkar's thought is very sophisticated philosophically, inevitably metaphysical speculation is always derivative of a deeper level of spiritual experience. Panikkar's strategy here seems again to be on target, since it corresponds to the priorities of the Eastern religions to which he is attempting to relate; for these religions and their theologies are rooted in a decisive and self-conscious way in deep spiritual experience.

Panikkar's spirituality-based theology may herald a new trend in Christian theology. Over the last centuries, and throughout its history, Christian theology has been closely tied to the philosophical trends of Western culture; this has been especially true of academic and university-based theology. This may be radically altered by the influx from the East. Stimulated and challenged by the power of Eastern religious experience, the experiential underpinnings of Christian theology may surface, free themselves from the fluctuations of Western philosophy, and become much more autonomously self-conscious within this larger horizon. This could bring about a paradigm-shift in theological methodology that would amount to a Copernican revolution. In this context theology could take the lead rather than timidly trying to adapt itself to philosophy and secular culture. In this context Panikkar's theological methodology deserves serious consideration from the theological community.

A fifth characteristic of Panikkar's theology—and perhaps its most profound—it that at its base and permeating its entire structure is a remarkable concidence of opposites: of the void and fulness. These two primordial archetypes provide the ultimate base and the all-penetrating logic of his thought—uniting transcendence and immanence, detachment and involvement, simplicity and complexity. His theology is profoundly apophatic, in the classical Eastern and Western spirit of the term. Yet his apophatism is accompanied by an affirmation of the created world. He combines the Buddha's experience of emptiness with Francis of Assisi's joy in the fulness of creation. The spirit of Francis' Hymn of Brother Sun permeates his thought. He has extended Francis' cosmic sense into the religious experience of humankind. He sings a Franciscan hymn to the fulness of creation, but he has transposed it to another key. His hymn of praise is not through Brother Sun and Sister Moon, but through Hinduism, Buddhism, Christianity, and the other great religions of the world. He rejoices in the varieties of religious experience with the same gusto with which Francis rejoiced in the varieties of flowers, animals, and birds. And this joy extends to the varieties of cultures and languages, and into natural sciences and the forms of secular culture.

Panikkar has found a ground and expression for both the archetype of the void and of fulness in the Christian doctrine of the Trinity and Christ. The silence of the Father is balanced by the fulness of the Logos, the transcendence of the Father by the immanence of the Spirit. Christ is the center of creation and the ground of pluralism, but at the same time he is the one who empties himself completely in his incarnation, death, and resurrection. Thus through the central Christian doctrines of the Trinity and Christ, Panikkar awakens the coincidence of opposites that forms the matrix of the new multi-dimensional consciousness.

WHAT REMAINS TO BE DONE

After we have pointed to the building blocks of this new systematic theology and sketched the outline of its structure, we face the question: What remains to be done? From the standpoint of Panikkar's own project, I see the following steps. These building blocks must be brought together by Panikkar or by others and assembled according to the classical blueprint of systematic theology. In general, I believe that his work on the Trinity is in its fundamental lines complete, but it must integrate the element of the power of the Father which already exists in *The Unknown Christ of Hinduism*, into his Trinitarian model of the silence of the Father. This enlarged model must be analyzed in greater detail against the two great strands of Trinitarian theology as studied by Théodore de Régnon: the Greek model with the Father as fountain-source, and the Latin model based on the divine substance and relations. This must be enriched by material drawn from the Christian mystical tradition on the Trinity, especially from the Pseudo-Dionysius and Meister Eckhart. When this material is brought into dialogue with the Trinitarian vestiges in world religions, there should ensue an enlargement of the Christian understanding of the Trinity not only in depth but in technical refinement. In the Christological pole of his thought, Panikkar must complete his Logos Christology and, much more importantly, express in writing and develop his incarnational Christocentricity. The theology of creation, human persons, redemption, and salvation implicit in his Christology must be made explicit by him or others and brought into harmony with his explicit treatment of these themes throughout his writing. This entire cluster of themes must be thoroughly developed, interconnected, and concretely related to world religions throughout.

His fundamental theology must be drawn together from his writings on revelation, the church, hermeneutics, and the philosophy of religion. This must be explicitly related to his dogmatic theology and developed in the light of this relationship. Finally, all the elements must be assembled in the interlocking structure of the classical genre of systematic theology. In the process, there should be a constant dialogue with the major Christian theological syntheses on how the genre is being transformed as it passes across the gap of the present into the global context of the mutational age.

In the process of building such a theology, one should not hesitate to draw on new resources from the history of religions never before used by Christian theologians. I would like to recall here a specific suggestion I made above—namely, that we use resources from shamanism to develop the epistemology of this new systematic theology. In primitive religions, the shaman has the power to leave his body in spirit and travel to distant place, acquire knowledge, and return to pass this on to the community. I hold that we all have a "shamanistic faculty" whereby we can leave, as it were, our distinctive forms of consciousness and enter by way of empathy into the consciousness of others. In so doing we enter into their value world

and experience this from the inside. Then we return enriched, bringing into our own world these values and a larger horizon of awareness. All of this we can attempt to share with those who belong to
our own world. What I am suggesting here is a radical break with
the epistemology that has dominated Western philosophy since the
time of Descartes. In the new global environment, Western theologians may find that they have powers of consciousness that they
have anesthetized for centuries but which may be awakened if they
are to meet the challenges of the future.

I believe that it is precisely this shamanistic epistemology that
Panikkar employs in his work on religion. I would suggest that in
his fundamental theology he explore this epistemology critically and
systematically. I would further suggest that he bring to bear on this
issue the recent extensive research on consciousness and especially
the speculative thought of Charles Tart based on this work. In an
extended essay in *Transpersonal Psychologies*, Tart proposes the model
of specifically different states of consciousness.[64] These distinct forms
of consciousness, which he suggests are exemplified in the great
traditions of spirituality, have their own sciences which he terms
"state-specific" sciences, containing their own logic and hermeneutics, and, I would underscore, their own epistemologies. This
work in consciousness could be very fruitful for constructing a
fundamental theology related to world religions.

In conclusion, I realize that the systematic theology I am proposing here may appear like science fiction. It is more imaginative —
even utopian — than empirical. If, however, we are in the mutational
environment that Leclercq describes, it is precisely this type of
imaginative projection that is called for. Besides in predicting future
scientific developments over the last hundred years, science fiction
writers have been conservative. Be that as it may, I believe that my
projection has more fact than fiction, because, as I have attempted
to establish, Panikkar has already produced the Christian systematic
theology of the future, at least in its fundamental elements. Of
course, much remains to be done. To build the Christian systematic
theology of the future is not the task of a single theologian; it is the
work of the Christian theological community. As a pioneer of the
future, Panikkar has charted the way and has brought back the early
maps of this new country. He now beckons others to follow and to
strike out on their own. Although he has made many contributions
to intellectual culture and specifically to the study of religion, his
most original work and ultimately his greatest contribution may
well be towards the construction of the new Christian systematic
theology of the Second Axial period.

V

Dialogic Dialogue:
Journey into Global Consciousness

Having examined Panikkar as a case study of the new global religious consciousness, we now face the question: What does this mean for us? In a striking way Panikkar has made the quantum leap into the future. We might even say that he was born in the future in the cross-cultural, interreligious environment of his Indian-Spanish, Hindu-Christian family; and his talents were nurtured by a multi-dimensional education that encompassed not only the religions of East and West, but the disciplines of science, philosophy, and theology. For others still immersed in the limits of their own culture, he can serve as a model and guide. He can assist them to make the passage into the new complexified consciousness. Having identified a model and the goal, we now must explore the path. We must map the journey and plan the itinerary that will take us into the realm of global consciousness, where Panikkar has been living and working and into which he beckons us. In what follows I will attempt to sketch a process through which we can make that journey.

I will take my point of departure within Christianity which has been the dominant religious force in Western culture. Although the West has been deeply affected by secularization, Christianity remains the major religious background for the majority of those who will be exposed to world religions in Europe and the Americas. I will describe a process involving three stages: (1) the encounter, in which a person with a Christian cultural background meets another religion; (2) the "passing over" into the value consciousness of the other religion and the "coming back" to one's own roots, enriched by the other religion; (3) the mapping of the journey, which attempts to develop a theory—cultural, philosophical, or theological—of the interrelation of world religions. I believe that it is crucial to distinguish these stages. To blur them could cause a major confusion. To ignore one would jeopardize the effectiveness of the process as a whole; in fact, to eliminate the second could lead to negative education, producing truncated knowledge and distorted value perception. To reverse their order could be disastrous for it could lead to imposing a preconceived theory on the experience of another religion.

ENCOUNTER

The first stage of the process involves the encounter with other religions. The Christian must be brought in touch with the reality of other religions in a comprehensive and vital way. From the standpoint of content, one might begin by viewing a panorama of humankind's religions in historical perspective, beginning with the religions of primitive peoples, tracing the development of the great world religions in the ancient civilizations of Asia, Europe, and Africa, to their encounter with modernity and their move into global consciousness. This involves gathering the basic data of the religions: information on the founders, sacred books, doctrines, moral precepts, rituals, spiritual practices, social structure, relation to culture, subsequent history. On these subjects an increasing amount of material has been made available over the last two decades: general surveys, translations of sacred texts, monographs, movies, video tapes, film strips. In the United States, the book by Huston Smith, *The Religions of Man*, published first in 1958, has become a classic of this genre, influencing a generation of students in colleges and high schools.[1] With the wealth of material being produced, we by no means face a poverty of resources, but the task of choosing judiciously.

Although material abounds, the very material itself poses a problem: it can entrap us in the objectivity of the data, preventing us from opening to the inner vitality of the religions. We may spend all our time studying historical facts, analyzing sacred texts on a verbal level, examining the externals of rituals yet never penetrating to their meaning, never tapping the living religious experience from which these manifestations flow. It is precisely this experience that is the substance of religion and it is precisely the discovery of this religious experience that can enrich our lives on a significant human level. The success of Huston Smith's book lies here. In his preface he describes the need he perceived for the type of book he wrote. Speaking of his television program in St. Louis which was the origin of his book, he writes that the response revealed "the need for a different kind of book on world religions, a book which without sacrificing depth would move more rapidly than the usual survey into the *meaning* these religions carry for the lives of their adherents."

He continues: "Despite innumerable masterful books in the field, I knew of no one which took this as its single object; against the backdrop of critical scholarship to carry the intelligent layman into the heart of the world's great living faiths to the point where he might see and even feel why and how they guide and motivate the lives of those who live them. This is the book I have tried to write."[2]

PASSING OVER

This leads us to the second stage of the process: "passing over" into the value consciousness of the other religion and "coming back" into our own, enriched by the other religion. Huston Smith's book provides a bridge between the first and second phase: between the encounter with data and the passing over into the meaning of the other religions. In his book *The Way of All the Earth*, John Dunne describes this process. He writes in his preface: "Is a religion coming to birth in our time? It could be. What seems to be occurring is a phenomenon we might call 'passing over,' passing over from one culture to another, from one way of life to another, from one religion to another. Passing over is a shifting of standpoint, a going over to the standpoint of another culture, another way of life, another religion." According to Dunne, passing over leads to a return: "it is followed by an equal and opposite process we might call 'coming back,' coming back with new insight to one's own culture, one's own way of life, one's own religion." Dunne sees this process as characteristic of our time: "Passing over and coming back, it seems is the spiritual adventure of our time. It is the adventure I want to undertake and describe in this book."[3]

I strongly agree with Dunne that passing over and coming back is the spiritual adventure of our time. How can this be done? By finding a stepping stone, a path, a road to take us across the cultural distance. Any of the data—the historical facts, a passage from the sacred text, an event in the life of the founder—can provide such a stepping stone. A book, such as Huston Smith's which focuses beyond the data to the underlying meaning can be a major help. Ideally we should come in firsthand contact with believers in the other religion in their indigenous cultural setting. The ideal journey then, would consist of a pilgrimage to the major centers of world religions: e.g., Varanasi, Kandy, Kyoto, Jerusalem, at the time of religious feasts so that we would be present at prayer and rituals in temples, mosques and synagogues; we would also be exposed to the everyday religious life of the people and have the opportunity to meet religious leaders and discuss with theologians. This of course, is only a dream; but it can be approximated by visiting religious centers—mosques, ashrams, zendos—which are increasingly found in large cities in the West. In a similar vein, one can meet members of other religions who might reside in the area. The personal contact with these believers, with the power that accompanies, for example, a Muslim's personal expression of his faith, would serve as a catalyst to draw us into the religious experience of the Muslim tradition.

I would like to illustrate the process of passing over and coming back with a personal experience. Some thirty years ago, while I was engaged in theological studies in Kansas, I served as a catechist at a small Catholic mission church on the Pottawatomie Indian Reservation. From the beginning, I was aware of the cultural difference between the Indians and the whites, but this was not so visible since the Pottawatomies had been largely assimilated into white culture, at least in the externals of language, dress, and occupation. After two years with the Pottawatomie, I spent two summers with the Sioux Indians on the Rosebud Reservation in South Dakota. I worked at a Jesuit mission, with both whites and Indians, as a handy man and amateur cowboy. From the moment I stepped off the train, I sensed that I was in a different cultural environment. The land was traditional Sioux territory, with soft rolling hills and eroded canyons that suggested a moon landscape. But the human environment was more dramatically different; for I heard the Lakota language spoken more than English, and as the days went on and I mingled more with the Indians, I sensed that they experienced the world in a radically different way from the whites. Although I did not realize it fully at the time, I had entered a world of primal consciousness, whose culture is classified as Neolithic and whose experience of such basic things as space, nature, and the animal world, time, family, and tribe was decisively different from my own.

I remember the day, while I was talking to a group of Sioux, that I felt my consciousness, as it were, extend itself out of my body and pass over into their consciousness. From that moment I felt I could see things from their perspective and experience their values from within their world. Also I could look back at my own world and see its values in a clearer light—but also its limitations! The insight of the moment grew over the following weeks. I became increasingly aware of human values that the Indians preserved and that we had lost: their love of the land, their organic harmony with nature, their strong tribal ties, their sense of time as a flowing process rather than a static continuum to be divided into endless schedules, their immersion in myth and ritual, whose language and dynamics they understood with a primordial wisdom. I perceived also their religious sensibility: their awareness of the presence of

Wakan tanka, or God, in nature and in their lives. Nature as a whole was sacred to them, as was life in all its dimensions. Certain areas, for example the Black Hills, were especially sacred to the Sioux. Through the sacred ritual of the Sun Dance, they participated in the cosmic harmony that bound together the entire realm of nature, the animal world—especially the buffalo—the tribe and Wakan tanka.

This passing over and coming back was decisive for me. It broke the invisible blinders of my own culture and opened an experiential world I had not even dreamed existed. For a while it alienated me from my culture, for I realized that I had been trapped within my culture without knowing it. I became aware that, while my culture had given me values that the Indians had not received, it also deprived me of values that were theirs. Only some five years later was I able to resolve this tension, by traveling to Greece and perceiving how the self-reflective consciousness of Greek culture had emerged out of primal consciousness.

It was decisive academically as well. Since I had discovered a new world of experience through the Indians, I realized that there existed many other such worlds beyond the horizons of my culture. These I hoped to explore in future years. At the moment, however, I was engaged in theological studies and found that the passing over into the Indian world produced a revolution in my approach to theology. The method employed in our classes was primarily textual analysis, with some cognizance of the historical context. However, we never used the method of passing over into the total experiential world out of which the text emerged. For practical purposes, we presupposed only one cultural experiential world, namely our own Western world of the twentieth century. For example, we did not even ask the question whether the experiential world expressed in the Nicene Creed might be distant from ours so that our only access to the meaning of the creed might be by passing over into that experience, as I had passed over into the experiential world of the Sioux Indians. Although our approach to theology did not acknowledge this, I tried to develop a method in which the basic element was passing over, although I did not use John Dunne's term at that time. During my studies I worked on this method in a rudimentary way and later, while teaching Christian theology, I developed it more fully, formulating it in an article entitled "Models and the Future of Theology."[4] Thus my passing over into the American Indian world has had a decisive effect on my approach to Christianity.

In my theoretical study of method, I became aware that we must investigate more technically what is involved in this passing over. Behind much of the study of comparative religion is an empirical presupposition: that our knowledge is circumscribed by our sense perception. Only what comes to us directly in sense data and can be referred back to sense data is to be taken seriously. As mentioned above, we may become entrapped in the limits of this position, at least methodologically if not philosophically, if we view the encounter with the other religions on an exclusively objectified level. It is possible to break through this impasse by another philosophical position, namely that of phenomenology, which focuses not on the sense data as such, but on the structures of consciousness that stand behind our sense perceptions. This is the method employed by Rudolf Otto in his classic study of religious consciousness: *The Idea of the Holy*.[5] In a masterful analysis, he studies the components of our consciousness when we are aware of the sacred. Valuable though this approach is, it must be extended to deal with the phenomenon of passing over. The phenomenological movement itself has given us the key in its concept of empathy, whereby we can share in the consciousness of another. However, I believe that the study of world religions calls for a more emphatic and nuanced statement of the issue; for we are not talking merely about sharing in the consciousness of another in our own culture, but of passing over into the consciousness of others who, like the American Indians, have a radically different form of consciousness from our own. This has led me to formulate what I have called above "shamanistic" epistemology.[6] I believe that we all have a faculty whereby we can pass over into the consciousness of another religion, gather new insight and return enriched to our own. Before the emergence of global consciousness, this faculty lay largely dormant, since it did not have to be activated as long as people lived exclusively within the experiential world of their own culture. But at the present time, with the encounter of cultures and religions, this shamanistic faculty must be cultivated by religious education. It must be clearly identified and made a basic element in the religious educational process. Techniques must be developed to activate and enhance it. An epistemology and philosophy of education must be formulated which can clarify the nature of this faculty and provide the theoretical groundwork for its function in a comprehensive program of religious education.

PASSING OVER INTO ISLAM

In my encounter with the Sioux Indians, I passed over chiefly into their general cultural world. Although my primary concern was not their religion as such, I did contact their religious values within the total cultural context. This was the beginning of my contact with non-Christian religions. Among the Sioux I perceived the survival of their traditional tribal religion within the Christianity they had embraced when they came to the reservation in the last century. However, when I returned to the Pottawatomies in Kansas, I had direct contact with the traditional tribal religion among the group that had never become Christian and who in Christian terms were pagan. According to some anthropologists, this Pottawatomie religion is one of the most ancient religions surviving into our times. I often attended their rituals which were held four times a year at the change of seasons, and I had extensive dialogues with religious leaders about their belief and practices.

Because of the rich results I had garnered from this passing over, I planned some years later a journey into the Muslim world along the same route. This took place in 1972–73, when I lived nine months with my family at the Christian ecumenical institute in Jerusalem called Tantur. One of my research projects consisted in passing over into the religious world of Islam, using the techniques I had learned among the Indians: in this case, to share in the everyday life of the Muslims by living in a village and praying with them in mosques. After some unsuccessful attempts to make contacts, I met a young Muslim named Abdul Jaleel, who invited me to spend time with his family in their tiny village in the mountains outside Hebron. For some five months he took me to mosques in Jerusalem, Bethlehem, Hebron, Gaza, and small villages to pray with the people and to discuss theology with the sheiks. We also discovered Sufi groups, who invited us to attend their special prayers and devotions.

My passing over followed the same route as with the Indians. I first became immersed in the everyday world of Arabic culture in the Middle East. As with the Indians, I felt that I passed over into the value experience of that world and could look back both critically and sympathetically on my own world in a new light. I remember very sharply the day on which I passed over into the religious experience of Islam. It was less than two weeks since I had met Abdul Jaleel. After spending the night at our apartment at Tantur, he invited me to attend the Friday service at the mosque in Bethlehem. Since Friday is the Muslim holy day, the service was longer than usual and attracted a large number of Muslims. Over the period of an hour, I joined in the prayers with several hundred men and listened to the chanting of the Koran by a blind sheik. The intensity of the prayer mounted as the group bowed down repeatedly, touching their heads to the ground in submission to Allah the all-powerful. At the peak of that intensity, I felt that I passed over into the heart of their religious experience. I shared with them their sense of the transcendence of God—of his power and majesty—

which calls forth a response of worship, so dramatically expressed in the Muslim's bowing to the ground.

This experience of God's transcendence is central to Islam. It is what we, in passing over, must contact as the primary element of the Islamic religious consciousness. Our method must be that of passing over rather than mere analogy to the Christian experience of God's transcendence. We must be cautious not to see Islam as a truncated Christianity or assume that God's transcendence is identical in both Islam and Christianity. In the latter God's transcendence is bound up with his immanence in the Incarnation, a distinct form of immanence which Islam strongly rejects. It is very difficult for Christians to disengage the Incarnational dimension from their religious consciousness. Only by passing over into Islam as a total structure of consciousness, can Christians grasp the pure transcendence that lies at the heart of Islam. And they must grasp this as a value, in fact, as the highest value, just as Muslims do. Only in this way will Christians understand the meaning of such images as being a slave of Allah and of submission to the will of Allah. If we penetrate deeply enough into the experience of Islam, we will discover the positive—even liberating—meaning these images have for Muslims, in spite of the fact that within the structures of Christian consciousness, with its images of freedom, they would seem repressive.

Having passed over into the central experience of Islam, Christians can come back to their own religion enriched with values perceived in Islam. If, like Muslims, they can grasp the value of God's pure transcendence, they might be liberated from some of the negative aspects of their own belief in God's transcendence. Since Christianity focuses so centrally on God's immanence in the Incarnation, transcendence may become a problem for Christians. They might so emphasize God's intimate loving presence in the human sphere in Jesus of Nazareth that they ignore or reject the dimension of God's transcendence that Christians share with Islam. Transcendence may appear only in a negative light, as God's detached distance from the world or his overwhelming power which threatens the creature's autonomy. By grasping the value of God's transcendence in Islam— unrelated to the Incarnation—Christians can discover a dimension of their own tradition that might otherwise remain submerged or rejected.

Having passed over and come back, Christians can return to a point midway between the two religions and observe them both. From there they will discern similarities and differences. The first difference they will observe will undoubtedly be the one we have alluded to: the presence of the Incarnation in Christianity and its lack in Islam. However, they may observe another difference which is not so obvious. It is related to the doctrine of the Incarnation and Redemption but not identical with it. At the core of this Christian doctrine is what can be called the archetype of transformation, expressed in the death and resurrection of Christ. This in turn is rooted in the Exodus of the Jews, who were delivered from slavery to freedom. Christians have seen this transformation archetype functioning in the structure of the cosmos and the dynamics of history. They participate in it ritually in the Eucharist, where bread and wine are transformed into sacramental manifestations of a new presence of Christ. They look upon spiritual growth as a progressive transformation into the life of Christ and death itself as a transformation into union with God.

It is striking to observe that the transformation archetype does not play a central role in Islam. Although the Exodus is recounted in the Koran, it is not subsumed as a foundational element, as it is in Judaism, or as a prefiguring of Christ's death, as it is in Christianity. Islam has no ritual comparable to the Jewish Passover, which celebrates the Exodus, or the Christian Eucharist, which commemorates the death and resurrection of Christ. What does this mean? It means that Islam's theology of history differs from that of Judaism and Christianity, for it lacks the transformation archetype which is basic to the Jewish and Christian reading of history. Islam's view of history is grounded much more directly in God's power and providence without discerning a primordial pattern of transformation in the cosmos and history. To come to this awareness, which is by no means obvious, is made possible by the process of passing over and coming back.

This awareness not only clarifies differences between Islam and Christianity, but throws light on the relation of Christianity to Judaism. On the matter of the transformation archetype, Judaism and Christianity are intimately related. We can observe how Christianity could emerge organically out of Judaism since it inherited the transformation archetype from its Jewish origins. Yet this emergence is not without a mutation, for the Incarnation presents a rupture from the Jewish doctrine of God's transcendence. While Judaism and Islam share a doctrine of God's transcendence that negates Incarnation, Judaism and Christianity share the centrality of the transformation archetype, which is at most peripheral in Islam. Thus passing over and coming back yields not only new knowledge of other religions, but a clearer understanding of one's own religion and its complex relationships to other religions.

PANIKKAR AND THE TRINITY

We can return to Panikkar's Trinitarian approach to world religions and view it as a passing over and coming back.[7] Grounding himself in the Christian doctrine of the Trinity, he passes over into the Buddhist experience of silence and the Hindu experience of undifferentiated unity. He comes back to a much deeper level of the mystery of the Trinity than Christians usually discern. In the Buddhist experience of *nirvāna*—of emptiness and absolute silence—he touches a level that resonates with the silence of the Father in the Trinity: the abyss of the divinity out of which the Father speaks his eternal Word. Throughout Christian history, theologians have focused primarily on the Father's fecundity, his power to generate his Son, who is his Image and Word. Presupposed in this fecund power is the abyss of silence out of which the Father speaks his eternal Word. This abyss of silence has been touched by Christian mystics who have experienced the unfathomable depths of the divinity at the ground of the divine processions. For two-and-a-half millennia Buddhists have followed the path of silence to arrive at that realm which they call the void and which can be experienced only in the most profound silence. By passing over into that silence and coming back, Panikkar has opened a dimension of the Christian Trinity which has been largely obscured through the centuries. At the same time, he has established contact with one of the world's great religions, which can be approached only by passing over into the depths of silence and not by building a bridge of words, concepts, or doctrines.

Panikkar also passes over into the Hindu experience of unity, where he focuses on the undifferentiated unity of the Hindu nondualistic *vedanta* tradition. In this experience the Hindu perceives no difference between his *atman*, soul, and *Brahman*, divine reality. This experience of unity resonates with the Christian experience of the Spirit, who is the unity of the Father and Son in the Trinity and who unites himself to the Christian's soul in grace. However, the Christian experience is differentiated and mediated through the Son. Although not the same, it nevertheless approximates and points to the Hindu's experience of non-differentiation. Having passed over and come back, the Christian has a much deeper appreciation for the mystery of unity in Christianity: of the unity of the Father and Son in the Spirit and the unity of the soul with the divinity through the Spirit. And the Christian has found a way of making contact with the nondualistic Hindu: along the path of unity which is the only road on which the two can meet.

Having passed over into the silence of Buddhism and the unity of Hinduism, Christians can gain a much clearer understanding of the central role of the Word in Christianity. According to Panikkar Judaism, Christianity, and Islam are religions of the Word. They claim that God has revealed his Word to them, to which they should respond in faith, obedience, and love. This is a personalizing and individuating Word, evoking a personal response and commitment. In the West we are, indeed, people of the Word not only religiously, but in our secular past and present. For the pre-Christian Greeks, *logos* was central: as word, concept and meaning. As Christians worshiped the Word of God, so the Greeks reverenced the *logos* in all aspects of life. Thus the Word, or *Logos*, with a capital and small *l*, provides an all-pervading atmosphere for Western culture. In both religion and secular culture, we live and breathe Logos. It should not be surprising, then, that in the Christian doctrine of God, the Word is central: as the eternal expression of the silence and fecundity of the Father and as the focus of union in the life of the Spirit. It is precisely this experience of the Word which is not central in Buddhism or Hinduism, or for that matter, in the culture of the orient in general. Thus Panikkar's passing over through the Trinity can liberate us from absolutizing the Word by opening up other dimensions of consciousness, such as silence and unity, which we share with Buddhism and Hinduism, but in a non-central way.

MAPPING THE JOURNEY

Panikkar's approach through the Trinity leads us to the third stage of the process of moving into global religious consciousness: mapping the journey, which seeks to develop a theory of the interrelation of world religions. I have situated this in the third position because if we were to begin here or place it before passing over, we might project our Western and Christian presuppositions on other religions or deal with the issue in an abstract way that would draw us far from the depth and diversity of world religious experience. For example, in a desire to be ecumenical Christians might move from the particularity of Christ's humanity to his existence as divine Logos present throughout the universe and the entire human community. In this perspective, which was employed effectively by the early Greek theologians, they can see all religions related to Christ. Valuable though this is from a Christian standpoint, it ignores the deeper difference with Buddhism and Hinduism, pointed out by Panikkar. These traditions bypass logos in all of its forms to arrive at a silence and unity which, on their own terms, cannot be subsumed under a divine Logos, no matter how universalized it be. In the spirit of the Enlightenment, others might seek a least-common-denominator among religions based on a common human nature which is open to transcendence. Although this perspective is valuable, we must beware of a too facile abstraction which ignores the fact that religions view human nature differently. For example, the Buddhist tradition teaches that the individual self, which others hold as a common ground, is merely an illusion.

At this point in the emergence of global consciousness, I believe that it is too early to formulate a definitive theory of the integration of world religions. Yet we cannot ignore the issue theoretically or practically, for it will inevitably surface in exploring world religions. The wisest strategy at the present is to be pluralistic in two senses: (1) to look at world religions from many standpoints, e.g., humankind, the universe, the divine; (2) within each standpoint, to view the matter from the different perspectives of the world religions, e.g., humankind seen from the Christian doctrine of the image of God and from the Buddhist doctrine of no-self. As we proceed, we must realize that our perspectives are regional—not comprehensive or absolute—and that our theories are tentative: to be nuanced, revised and perhaps supplanted as we become more accustomed to the complexities of global consciousness. On the practical level, in our search for a pluralistic starting point we might survey the ways in which the world religions themselves throughout their history have related positively and negatively to other religions as well as the theories each has developed on the interrelation of religions.

As we explore these approaches, we must not confuse stage two with stage three: passing over with theories of interrelation. For example, in basing himself on the Christian doctrine of the Trinity, Panikkar does not intend to create a universal theory of world religions which Buddhists and Hindus would accept. Rather his approach should be situated primarily in the stage of passing over. If we pass over into the depth of another religion, we will discover levels of our own religion which might have been hidden from us, such as the silence of the Father, and which can now be drawn into our theories of interrelationship. As indicated above, this in-depth passing over, in which we discover deeper dimensions of ourselves Panikkar has call the "dialogic dialogue," to distinguish it from the dialectical dialogue which is concerned with defending one's own position against the other. He describes the dialogic dialogue as "a way of knowing myself and of disentangling my own point of view from other viewpoints and from me, because it is grounded so deeply in my own roots as to be utterly hidden from me. It is the other who through our encounter awakens this human depth latent in me in an endeavor that surpasses both of us. In authentic dialogue this process is reciprocal."[8] This last point is crucial. We must remember that in the emerging global consciousness passing over should not be a one-way process, but mutual, that Hindus and Buddhists must, themselves, pass over into Christianity and return to their positions enriched. Results of this reciprocal passing over must then be channeled into theories of the interrelation of religions.

The most decisive—and the most problematic—element to be channeled into these theories is the absolute and exclusive claims of the religions. Each religion makes a claim that its ultimate position is absolutely true and, in some sense, exclusively true. For example, the Hindu non-dualist claims that undifferentiated unity is absolute and that all other approaches must be subordinated to this; the Buddhist, that the void is absolute and that silence is the exclusive way; the Christian, that Trinitarian differentiation is absolute and that differentiated union is the ultimate norm. Although this Trinitarian position seems most tolerant since it integrates the other two, it fails to include precisely the other's claim to possess absolute-exclusive dimensions beyond Christian differentiation. All involved in the dialogic dialogue must be cautious neither to hide their absolute-exclusive claims nor to allow themselves unconsciously to subordinate the absolute-exclusive claims of the others. In the dialogic dialogue these claims should not be masked or submerged out of a naïve liberalism or irenic tolerance. Absolute-exclusive claims must be part of the substance of the dialogue; they cannot be left under the table. If they are brought forward and faced squarely in the dialogic atmosphere of mutual passing over and coming back, then the participants in the dialogue can discover concrete interrelations among themselves that will provide new elements for a comprehensive theory.

In the meantime, what are we to do? I would suggest that we proceed through the first two stages of encounter and passing over, as described above. In order to move into the beginning of the third stage, I would suggest that we explore theories of interrelation pluralistically, as outlined above, and that we develop ways of seeing the mutual dimension of the dialogue: for example, how a Hindu or Muslim would pass over into Christianity and return enriched. We can observe how the absolute-exclusive claim of each religion surfaces in the process and how the very theories of universality in each religion are colored by this claim. Realizing the complexity of the issue, we will acquire a sophisticated tolerance which will not attempt to reduce all religions to a least-common-denominator nor naïvely subordinate all absolute-exclusive claims under our own. In this way we will be doing much more than merely assimilating data on world religions, even much more than enriching our religious consciousness by opening to the values of other religions and deepening our own. We will be evoking and nurturing the complexified form of religious consciousness that will be characteristic of the global community of the future. We will discover that this kind of interreligious dialogue is itself a spiritual process, it is the characteristic collective journey of our time.

ACADEMIC STUDY OF MYSTICISM

In addition to the process of interreligious dialogue described above, the academic study of mysticism has contributed to the emerging global consciousness. It has done so by retrieving the heights of mystical experience of the Axial religions and by engaging in comparative studies across religious lines. In the West there has been a steady stream of interest in mysticism since the beginning of the twentieth century. In the United States, for example, this was given expression in the work of William James, especially in *The Varieties of Religious Experience*.[9] Interest during this period can be explained in part as a reaction against the scientific mentality of the era or an attempt to bring mystical experience under scientific scrutiny. However, in the sixties, interest in mysticism emerged more solidly on its own terms in the United States when spiritual teachers came from the East to impart methods of meditation and to alert the secularized masses to the reality of the spiritual journey. Their arrival coincided with the growing interest in the history of religions in academic circles. The publishing world followed suit, and works of the mystics began to appear more widely in print.

In addition to the major series of mystical texts that I spoke of earlier, a number of studies of mysticism have appeared: for example, a collection of essays on mysticism entitled *Understanding Mysticism*, edited by Richard Woods; *Mysticism and Philosophical Analysis*, followed by *Mysticism and Religious Traditions*, both edited by Steven Katz.[10] In 1978 Peter Berger, the sociologist of religion, launched a research seminar to explore mysticism in world religions. The seminar grew out of his book *The Heretical Imperative*, whose last chapter, entitled "Between Jerusalem and Benares: The Coming Contestation of Religions," presented a typology for the cross-cultural study of mystical experience.[11] Berger invited some fifteen academic specialists in the major religions to gather several times a year to present papers and to discuss religious experience — specifically mystical experience — in an interreligious context. Out of this collaborative research, in which I was privileged to participate, came the book: *The Other Side of God: A Polarity in World Religions*, edited by Peter Berger.[12]

A RESEARCH MODEL

The design developed by Peter Berger in this seminar contains, I believe, essential elements for research into mysticism in a global setting at the present time. Such research, it is true, must be solidly grounded in sources, precise in analysis, critical in interpretation according to the highest standards of the academic world. But it must also be cross-cultural and interreligious. This is imperative not only because we now dwell in a global environment, but in order to understand each tradition more accurately and the nature of mystical experience more deeply. In the study of mysticism typologies are crucial. Yet the researchers must be critical about the typologies they choose. These must be tested within the context of a broad horizon of data. Since the data of humankind's mystical experience is largely available at the present time, this data must be taken into account. But who is personally equipped to handle this data? The academic world has not yet produced—and may never do so—a group of scholars each of whom is simultaneously a specialist in all the major world religions, as well as in surviving and nonsurviving primal traditions. How to resolve the dilemma? As Peter Berger did, by bringing a group of specialists together in collaborative work. It is this model of collaborative research in mysticism that I would like to explore as a path into global consciousness.

The Peter Berger seminar met about five times a year, first in New York and then in Boston, to explore mystical experiences in Hinduism, Buddhism, Judaism, Christianity, and Islam, both on their own terms and in comparison among themselves.

Although much clarification issued from this research, I felt it was necessary to supplement it by a more controlled project, using a common methodology whose presuppositions would be brought to light at the outset. On a trip to India in 1983 I met Professor R. Balasubramanian, who was then the director of the Dr. S. Radhakrishnan Institute for Advanced Study in Philosophy of the University of Madras. I discovered that he had been using in his study of Hindu mysticism the same method—phenomenology—that I had been using to study Christian mysticism. So I proposed to him that we collaborate on a joint project in the cross-cultural, interreligious study of mysticism from which would come a book entitled *Mysticism: Hindu and Christian.* He would write chapters on Rāmānuja and Śankara, and I would do chapters on Bonaventure and Eckhart. We would agree in the introduction on a common methodology and collaborate on a conclusion. He accepted and invited me to deliver five lectures at the University of Madras in January 1984. During these talks, I laid out my position on method and applied it to

Bonaventure and Eckhart; then the two of us had a dialogue on their relation to Rāmānuja and Śankara.[13] He agreed with my presentation of the method to the point of saying that we could work out a statement of method in our first chapter to which both of us would sign our names. He invited me back to give three more lectures at the University of Madras in 1985, and I invited him to New York for a month in the fall of 1985, during which time we hoped to advance our project substantially. Since then we have met once or twice a year somewhere around the world, usually at conferences, and have pursued our joint enterprise.

This project is in the tradition of Rudolph Otto's book, *Mysticism East and West*, but differs on major points.[14] Instead of a Western scholar studying a Hindu and a Christian mystic, we have two scholars, one from an Indian Hindu background. Such a configuration has many advantages, since it is more likely than Otto's approach to be authentically in touch with the Hindu materials. Furthermore, it reflects the present climate of cross-cultural studies of religion, which is more dialogic and interreligious than in Otto's generation, as is witnessed by the cross-cultural representation in Peter Berger's seminar. It begins by clarifying a common method and examining critically its cross-cultural dimensions. Of course, Otto's book, *The Idea of the Holy*, which uses phenomenology, could be looked upon as supplying this statement of method, but it is not specifically oriented to cross-cultural studies.

METHODOLOGY FOR MYSTICISM

The method I have proposed to Professor Balasubramanian is akin to the phenomenology of Edmund Husserl, in that it proceeds by describing the contents of consciousness. However, it does not bracket and hold in abeyance the metaphysical content of the consciousness it is studying, although the observer may be called upon to bracket his or her own metaphysical presuppositions. Nor does the method adopt the model in which all intellectual content is derived from the interpretation of raw experience by subjective consciousness. On the contrary, this method is open to the possibility that the intellectual content of the experience can come from the very object of consciousness.

I propose the following as stages of a journey into the study of mystical consciousness:

The first stage is to encounter mystical consciousness. This may be a personal experience of the investigator that is reflected on later. Or it may be the experience of another that is described to the investigator, either personally by the subject or through writings. The investigator might even be present during the mystical experience of the subject or learn of it later. Or in the usual academic context, the investigator studies classical texts. Even here there is a variety of genres. Some mystical writings recount personal experience, for example, those of Augustine, Bernard of Clairvaux, and Julian of Norwich. Others record the experience through a biographer—like the ecstatic experience of Francis of Assisi, when he received the stigmata. Or they may be works giving instruction on the stages of mystical contemplation, for example, Bonaventure's *The Soul's Journey into God*, or sermons like Eckhart's, intended to evoke in the listener levels of contemplative and mystical consciousness.

The second stage of the method is to enter into the consciousness of the mystic. Many elements fall within this stage: for example, in the case of nature mysticism, the mystic's experience of sense objects or the universe as a whole. I would like to focus here on one, a distinctive and crucial dimension; that of the divine, absolute reality. I realize that I am speaking of a specific type of mysticism, namely, God mysticism or theistic mysticism. However, I do not want to take theism in a narrow sense of a personal God, but of absolute reality, differing in ontological status from all other things and designated in some positive or affirmative fashion, not merely by silence or negative judgments. I will deal with the problem of negative and positive approaches later. The point I wish to make here is that the ontological status of this reality must be taken into account seriously in dealing with the mystical experience.

I propose that intentionality is the perspective from which to view mystical experience. Husserlian phenomenology drew the Aristotelian notion of the intentionality of consciousness from Franz Bretano. According to intentionality, our consciousness "intends," in the Latin etymological root meaning of "stretching toward" an object. It is consciousness of something.

What is the intentionality of God mysticism? What is the object of consciousness? I claim that it is the reality of the divine—with all the divine attributes that the classical theologies have affirmed. This ontological affirmation cannot be bracketed, nor can it be said to be merely the mystic's subjective interpretation. What makes God mysticism, what constitutes its distinctive character, is precisely the experience of God as the real, as that which is. This is not a mere interpretation of the experience; it constitutes the very essence of the experience.

Intentionality also can help answer the question that has been recently raised again by Steven Katz and others: Is there one form of mystical experience or many?[15] I believe that there has been a lack of critical reflection in posing the question, which has been formulated in terms derived from the finite realm of multiplicity. Instead, if it is explored through the very intentionality of God mysticism, then the ontological status of the object—the unique divinity—can provide the basis for the claim of unity. If God is perceived as being the one without a second, then, when mystics touch that reality, they realize that they have reached the same realm that all other God mystics have reached. In this sense, at least, there is only one experience of the divine, since the divine is the uniquely one, although there may be diversities in the subjective paths, and even among the divine attributes. But even in the diversity of the divine attributes, the mystics perceive the divine nature, which is the point where the intentionality of their experience converges.

Once we employ this empathetic phenomenology, we begin to see the importance of typologies in the study of mystical experience. For the typologies emerge from analysis of the structure of consciousness of the mystic. Whether there is ultimately only one form of mystical experience or whether there is a principle of unity within divergent forms are questions which must logically follow a study of the varieties of mystical experience. These varieties can be based on the experience of the subject: affective or intellectual, as prophetic encounter or harmonious relation with the cosmos; on where he or she perceives the mystical dimension: in nature, in the soul, in God; on the perception of ultimate reality: as being, energy, love, intelligibility, beauty, power, oneness, darkness, silence. Once we become aware of this variety, certain questions arise: is the mystical experience one and the variety due to non-mystical elements? To language, to concepts, to affective states? I believe that we should not begin with an affirmative assumption here, but keep the issue open at the start, at least the possibility that the variety might be part of the mystical experience itself.

A similar question arises over the intellectual content of certain mystical experiences: Is mystical experience devoid of intellectual content, which comes merely from our interpretation of the experience? Such a model is widespread in academic circles, acknowledging only a non-intellectual experience with all intellectual content derived from human interpretation. Again, I believe that one should not begin with such an assumption. In fact, I believe that there is convincing evidence that certain forms of mystical experience have intellectual content given within the experience. This raises two closely-related questions: What is the relation between mystical experience and metaphysics? Can metaphysics merely attempt to give a theoretical explanation of mystical experience or can it be part of the mystical experience itself? I believe that it can be part of the experience. On the other hand, when examining mystical experience the researchers should be careful not to impose their own metaphysics on the experience but examine the experience on its own. My methodological strategy, then, is to examine phenomenologically the experience on its own terms and see what typology emerges and what metaphysical perception may be given within the content of the experience.

This strategy must control the entire investigation. It must be firmly kept in mind that mystical experience is not ordinary, everyday experience. If one holds that in ordinary consciousness knowledge of God can be had only analogously with our knowledge of creatures, this position must not be carried over as an uncritical assumption in investigating mystical experience. In fact, mystics claim to experience God directly. In phenomenological investigation such a claim must be taken seriously and the content of such consciousness explored on its own. Throughout the investigation care should be taken not to impose the structures of everyday consciousness on mystical experience unless the experience itself yields such evidence.

BONAVENTURE AND MYSTICAL EXPERIENCE

I would like now to turn to case studies of Christian mysticism, which form the basis for our collaborative investigation of mysticism, Christian and Hindu. I will choose as my cases for investigation Bonaventure and Eckhart, two major authors of mystical writings in the medieval period, whose works have become classics in the field. While representing a common Christian tradition, they express considerable divergences. Bonaventure was a Franciscan who emphasized the affective approach to God, following Francis of Assisi in devotion to the humanity of Christ. Eckhart was a Dominican, who moved to God through the intellect, not through affectivity or devotion to Christ's humanity. Like Francis of Assisi, Bonaventure experienced the created world as a ladder on which he could climb up to God as its fountain-source. Eckhart counseled radical detachment from creatures which would lead ultimately to "the desert" of the Godhead.

These two Christian authors can fruitfully be studied in relation to the Hindu spiritual writers Rāmānuja and Śankara; for Bonaventure represents the devotional, or *bhakti*, approach of Rāmānuja, and Śankara the intellectual, or *jnana*, approach of Eckhart. Like Rāmānuja, Bonaventure focuses on the personal aspects of God; and like

Śankara, Eckhart focuses on the transpersonal dimensions of the divinity. Rāmānuja has been studied in relation to Bonaventure and Eckhart in relation to Śankara.[16] But a study of the four authors together can reveal the variety of mystical experience, the diversity of mystical paths, and underlying patterns of unity. I believe that such cross-cultural study can help clarify issues within each tradition. For example, if Bonaventure is viewed as pursuing the way of *bhakti* and Eckhart the way of *jnana*, their own interrelation can be clarified in the light of this Hindu polarity. A study of these two ways in the West, free from the controversies between the Hindu schools, can throw light on the diversity and interrelation of Hindu mystical paths.

In studying the two authors, I will focus on Bonaventure's treatise *The Soul's Journey into God* and Eckhart's sermons.[17] These works are not in the genre of autobiography or spiritual journal; hence they do not intend to give descriptions of the author's experience. However they do intend to guide others to mystical contemplation and even to mystical ecstasy. Hence they describe and evoke varied levels of mystical experience. By entering into the texts, then, we can clarify through phenomenological analysis the structure of consciousness that they describe and evoke. In this way we will be studying not Bonaventure's mystical experience in a restricted sense, but the mystical experience he wished to evoke in his readers. Hence he, like Eckhart, presents structures of mystical consciousness, not as personal to himself, but in their more universal modality as these can be shared by many who read this work.

THE PATH OF LOVE

In *The Soul's Journey into God*, Bonaventure sketches the map of the mystical journey. One proceeds through the following stages: contemplation of God in the material world, in our activity of sensation, in the faculties of our soul, in these same faculties reformed by grace, in God himself as Being and as the Good. Although the path involves much intellectual contemplation, even metaphysical analysis, Bonaventure gives primacy to devotion and affectivity. His path through knowledge involves an intellectual perception of the hierarchical structure of reality with matter at the bottom, then spirit, then God. By contemplating this structure and by ascending the metaphysical ladder, one could reach contemplation of and even union with God himself. Granted that this provides the landscape of Bonaventure's journey, his point of departure, his motivating force throughout, and the goal which he reaches is permeated with love and devotion. For example, in the prologue immediately after the passage quoted above, Bonaventure states: "There is no other path but through the burning love of the Crucified, a love which so transformed Paul into Christ when he *was carried up to the third heaven* (2 Cor. 12:2) that he could say: *With Christ I am nailed to the cross. I live, now not, I, but Christ lives in me* (Gal. 2:20)." He goes on to describe how this love permeated Francis of Assisi: "This love also so absorbed the soul of Francis that his spirit shone through his flesh when for two years before his death he carried in his body the sacred stigmata of the passion." In the same vein Bonaventure invites the reader to prayer and devotion to Christ's passion "so that he not believe that reading is sufficient without unction, speculation without devotion, investigation without wonder, observation without joy, work without piety, knowledge without love, understanding without humility, endeavor without divine grace."[18]

When Bonaventure contemplates the Trinity, he sees it not primarily as the mystery of the divine differentiation, but of the divine self-diffusion. Proceeding along the lines of Anselm's ontological argument, he states: "See, then, and observe that the highest good is without qualification that than which no greater can be thought. And it is such that it cannot rightly be thought not to be, since to be is in all ways better than not to be."[19] He then applies this notion of the good as perfection to the Trinity. For according to Bonaventure, the highest perfection is self-diffusion, that is, the spontaneous self-communicating within the divine life. "For the good is said to be self-diffusive; therefore the highest good must be most self-diffusive."[20] This leads him to the Christian doctrine of the Trinity, for there must exist within the divinity a self-diffusion that is eternal, intrinsic to the divinity, totally actualized, and perfect. This means that there must be an eternal self-communication from the Father to the Son in the unity of the Spirit. The divine self-communication in creation is unable to give adequate self-expression to the immensity of the divine fecundity. Elsewhere Bonaventure treats the Father in the Trinity as fountain fulness (*fontalis plenitudo*); this is a mystical image of the fountain of divine energy ever flowing in its creative, self-diffusive love.[21]

I propose that the affectivity of Bonaventure—and of the early Franciscan tradition—was based on a contemplative and mystical experience of the divinity as the self-diffusive, fountain fulness. In *The Idea of the Holy* Rudolf Otto gave a phenomenological analysis of the elements in the religious consciousness of the sacred.[22] He sought the intentionality of this consciousness: the object to which it was directed. This he called the *numen* and analyzed it as containing the elements of *mysterium tremendum et fascinans*. Using the same phenomenological method, I would like to identify the elements in Bonaventure's most characteristic mystical experience, the intentionality of his contemplative consciousness. This is *bonum divinum: perfectum et diffusivum sui*. That is the divine good: perfect and diffusive of itself. In the hierarchy of perfection, for Bonaventure, the highest good coincides with self-diffusion; hence we can describe the intentionality of his mystical consciousness as directed toward the divine fountain fulness: *divina fontalis plenitudo*. If this is the object of the consciousness, what is the subjective correlative of the consciousness? Otto presented the subjective correlative of the numinous as consciousness of oneself as a creature. In the case of Bonaventure the corresponding subjective correlative is affectivity, but affectivity of a complex kind. There is love and awe at the divine perfection in general, but a special kind of love and awe before the *divina fontalis plenitudo*, for this involves a sharing in the divine self-diffusion. This is a complex experience of God's love for us, of grace, and of participating in his divine energy and interpersonal love.

Granted this, it is not surprising that immediately after contemplating God in this fashion, Bonaventure turns to the humanity of Christ as the expression of this self-diffusive love and of the passage back to its source. Just as devotion to the humanity of Christ was the energy that inaugurated the soul's journey, so devotion to the humanity of Christ is the vehicle of our passage from contemplative to ecstatic consciousness, that is, from the sixth to the seventh stage of the journey. As Bonaventure says, "In this passing over, Christ is *the way and the door*; Christ is the ladder and the vehicle."[23] This final state of ecstasy is a state of love, in which intellectual contemplation has been left behind: "In this passing over, if it is to be perfect, all intellectual activities must be left behind and the height of our affection must be totally transferred and transformed into God."[24] He concludes with the image of divine fire:

> But if you wish to know how these things come about, ask grace not instruction, desire not understanding, the groaning of prayer not diligent reading, the Spouse not the teacher, God not man, darkness not clarity, not light but the fire that totally inflames and carries us into God by ecstatic unctions and burning affections. This fire is God, and his furnace is in Jerusalem; and Christ enkindles it in the heat of his burning passion.[25]

ECKHART AND THE PATH OF KNOWLEDGE

Like Bonaventure, Eckhart in his sermons leads his hearers along a spiritual path that moves from creatures to God, but the route and the goal are different. He proceeds by way of knowledge rather than love; he uses negation rather than affirmation; and he arrives ultimately at "the desert" of the Godhead rather than the ever-flowing fountain of divine fecundity. We must introduce a caution here. Eckhart does not reject the way of affirmation, for he affirms that God is reflected in creatures. Nor does he reject the notion of God as fountain of fecundity, for he acknowledges that in his treatment of the Trinity. But when he sketches the map of the spiritual journey, he directs his followers along a different path. Since he follows the path of negation, it is not surprising that he moves by way of intellect rather than affectivity. By penetrating intellectual analysis, he attempts to liberate his hearers from attachment to creatures, even from God himself. In his works we do not find meditation on the humanity of Christ, with its corresponding devotion and affectivity, as we do in Bonaventure and the Franciscans.

In a sermon on poverty, he distinguishes two kinds of poverty: external and internal. After glossing over external poverty, which he approves, he directs his attention to internal poverty. "A poor man," he says, "wants nothing and knows nothing and has nothing." Although poverty is the central Franciscan virtue, Eckhart moves beyond the usual Franciscan position by advising a radical internal poverty that ultimately strips one of God himself. He points out how "people say that a man is poor who wants nothing but they interpret it in this way, that a man ought to live so that he never fulfills his own will in anything, but that he ought to comport himself so that he may fulfill God's dearest will." But Eckhart says that such are not poor men. "If a person wants really to have poverty," Eckhart says, "he ought to be as free of his own created will as he was when he did not exist." He goes on to say: "So long as you have a will to fulfill God's will and a longing for God and for eternity, then you are not poor; for a poor man is one who has a will and a longing for nothing."[26]

Eckhart then proceeds in his radical analysis, saying that we must be free from God himself. He speaks of his existence in his first cause, saying that there he had no 'God.' "I wanted nothing, I longed for nothing, for I was an empty being. But when I went out from my own free will and received my created being, then I had a 'God,' for before there were any creatures, God was no 'God,' but he was what he was." He concludes: "So let us pray to God that we may be free of 'God,' and that we may apprehend and rejoice in that everlasting truth in which the highest angel and the fly and the soul are equal—there where I was established, where I wanted what I was and was what I wanted."[27]

Eckhart's position sounds radical within the classical Christian tradition and has been a matter of controversy since his own lifetime. Part of the problem has stemmed from the fact that Eckhart spoke in metaphysical terms which seemed to go counter to the established metaphysical and doctrinal terms of the tradition. If we use the method of phenomenology, we may be able to reach the heart of the mystical experience he was evoking in his hearers and determine what metaphysical insights are contained in the experience itself. Ultimately the question comes to this: What was Eckhart's distinctive experience of God?

It is most accurate to say that Eckhart's experience of God was multi-dimensional. For there is abundant evidence that he shared Bonaventure's experience of God as flowing fountain of fecundity. For example, he says: "The Father speaks the Son out of all his power, and he speaks in him all things. All created things are God's speech. The being of a stone speaks and manifests the same as does my mouth about God. . . . Therefore the Father speaks the Son always, in unity, and pours out in him all created things. They are all called to return into whence they have flowed out. All their life and their being is a calling and a hastening back to him from whom they have issued."[28]

Granted this, Eckhart's characteristic experience is not of the divine fountain but of the divine desert. It is the divine silence that precedes speech, and out of which divine speech flows; it is the divine abyss of emptiness that is the ground of the divine fulness; it is the divine darkness that is the origin of the divine light. Eckhart evokes the mystical experience of the divine desert in the following statement:

> I speak in all truth, truth that is eternal and enduring, that this same light [the spark of the soul] is not content with the simple divine essence in its repose, as it neither gives nor receives; but it wants to know the source of this essence, it wants to go into the simple ground, into the quiet desert, into which distinction never gazed, not the Father, nor the Son, nor the Holy Spirit.[29]

In another passage, Eckhart evokes the same experience:

> But if all images are detached from the soul, and it contemplates only the Simple One, then the soul's naked being finds the naked, formless being of the divine unity, which is there a being above being, accepting and reposing in itself. Ah, marvel of marvels, how noble is that

acceptance, when the soul's being can accept nothing else than the naked unity of God![30]

At this point we must apply the phenomenological method to the experience that Eckhart is attempting to evoke in his hearers. What is the intentionality of the experience; what is its object? As Eckhart describes it, it is an experience of unity on the absolute level of reality. It might be more accurate to say that it is an experience of non-differentiation since this is the characteristic way in which Eckhart speaks, claiming that this desert is beyond the differentiations of Father, Son, and Holy Spirit. Following the suggestion of Rudolf Otto, we should examine this experience on its own terms, not applying analogies from other spheres, for example, from sense experience. In many respects, it is more subtle to describe phenomenologically than that of Bonaventure's flowing fountain of divine fecundity. For it seems to be a mere negation, and is largely so on the linguistic level or the general level of ordinary consciousness. But if our awareness on the absolute level is evoked, then on this level the experience is not of negation, but of reality itself in its deepest form. I believe that Eckhart's metaphysical statement about God, creation, and the spiritual path of radical detachment are all to be read from this ultimate experience of the desert of the Godhead. In a seminal sense they are all contained in the experience. As with Bonaventure, we can ask the question: What is the subjective correlative of this intentionality of consciousness? Since the experience of the desert of the Godhead is a mystical experience of emptiness on the highest level of reality, it has as its correlative on the level of subjective consciousness the radical detachment which Eckhart inculcates.

FULNESS AND EMPTINESS

Having done a phenomenological analysis of the mystical experience of both Bonaventure and Eckhart, we are faced with the question: Can these mystical experiences be reconciled? Are they so divergent that there is no basis for integration? Or can the same mystic have these two diverse experiences in such a way that they are compatible? These questions can be approached theoretically by exploring the structure of each experience to determine compatible or incompatible dimensions. Or they can be approached practically by asking whether the mystics themselves experienced both types. Following the second approach, we can find little evidence that Bonaventure had the mystical experience of the desert of the Godhead, such as

Eckhart describes. The chief strand of positive evidence is found in the seventh chapter of *The Soul's Journey into God*, from which we quoted above. However, love predominates in this stage and, in fact, reaches its climax. Eckhart's desert of the Godhead seems to stand beyond affectivity. There is reason to think, as we indicated above, that Eckhart shared Bonaventure's mystical experience of the divine fountain of fecundity. If this is the case, then at least Eckhart offers an example of a mystic who shared the two experiences.

Granted this, we now turn to the theoretical question: Can the two experiences be reconciled according to their internal structure? I believe that in Eckhart's case they were, for he describes a flow of energy from the desert to the fountain and from the fountain to the desert. It is here that the doctrine of the Trinity can mediate the two experiences. For the person of the Father can be seen to have two aspects: that of the fountain of creative energy out of which the Son as Word is generated and the Holy Spirit breathed forth; and that of the desert or the abyss out of which the creative energy flows. Since Christians believe that every aspect of the Trinity is fully divine, there is an ontological equality on the level of the divinity, but a differentiation in terms of the dynamic process of ebb and flow of the divine life from the desert to the fountain and back again.

If this is the case, then the other divergent elements can be reconciled: the path of affirmation and the path of negation, the way of affectivity and the way of understanding. If they are reconciled, then we must be cautious not to use one against the other. We can use a perspectival approach to the spiritual paths and their respective goals. From the perspective of the path of love and the personal dimension of the divine, there may seem to be no coherent link with the desert of the Godhead, and vice versa. However, they would be compatible from the standpoint of a coincidence of opposites, such as described in Eckhart's experience and our theoretical analysis of the two structures of consciousness. This suggests that there are two ultimate categories of mystical experience: fulness and emptiness. These are present on the level of the absolute and on all levels of reality, forming the essential structure of the spiritual paths. In a separate study, I have attempted to view Bonaventure and Eckhart precisely from the standpoint of the coincidence of fulness and emptiness.[31] The results were sufficiently enlightening to suggest further use of these categories in the study of mystical experience.

After studying Bonaventure and Eckhart, we come to the phase of the research that involves the cross-cultural comparison with Rāmānuja and Śankara. The general lines of the comparison are clear: the similarity of Bonaventure and Rāmānuja in following the path of devotion and arriving at the personal dimension of the divinity; the similarity of Śankara and Eckhart in the path of knowledge and arriving at the non-differentiated, transpersonal dimension of the divinity. For those familiar with the two Hindu theologians, many other points will appear pertinent. Furthermore, the Christian paths can be seen with greater refinement in the light of the precision of Hindu thought; and the relation between the Hindu schools can be clarified by Eckhart's comprehensive vision. Having come after the affective approach the Franciscans had developed, his mysticism seems open to including it within a larger whole. Beyond this general observation, the model that I am proposing prevents me from proceeding further. For I am not a specialist in Hindu mysticism, philosophy, or theology. Therefore what is required is a continuation of my collaborative venture with R. Balasubramanian.

My dialogue with Balasubramanian has been primarily over Eckhart and Śankara since my colleague is a specialist in Śankara's non-dualism. We have come to a common understanding that the crucial philosophical, theological, and mystical question, both in Hinduism and Christianity, is how to reconcile the abyss with the fountain.

While dialogue between polar opposite positions such as this can be very challenging and fruitful, I have pursued a dialogue of similar traditions in an interreligious exploration between the spiritual path of love in Christianity and Hinduism held yearly since 1988 at St. Bonaventure University. This, too, has been very fruitful, yielding more similarities than either side had anticipated. Such precise academic dialogue is one of the many paths on the journey into global consciousness.

VI

Guides for the Second Axial Period: Francis of Assisi, Bonaventure, Eckhart

Earlier in this book I made the claim that in moving into the Second Axial Period the world's religions should retrieve the fulness of their First Axial heritage. At the same time, however, they are caught up in a transformation from individual to global consciousness. I gave the example of Raimundo Panikkar as a person who has already made this transition and who as a guide to the future has illumined the way for others to make the passage, especially in respect to what I called the horizontal level of global consciousness: namely, interreligious dialogue.

But there is another dimension of global consciousness, which I called the vertical level, where spirituality is rooted in the earth and matter. The First Axial transformation of consciousness tended to disengage spirituality from matter. The Second Axial Period faces a major challenge of discovering a new spirituality of matter—or more precisely a new holistic spirituality that integrates in an organic way matter, the human, and the divine.

Who are the teachers of this new spiritual wisdom? I have proposed earlier that the richest source is the spirituality of primal peoples. It was from them that First Axial spirituality emerged; it was from them that First Axial religions inherited a rich legacy of ritual and archetypal symbols; and it is by the wisdom of the millions of primal people around the world today that we can be guided in a special way into the holistic spirituality of the Second Axial Period. At the present time the relation of primal spirituality to First Axial religions is being intensely explored in the ecological movement. It is a major concern of the series World Spirituality: An Encyclopedic History of the Religious Quest, and is the object of a three-year research program organized by the Confucian scholar Wei-Ming Tu at the Institute of Culture and Communication at the East-West Center in Honolulu.[1]

But there are also other guides—spiritual teachers from the history of First Axial religions who are especially relevant at the present time. In their mystical experience or in their theoretical vision they witnessed to a holistic spirituality even in the First Axial context. Thus they can serve as guideposts and models for moving into the transformed global consciousness of the Second Axial Period. In this and the subsequent chapter I will single out some such guides from the Christian tradition, beginning here with Francis of Assisi and Bonaventure. But before doing this, I would like to highlight some of the issues involved in the transition by drawing from the series World Spirituality.

PRIMAL AND AXIAL SPIRITUALITIES

Although it was not designed with this explicitly in mind, the series is organized in such a way that it reflects the Pre-Axial, the First Axial, and the Second Axial Periods. There are five volumes on the spirituality of primal peoples—the archaic spirituality of Asia, Europe, Africa and Oceania, North America, South and Meso-America. These are followed by volumes on the major traditions, usually two per tradition: Hindu, Buddhist, Taoist, Confucian, Jewish, Christian, and Islamic. The series includes also Zoroastrianism, Jainism, and Sikkhism, as well as traditions which have not survived as such: for example, the Sumerian and Hittite, Egyptian, Greek, and Roman. To these are added a volume on modern esoteric movements and one on the secular spiritual quest. The last three volumes deal with the interrelation of spiritualities. Volume 23 treats the encounter of spiritualities past to the present and explores those archetypal symbols and practices which are the basis for a creative encounter. Volume 24 is on the encounter of spiritualities present to the future; it will contain a forum of articles by the volume editors on the present and future state of spirituality as they see it from the standpoint of their traditions and from their own perspectives. Volume 25 is a dictionary of spiritual terms drawn from all the traditions. It is not a mere listing of definitions but a view of world spirituality in its diversity and interrelatedness through its technical vocabulary.

Since World Spirituality is global in scope, it was necessary to formulate a working definition of the term that would be acceptable to all traditions. This was all the more challenging since not all of the traditions have a term that corresponds to "spirituality." The following is the formulation which was distributed to the editors at the beginning of the project to serve as a guideline for them and their contributors. Since certain traditions, like the Buddhist, do not speak of the divine, it seemed best to formulate the meaning in terms of the human person:

> The series focuses on that inner dimension of the person called by certain traditions 'the spirit.' This spiritual core is the deepest center of the person. It is here that the person is open to the transcendent dimension; it is here that the person experiences ultimate reality. The series explores the discovery of this core, the dynamics of its development, and its journey to the ultimate goal. It deals with prayer, spiritual direction, the various maps of the spiritual journey, and the methods of advancement in the spiritual ascent.[2]

I believe that the above definition applies to the spirituality of Axial religions and not to that of primal peoples. As we will see later, the focus on the individual person and his or her ascent to the transcendent is characteristic of the religions of the Axial Period and not of primal peoples. "Holistic" would be a better way to describe primal spirituality, indicating the experience of an integral relationship between the cosmic, the human, and the transcendent. It is this holistic quality that is presented in the following statement by Lame Buffalo, an American Indian of the Sioux tribe:

> The Native Indians of this land offer to humanity a unique expression that belongs among the great spiritual traditions of mankind. Just as other traditions have their specific glory, the members of the Native Indian community have their own special form of Nature Mysticism. Being aware of the presence of the Great Spirit throughout the entire cosmic order establishes among these peoples one of the most complete forms of spirituality known to man. The cosmic, human, and divine are present to one another in a way that is unique.
>
> The Native Indian is profoundly religious in his character. The formalities of his life are religious formalities. His mode of life, his thought, his every act are given spiritual significance. His most deliberate words and deeds revolve upon religious considerations. He has a highly developed sense of the sacred, and understands clearly that his view of himself and the world is preeminently a religious view.
>
> From the very first, the Native Indian has centered his life in the Natural World. He is deeply invested in the earth—committed to it in his consciousness and in his instinct. Only in reference to the earth can he persist in his true identity. This is why the Native Indian conceives of himself in terms of the land. In his view the earth is sacred. It is a living entity in which living entities have origin and destiny—the Native Indian is bound to the earth in his spirit. By means of his involvement in the Natural World does the Indian insure his own well-being.[3]

In the history of Christianity, perhaps no saint has exemplified the spirituality of the earth more seminally than Francis of Assisi. Although living in the First Axial context of medieval Europe eight centuries ago, St. Francis gave expression to a holistic spirituality that finds resonances in primal peoples and in the global spirituality of the future. Francis did not sever the human from nature or nature from the human. He called the sun his brother and the earth his sister and mother; he spoke as a friend to birds and to the wolf of Gubbio. Because he felt himself part of the family of creation, he did not exploit or dominate nature, but rather humanized nature and naturalized the human. At the same time, he cultivated distinctly human ideals by imitating the humanity of Christ in radical literalness. In spite of Francis's influence, the split between nature and the human widened in Western culture, reaching a climax in the ecological crisis of our time.

FRANCIS AND NATURE

With a penetrating spiritual insight, Francis saw an organic relationship between nature, the human, and God.[4] For him nature was not something separate from God and human beings: an autonomous given, standing on its own apart. Nor was it humanity's footstool on which they could lift themselves above, trampling and exploiting nature in the process. For him nature was sacred, an expression of God himself; it was a divine gift which bore God's imprint. According to Bonaventure and Francis's other biographers, he saw God reflected throughout creation. Although he was aware of God's reflection in the universe as a whole, he focused, in characteristic fashion, on specific creatures: the sun, the moon, and the stars; an earthworm, a lamb, a flock of birds. Bonaventure sums up his attitude as follows: "Aroused by all thing to the love of God, he *rejoiced* in all *the works of the Lord's hands* (Ps. 91) and from these joy-producing manifestations he rose to their life-giving principle and cause. In beautiful things he saw Beauty itself and through his vestiges imprinted on creation he followed his Beloved everywhere (Job 23:11; Cant. 5:17), making from all things a ladder by which he could climb up and embrace him who is utterly desirable (Cant. 5:16)." After sketching this attitude towards creatures as a whole, Bonaventure points out the joy he felt in each creature as he saw it flowing from the fountain of the divine fecundity: "With a feeling of unprecedented devotion he savored in each and every creature— as in so many rivulets—that Goodness which is their fountain-source." Having described Francis's seeing Beauty and tasting Goodness, he describes his hearing the heavenly music that emerges from the harmony of creatures: "He perceived a heavenly harmony in the consonance of powers and activities God has given them, and like the prophet David sweetly exhorted them to praise the Lord."[5]

In the final line above, Bonaventure is referring to Francis's composing *The Canticle of Brother Sun*, which has become the classical expression of his feeling towards nature. In 1225, about a year and a half before his death, Francis composed a *cantico* or song in his Umbrian dialect, along with a melody, which has been lost. In this *cantico* Francis praises God by and through creatures: the sun, moon, and stars, along with the four elements: earth, air, fire, and water. He sings of Sir Brother Sun, who in his beauty images God: "He is beautiful and radiant with great splendor, and bears the signification of you, Most High One." He proceeds through the four elements, praising God, for example, by, for, and through "Sister Water, which is very useful and humble and precious and chaste"; and "Brother Fire, by whom you light the night, and he is beautiful and jocund and robust and strong." Finally, he closes his hymn with an exhortation to all creatures: "Praise and bless my Lord and give him thanks, and serve him with great humility."

Because of its richness and complexity, I would like to present the entire text of *The Canticle of Brother Sun* in the original Umbrian Italian along with an English translation.[6]

IL CANTICO DI FRATE SOLE

1 Altissimu onnipotente bon signore,
2 Tue so le laude, la gloria e l'onore et onne benedictione.
3 Ad te solo, altissimo, se konfano,
4 Et nullu homo ene dignu te mentovare.

10 Laudato si, mi signore, per sora luna e le stelle,
11 In celu l'aì formate clarite et pretiose et belle.

5 Laudato sie, mi signore, cun tucte le tue creature,
6 Spetialmente messor lo frate sole,
7 Lo qual'è iorno, et allumini noi per loi.
8 Et ellu è bellu e radiante con grande splendore,
9 De te, altissimo, porta significatione.

12 Laudato si, mi signore, per frate vento,
13 Et per aere et nubilo et sereno et omne tempo,
14 Per lo quale al e tue creature dai sustentamento.

15 Laudato si, mi signore, per sor aqua,
16 La quale è multo utile et humile et pretiosa et casta.

17 Laudato si, mi signore, per frate focu,
18 Per lo quale enn' allumini la nocte,
19 Ed ello è bello et iocundo et robustoso et forte.

20 Laudato si, mi signore, per sora nostra matre terra,
21 La quale ne sustenta et governa,
22 Et produce diversi fructi con coloriti flori et herba.

23 Laudato si, mi signore, per quelli ke perdonano per lo tuo amore,
24 Et sostengo infirmitate et tribulatione.
25 Beati quelli ke 'l sosterrano in pace,
26 Ka da te, altissimo, sirano incoronati.

27 Laudato si, mi signore, per sora nostra morte corporale,
28 Da la quale nullu homo vivente po' skappare.
29 Guai a quelli, ke morrano ne le peccata mortali:
30 Beati quelli ke travarà ne le tue santissime voluntati,
31 Ka la morte secunda nol farrà male.

32 Laudate et benedicete mi signore,
33 Et rengratiate et serviateli cun grande humilitate.

THE CANTICLE OF BROTHER SUN

1 Most high omnipotent good Lord,
2 Yours are the praises, the glory, the honor and all blessing.
3 To you alone, Most High, do they belong,
4 And no man is worthy to mention you.

5 Praised be you, my Lord, with all your creatures,
6 Especially Sir Brother Sun,
7 Who makes the day and through whom you give us light.
8 And he is beautiful and radiant with great splendor,
9 And bears the signification of you, Most High One.

10 Praised be you, my Lord, for Sister Moon and the stars,
11 You have formed them in heaven clear and precious and Beautiful.
12 Praised be you, my Lord, for Brother Wind,
13 And for the air—cloudy and serene—and every kind of weather,
14 By which you give sustenance to your creatures.

15 Praised be you, my Lord, for Sister Water,
16 Which is very useful and humble and precious and chaste.

17 Praised be you, my Lord, for Brother Fire,
18 By whom you light the night,
19 And he is beautiful and jocund and robust and strong.

20 Praised be you, my Lord, for our sister Mother Earth
21 Who sustains and governs us,
22 And produces various fruits with colored flowers and herbs.

23 Praised be you, my Lord, for those who give pardon for your love
24 And bear infirmity and tribulation,
25 Blessed are those who endure in peace,
26 For by you, Most High, they will be crowned.

27 Praised be you, Lord, for our Sister Bodily Death,
28 From whom no living man can escape.
29 Woe to those who die in mortal sin.
30 Blessed are those whom death will find in your most holy will,
31 For the second death shall do them no harm.

32 Praise and bless my Lord and give him thanks
33 And serve him with great humility.

Francis, it is true, saw nature intimately linked with God as an expression of the divine. But he also saw nature intimately linked with himself. He did not consider himself as a mere spectator observing a distant panorama, nor as an actor on the stage of the world, with nature providing a beautiful setting. Rather he was part of the setting himself, and nature and he were actors together in the drama of creation. This is crucial for the issue of ecology. The Franciscan attitude involves two basic elements: (1) a sense of reverence derived from the fact that the world is sacred as God's expression of himself; (2) a sense of intimacy with the physical universe: the inorganic, vegetative, and animal realms. Reverence alone is not enough; we must feel ourselves part of the family of creatures. It is this family consciousness that crowns Francis's attitude toward nature.

When treating Francis's attitude toward creatures, Bonaventure situates it under the virtue of piety. At first this may seem strange; however the term "piety" did not carry the connotations of superficial religiosity that it does at present in English. Rather piety was a profoundly relational virtue, the ancient Roman *pietas* that provided the root of intimate relations in the family, in the clan, and in the state. It included love, devotion, affection, reverence, kindness, fidelity, and compassion. With this in mind, we can realize the significance of Bonaventure's observation: "When he [Francis] considered the primordial source of all things, he was filled with even more abundant piety, calling creatures, no matter how small, by the name of brother or sister, because he knew they had the same source as himself."[7] It is interesting to note that in his *Canticle of Brother Sun*, Francis was heavily influenced by Biblical sources, for example,

Psalm 148 and the *Canticle of the Three Young Men* in the Book of Daniel (3:52–90). However, these Biblical sources do not call creatures brother and sister, nor formulate the family relationship Francis felt. Although implicit in the Bible, the intensity of this family sense and its self-consciousness is uniquely Franciscan.

FRANCIS AND MYSTICISM OF THE HUMANITY OF CHRIST

Francis cultivated the human not only in relation to nature, but also in its own sphere. This he did through identifying with the humanity of Christ, imitating him in distinctly human virtues. Francis was the recipient of the most celebrated mystical experience of the Middle Ages: the ecstatic vision on Mount La Verna in 1224 of the Six-winged Seraph in the form of the Crucified, during which he received the stigmata. Yet this vision and his other mystical experiences were not characteristic of the mainstream Christian mystical tradition that preceded him both in the Greek East and the Latin West. For centuries the patristic and medieval periods were dominated by the speculative mysticism of the Neoplatonists, which had been given a Christian form by the Alexandrians in the East and Augustine in the West. The writings of the Pseudo-Dionysius became the handbook for this speculative mysticism, which reached its climax in the *via negativa*, negating all images in order to plunge into the divine darkness. Even in its *via affirmativa*, it did not cultivate visionary mysticism, but rather a metaphysical ascent of the Neoplatonic ladder of creatures.

The figure of the Six-winged Seraph in the form of Christ Crucified ushered in a major trend in the history of Western Christianity: devotion to the humanity of Christ, especially in his suffering and death. The very stigmata imprinted on Francis's flesh—the first recorded case in history—graphically displays his innovative Christ mysticism. In contrast to earlier mysticism which saw Christ as the eternal Logos and resurrected Lord, Francis focused on the incarnate Christ: on his birth at Bethlehem, his preaching and public life, and especially his passion and death. For Augustine, Christ was primarily the Logos as interior Teacher of wisdom; for Bernard of Clairvaux he was the interior Lover, the Bridegroom of the soul; for Francis he was his crucified Redeemer. With a profound intuition, Francis discerned the humanness of Christ and set out to imitate this humanness as a religious ideal. Francis represents a watershed in the history of Western Christianity. After him Western religious experience flows in two currents: speculative Neoplatonic mysticism gains vigor, reaching a culmination in the Rhineland mystics. But the devotional current flowing from Francis—with its focus on the humanity and passion of Christ—spreads throughout the people at large and becomes the characteristic form of Western religious sensibility for centuries to come.

In highlighting the humanity of Christ, Francis focused on his birth and death. This is not surprising since it is precisely our birth and death that establish us in the human situation. In 1223 in the town of Greccio he created a dramatic Christmas setting for midnight Mass. Although there had been cribs before, his dramatic flare and humanness infused the scene with a spirit that has become part of the sensibility of Western culture. According to Bonaventure, "he had a crib prepared, hay carried in, and an ox and an ass led to the place." The friars and congregation gather, carrying candles and singing hymns. Francis "stands before the crib, filled with affection, bathed in tears and overflowing with joy." At the solemn high Mass celebrated over the crib, Francis as deacon chants the Gospel. "Then he preaches to the people standing about concerning the birth of the poor King, whom, when he wished to name him, he called in his tender love, the Child of Bethlehem."[8]

In the crib at Greccio Francis evoked tenderness and joy at the newborn babe, awakening the cluster of human emotions we feel at the sight of an infant. These emotions were intensified and lifted to the religious plane by the fact that God himself was entering into the human experience of infancy, and through that into the entire ambit of human experiences, which culminated in death on the cross. Throughout his life Francis had an intense devotion to Christ's passion. Bonaventure describes a scene at an early stage of Francis's religious conversion when he began to pray in deserted places. While he was absorbed in prayer, "Jesus Christ appeared to him fastened to the cross. Francis's *soul melted* (Can. 5:6) at the sight, and the memory of Christ's passion was so impressed in the innermost recesses of his heart that from that hour, whensoever Christ's crucifixion came to his mind, he could scarcely contain his tears and sighs."[9]

His life-long devotion to Christ's passion was crowned by the vision which Francis received on Mount La Verna, two years before his death. He saw a Seraph descending toward him from heaven with six fiery wings and between the wings the figure of Christ crucified. "When Francis saw this," Bonaventure says, "he was overwhelmed and his heart flooded with a mixture of joy and sorrow. He rejoiced because of the gracious way Christ looked upon him under the appearance of the Seraph, but the fact that he was fastened to a cross *pierced his soul with a sword* of compassionate sorrow" (Luke 2:35).[10] Immediately after the vision disappeared,

Francis received the stigmata: the marks of Christ's passion, on his hands, feet, and side. As in the crib at Greccio, Francis gave dramatic expression to the humanness of Christ, this time manifesting his very wounds in his body. Focusing on the anguish of human suffering, Francis evoked compassion for Christ's suffering; through this compassion for the suffering of the God-man, he evoked compassion for the suffering of all of humanity. The same human sensibility that expressed itself in tenderness for the birth of human life now expresses itself in compassion for the suffering in the human situation that reaches its climax in death and its climactic expression in the death of Christ.

MYSTICISM OF THE HISTORICAL EVENT

This devotion to the humanity of Christ issues in a form of mysticism which I will call "the mysticism of the historical event." In this type of consciousness, one recalls a significant event in the past, enters into its drama, and draws from it spiritual energy, eventually moving beyond the event towards union with God. Of course, for Christians the significant events were those of the life of the historical Jesus, especially his birth at Bethlehem and his death and resurrection at Jerusalem. Although this type of consciousness was present in Christianity from the beginning, especially in the liturgy, it emerged in the thirteenth century in a new form and with new vigor. Under the impetus of Francis, it developed a specific form of meditation which became the characteristic form of Christian meditative prayer for centuries. In this form of prayer, one imagines the physical setting of the event—the place, the persons, the circumstances, for example the birth of Jesus in the stable at Bethlehem, with Mary and Joseph, an ox and an ass. However one does not remain a detached spectator, but enters into the event as an actor in the drama, singing with the angels, and worshipping the infant with the shepherds. This immersion in the event opens its spiritual meaning— for example its message of poverty and humility, draws us into its deeper archetypal significance, and leads ultimately to union with God. Cultivated in the Franciscan milieu, this form of prayer reached its culmination in *The Spiritual Exercises* of Ignatius of Loyola, where it was developed into one of the most systematic techniques of prayer in the history of Christian spirituality.

In a generic sense, the mysticism of the historical event belongs to that form of consciousness whereby we remember a past event, of our own lives or of our collective history. But it is more than merely recalling, for it makes us present to the event and the event present to us. This consciousness has a secular and a religious form. For example, when we visit a place where a great event occurred, especially a battlefield like Waterloo or Gettysburg, we can feel the power of the event—as a moment when thousands clashed and died and where the flow of history itself was altered. This experience of presence may be so strong that we feel ourselves swept up into the action of the event as if we ourselves were fighting in the battle. In and through our immersion in the event, we can discern its meaning as it reveals mankind's struggle for justice and power. If the event is religious, then its revelatory power is greater; for it manifests God's plan of salvation history and through salvation history God himself.

Some might argue whether this type of consciousness should be called mystical. I believe it is legitimate to designate it as such for two reasons. First, it is different from our everyday forms of consciousness, even different from our ordinary modes of recalling the past. In it we transcend the present moment and are transported into the past, entering into a unity with a past event that manifests its meaning. Such consciousness is analogous to nature mysticism, where we have a similar experience with regard to space. There is another reason to consider it mystical, because in its religious form it provides a path to another form of transcendence, namely, contact with God. The great religious events are seen as modes of God's manifestation to us and of our union with God. This is analogous to nature mysticism. In its religious form, our union with nature becomes a mode of God's communication of himself to us through his creation and of our union with him by perceiving his presence in the physical world.

FRANCIS'S ALCHEMICAL CONJUNCTIO

As a guide into the Second Axial Period, Francis has provided us with an example of deep nature mysticism in *The Canticle of Brother Sun*. He has cultivated a sensitivity to the human, especially compassion for human suffering, by dramatizing in his own person the life of Christ and awakening in Western culture the mysticism of the historical event. In his crowning mystical experience at La Verna, he saw the humanity of Christ fused with the six fiery Seraphic wings, symbolizing the integration of the human and the intensity of divine love. He has thus provided us with a paradigm of a holistic spirituality which integrates the cosmic, the human, and the divine. However, unlike Hildegard of Bingen, he does not provide us with an abundance of cosmic mandala symbols that express that integration. Yet the night before he composed the *Canticle* he perceived the alchemical symbol of the earth transformed into gold. This may contain Francis's most important lesson for us in our ecological crisis. For it reveals not only the integration that must take place but also the spiritual process that the human community must go through in order to reach the depths of harmony with nature that Francis achieved and which he expressed in the *Canticle*.

To grasp the dynamics of this spiritual process, we must understand the circumstances of the composition of the *Canticle*. Some six months previously Francis had had on Mount La Verna the vision of the Six-winged Seraph in the form of Christ Crucified, after which he had received the stigmata. At this time he was almost blind. The condition of his eyes had worsened to the point that they caused him intense pain. We fortunately have a very early account of the circumstances in the *Legenda Perugina*:

> St. Francis lay there [at San Damiano] for fifty days and could no longer see in the daytime the light of day, nor at night the light of the fire, but always remained in the house and in the little cell in darkness. Moreover, he had great pain in his eyes day and night so that at night he could scarcely rest or sleep, which was very bad for him and greatly aggravated the sickness of his eyes and his other infirmities. Also, if at any time he wished to rest or sleep, there were many mice in the house and in the little cell where he lay, which was a lean-to made of rushes attached to one side of the house, the mice ran backwards and forwards over him and around him, and so did not let him go to sleep. They even hindered him considerably at the time of prayer. Not only at night but even by day they so tormented him that even when he ate they got up on to the table, so that his companions and he himself considered it must be a temptation of the devil, as indeed it was.[11]

On one occasion Francis was so tormented by these sufferings that he prayed to God in his distress as the text tells us: "One night St. Francis was thinking about how many tribulations he had and began to feel sorry for himself, saying inwardly: 'Lord, come to my help and look on my infirmities so that I may be able to bear them patiently.' "[12]

At this point he heard God speak within himself, promising him eternal happiness in the kingdom of heaven. However God did not merely state this gift directly but expressed it through the image of the earth transformed into gold:

> Immediately it was said to him in spirit: 'Tell me, brother: if anyone were to give you for your infirmities and tribulations such a great and precious treasure that, if the whole earth were pure gold, all stones were precious stones, and all water were balsam [si tota terra esset purum aurum, omnes lapides essent lapides pretiosi, et tota aqua esset

balsamum], yet you would consider all this as nothing, and these sub-
stances as earth, stones, and water in comparison with the great and
precious treasure given to you, surely you would rejoice greatly?'[13]

The text continues:

St. Francis replied: 'That would be a great treasure, Lord, and worth
the seeking, truly precious and greatly to be loved and desired.' He said
to him: 'Therefore, brother, rejoice, and rather be glad in your infirmities
and tribulations, since henceforth you are as secure as if you were already
in my kingdom.'[14]

According to the text, when Francis arose in the morning, he told
his companions of the assurance God had given him and how he
should rejoice and give thanks to him. The text continues:

"Therefore I want for his praise and my consolation, and the edification
of our neighbors, to make a new song of praise to the Lord for his
creatures, which we use daily and without which we could not live. In
them the human race greatly offends the Creator and daily we are
ungrateful for such grace, because we do not praise our creator and giver
of all good things which we ought." Sitting down, he began to meditate
and afterwards began: "Altissimo, onnipotente, bon Signore." He made
a song on the creatures and taught his companions to recite it.[15]

INTERPRETATION OF THE SYMBOL

At first glance the image of the transformation of the earth may not
seem to be especially significant in this context. For it is not focused
upon directly, and on the surface it seems to function merely as a
comparison to highlight the greatness of the gift of the kingdom of
heaven. Yet from several points of view, it can be seen to play a
much greater role. From the standpoint of the psychology of C.G.
Jung, it can be seen as an archetypal symbol, employed by the
medieval alchemists, to signify the transformation of consciousness.
From this perspective the symbol can throw light upon the specific
type of nature mysticism Francis experienced and also highlight a
purification which he underwent to reach this nature mysticism at
the final stage of his life. It can also help relate his nature mysticism
to his visionary Christ mysticism which reached its climax in his
ecstatic experience on Mount La Verna.

On the structural-logical level, the symbol does establish a com-
parison/contrast between the earth and the gift of eternal life. However the comparison is more complex than one would expect. For
it really establishes a threefold hierarchical structure: the earth in its
natural state, the earth transformed into gold, and the kingdom of

God. If one were to take the transformation of the earth in its archetypal-psychological meaning, as we will soon see, the threefold structure of the comparison would correspond to the threefold hierarchical structure of the Neoplatonic universe: matter, spirit, divinity, which provides the fundamental structure of Bonaventure's *The Soul's Journey* and the basis of his interpretation of Francis's nature myticism through his metaphysics of exemplarism and epistemology of illumination.

C.G. Jung saw medieval alchemy as having a double concern: the chemical search to transform base metal into gold and the psychological transformation symbolized by the chemical processes, which paralleled Jung's own psychotherapeutical process of individuation. "The entire alchemical procedure," Jung wrote, " . . . could just as well represent the individuation process of a single individual, though with the not unimportant difference that no single individual ever attains to the richness and scope of the alchemical symbolism."[16] Such symbols as treasure (*thesaurus*), gold (*aurum*), stone (*lapis*), and water (*aqua*), found in the above text from the *Legenda Perugina*, feature prominently in alchemy, where they are part of the process of the transformation of consciousness.

The transformation of the base metals of the earth into pure gold symbolizes the process of the differentiation of what Jung calls the Self, the God image at the center of the psyche. This involves what the alchemists called *separatio*—the separation of the spirit from the material body through a process of purification or *mortificatio*. This is not a final state, but is followed by the *conjunctio*, in which the opposites are brought together in an integration.[17]

We find all of these elements in Francis's experience. In the affliction of his senses, especially sight, he suffers what could be called a "dark night," in the later terminology of John of the Cross, especially since it deprives him of his former mystical experience of the presence of God in the physical world. But it is also a purifying suffering since it can separate his spirit from his bodily senses so that he can experience God as pure gold in the depths of his soul. This is the way charted by Bonaventure in his *The Soul's Journey*.

The *separatio* reaches an extreme when Francis is assured of the kingdom of heaven, or the beatific vision of God. At this point we would expect Francis to rejoice in his liberation from the material world. If he were to compose a mystical melody, it should be in an apophatic key, using the negations of *The Mystical Theology* of the Pseudo-Dionysius, the "letting go" of Eckhart, or the *nada* of John of the Cross. On the contrary, Francis sings a kataphatic song, dancing up the ladder of creatures, rhapsodizing on God's presence in and through the sun, the moon, and the stars, earth, air, fire, and water, even calling upon all creatures to join in his song of praise.

We can find the resolution of this paradox in alchemical symbolism, for the final stage in the alchemical process is not *separatio*, but *conjunctio*: the coincidence of opposites: in this case spirit and matter, God and the world. After being assured of heaven, Francis returns to the earth, but it is an earth transformed into pure gold. Through his heightened consciousness, now transformed by the *mortificatio* and *separatio*, he can see the earth in its true reality—transformed by the *conjunctio* of the pure gold of the divine presence.

A further implicaiton of the *conjunctio* can be found if we compare the two poles of Francis's mysticism: his visionary mysticism of the Seraph and his nature mysticism of the transformed earth. The heavenly or sky realm of the Seraph is now joined to the pure gold of the transformed earth. At the center of this *conjunctio* is the figure of Christ Crucified, whose death on the cross is the symbol linking the two realms through the *mortificatio* and *separatio* of his death which is completed in the *conjunctio* of his resurrection.

What does this mean for Francis's nature mysticism? In the process of his life, it means that after the sky experience of La Verna he needed a further purification of his nature experience to bring his nature mysticism to its climax so that *The Canticle of Brother Sun* could stand in conjunction with the heavenly vision of the Six-winged Seraph.

What does this teach us about the Second Axial Period? Along with the other First Axial religions, Christianity has shared in the breakthrough into the transcendent realm. Francis's vision at La Verna of the humanity of Christ appearing in a heavenly form can symbolize this breakthrough. Rich though it has been, it calls for a *conjunctio* with the earth. But because of the loftiness of the breakthrough, our spirit must penetrate into the depths of matter to achieve an integral balance. As in the case of Francis, this can cause intense suffering. The earth itself has been suffering under our exploitation and pollution. We must free ourselves from our greed and domination in order to liberate our spirit and to find a new organic harmony with nature. This may well involve the greatest collective suffering in the history of the human community. But if we go through the alchemical process of *mortificatio* and *separatio*, we can achieve the *conjunctio*, and with Francis rise at dawn and sing the new *Canticle of Brother Sun* of the Second Axial Period.

The elements of Francis's spirituality coalesced into a holistic synthesis. Although he had integrated his devotion to the humanity of Christ with his attitude toward nature, these elements were often separated in the subsequent history of Western culture. Christian devotion focused on Christ, especially the suffering Christ.

Attention turned from creation to redemption in such a way that redemption of the human race from sin became an exclusive concern of Christians by the time of the Reformation. Although Western Christianity was turning away from creation and towards redemption, a counter current emerged within the Franciscan milieu. Flowing through Bonaventure and Scotus, this current formally linked the humanity of Christ to creation, thus drawing into a theological synthesis the primary elements of Franciscan spirituality. Bonaventure developed the concept of Christ the center: the center of the Trinity, the physical universe, the redemption, and the return of all things to the Father. Duns Scotus taught the primacy of Christ in creation, claiming that even if Adam had not sinned, Christ would have come.[18] Thus there emerged in the early Franciscan movement a medieval doctrine of the cosmic Christ. If this had prevailed in Western Christianity, then the split between creation and redemption—and between the cosmos and the human—would not have cut so deeply into Western consciousness.

FRANCIS AND GLOBAL CONSCIOUSNESS

Even if integral Franciscan humanism had prevailed in Western culture, would it offer resources for the present and future? The closed world of medieval Europe, in which Francis lived, broke out of its boundaries at the time of the Renaissance with the discovery of new continents and peoples. The process of expansion continued, through the increase in communication and population, producing in the twentieth century a new form of global consciousness. Within this context the religions of the world are meeting in an atmosphere of mutual respect and understanding. At the same time that they are coming to appreciate the classical spiritualities of other religions, all are confronting a common problem of the survival of this planet in the face of nuclear threat, the pollution of the environment, the depletion of natural resources, and the unequal sharing of the world's goods. Does Francis have something to say to these issues? Does integral Franciscan humanism have a place in the new global environment?

The answer to these questions is an emphatic yes. Francis's integral humanism can quite naturally—and on its own principles—be transposed to a global context. The joy he experienced in the diversity of creatures can be extended to the diversity of human experience. In the ecumenical climate of the twentieth century, his *Canticle of Brother Sun* can be transposed into a new key, so that it encompasses the variety of humankind's religious experience in its diverse spiritual journeys. In the spirit of Francis, Bonaventure saw the variety of creatures expressing the fecundity of God, a fecundity that reaches its ultimate expression in the Trinitarian processions. He spoke of the Father's fountain fulness (*fontalis plenitudo*) which expressed itself in the generation of his Son as Image and Word and in the procession of the Holy Spirit as Love. This fountain-fulness of fecundity overflowed in the creation of the world with all of its richness and variety.[19] Now in the twentieth century, when we have come to learn sympathetically of the diversity of religious experiences and spiritual paths in the world religions, we can see these, also, as an expression of God's fecundity, of the primordial fountain-fulness of the divine life.

Francis's attitude toward nature is even more relevant to the twentieth than to the thirteenth century. In the Middle Ages and into modern times, Westerners did not listen seriously to his *Canticle*. They failed to call water their sister and air their brother. In the global environment of the twentieth century, we have no choice. We must listen to Francis's *Canticle*—and sing its melody along with him—or we will perish from the earth. His humanism is relevant, not only in its relation to nature, but also in its distinctive human themes. Our global environment needs to be suffused with the joy in human life that Francis expressed in the crib at Greccio and with the compassion for human suffering he felt so profoundly at La Verna. In a world that is losing its natural resources, in which physical poverty is increasing, Francis's insight into poverty of spirit cuts to the heart of a critical issue. However we resolve the problem of the earth's resources, our spirit must not be imprisoned in the process. Following Francis's wisdom, we must be ready to empty ourselves on the deepest level so that we can be filled with the fulness of the universe, the human and the divine. Francis's radical emptiness reminds us that an integral humanism involves all three dimensions. To achieve that integral humanism with the global context of the twentieth century is the ultimate challenge of our time.

BONAVENTURE: GUIDE TO THE SECOND AXIAL PERIOD

Francis of Assisi can be a guide into the Second Axial Period largely by retrieving through his nature mysticism the immediate experience of nature that is found among primal peoples. In Bonaventure we find another type of guide. He gives us a classical example of First Axial consciousness, for he is a professional philosopher-theologian who draws from the Greek speculative tradition that emerged at the height of the First Axial Period. How, then, is he a guide into the

Second Axial Period? Although the First Axial religions moved away from nature and into the transcendent, they contained a compensating current that drew them back into the world. This movement is a characteristic mark of Bonaventure's philosophy and theology. He made a spiritual ascent into God, it is true, but there at the heart of the divinity he touched the fountain-fulness of the divine fecundity that caused God to overflow and express himself in the finite realm. In addition, Bonaventure was in touch with the great archetypal symbols that nourished primal peoples and flowed through a group of First Axial writers like Richard of St. Victor and Dante.

In the fall of 1259, two years after he had been elected minister general of the Franciscan order, Bonaventure retired to Mount La Verna, as he says, "seeking a place of quiet and desiring to find there peace of spirit."[20] His statement reflects the administrative problems he had to deal with as general, especially the tensions between factions within the order. Spiritually, his journey to La Verna seems to have been a search for his Franciscan roots. "While I was there," he says "reflecting on various ways by which the soul ascends to God, there came to mind, among other things, the miracle which had occurred to blessed Francis in this very place: the vision of a winged Seraph in the form of the Crucified."[21] In this meditation Bonaventure grasped a symbolic meaning of the vision. "While reflecting on this," he says, "I saw at once that this vision represented our Father's rapture in contemplation and the road by which this rapture is reached."[22] For Bonaventure the six wings of the Seraph symbolize the six stages of the soul's journey into God. In his own words: "The six wings of the Seraph can rightly be taken to symbolize the six levels of illumination by which, as if by steps or stages, the soul can pass over to peace through ecstatic elevations of Christian wisdom."[23] According to the prophetic vision of Isaiah (Is 6:1–13), which is the biblical source of Francis's vision, each of the Seraphim have three pairs of wings: two covering their feet, two covering their faces, and with two they hovered aloft. For Bonaventure the two lower wings symbolize the contemplation of God in the sense world; the two middle wings, the contemplation of God in the soul; the two upper wings, the contemplation of God in himself. Each of these stages is subdivided into two, making a total of six. For example, the two lower wings symbolize first the contemplation of God in the exterior material world, then the contemplation of God in the internal activity of sensation. The second pair symbolizes first contemplation of God in the natural faculties of the soul, then in these same faculties reformed by grace. The third pair symbolizes the contemplation of God as Being and as the Good. Bonaventure adds a seventh stage which corresponds to Francis's ecstatic experience on La Verna and in which the soul is lifted out of itself, beyond all symbols and concepts into a state of apophatic rapture.

Bonaventure developed this symbolic interpretation of the vision in *The Soul's Journey*. Written shortly after his meditation on La Verna, this brief treatise of about fifty pages presents in the condensed summa form of the thirteenth century a compendium of types of mystical experience. From one point of view, it can be seen as a typology of the major forms of mystical consciousness; from another, it can be seen as the map of the spiritual journey, in which these various forms of mystical consciousness are related to each other as stages on the way. Since the plan of the chapters provides the typology and the direction of the journey, it seems wise to list the chapter headings as Bonaventure presented them at the end of his prologue:

Chapter One
> On the Stages of the Ascent into God and on Contemplating Him through His Vestiges in the Universe

Chapter Two
> On Contemplating God in His Vestiges in the Sense World

Chapter Three
> On Contemplating God through His Image Stamped upon Our Natural Powers

Chapter Four
> On Contemplating God in His Image Reformed by the Gifts of Grace

Chapter Five
> On Contemplating the Divine Unity through Its Primary Name Which is Being

Chapter Six
> On Contemplating the Most Blessed Trinity in Its Name Which is Good

Chapter Seven
> On Spiritual and Mystical Ecstasy in Which Rest is Given to Our Intellect When through Ecstasy Our Affection Passes over Entirely into God.[24]

MYSTICAL TRADITION FRANCISCANIZED

What has Bonaventure accomplished here? He has subsumed within Francis's nature mysticism the whole of the Christian medieval spiritual tradition. In so doing, he has extended the scope of Francis's nature mysticism to include the entirety of human experience; and he has given a unifying perspective to the varieties of mystical experience. He has Franciscanized the tradition and traditionalized Francis. In a certain sense, *The Soul's Journey* is Bonaventure's *The Canticle of Brother Sun*, but instead of seeing God only through (reflected through) the outer world, he sees God reflected also in the inner act of sensation, in aesthetic experience, in the activities of memory, understanding, and will, and in the contemplation of Being and self-diffusive Goodness. He has integrated the mysticism of the inward way with the mysticism of the unifying vision; the nature mysticism of Francis with the soul mysticism of Augustine and Bernard of Clairvaux; the spontaneous mysticism of Francis with the speculative mysticism of the Pseudo-Dionysus; the kataphatic mysticism of the Divine Names of the Pseudo-Dionysius, with the apophatic mysticism of his *Mystical Theology*.

This integration can be seen by a systematic correlation of the chapters of *The Soul's Journey* with their sources in the tradition. Chapter One applies the vestige doctrine of Augustine to the nature mysticism of Francis: "From these visible things, therefore, one rises to consider the power, wisdom and goodness of God as existing, living, intelligent, purely spiritual, incorruptible, and unchangeable."[25] Chapter Two contemplates the reflection of God in sensation chiefly in the aesthetic experience of harmony: "Augustine shows this in his book *On True Religion* and in the sixth book, *On Music*, where he indicates the difference of numbers [harmonies] which ascend step by step from sensible things to the Maker of all so that God may be seen in all things."[26] Chapter Three bases itself heavily on Augustine's doctrine of the soul as image of the Trinity, with memory reflecting the eternity of the Father, intelligence the Son as truth, and the will the Holy Spirit as goodness: "See, therefore, how close the soul is to God, and how, in their operations, the memory leads to eternity, the understanding to truth and the power of choice to the highest good."[27] Chapter Four deals with the restoration of the soul as image of God after its fall into sin. Drawing from Bernard of Clairvaux, it describes the union of the soul with Christ its bridegroom: "Having recovered these senses [i.e. spiritual senses lost through sin], when it sees its Spouse and hears, smells, tastes, and embraces him, the soul can sing like the bride in the Canticle of Canticles, which was composed for the exercise of contemplation in this fourth stage."[28] Chapter Five reflects John Damascene and the general Aristotelian tradition that focuses on God as Being, and Chapter Six applies Pseudo-Dionysius's notion of self-diffusive goodness to the inner life of the Trinity: "Damascene, therefore, following Moses, says the *He who is* (Ex 3:14) is God's primary name; Dionysius, following Christ (Mk 10:18, Lk 18:19), says that the Good is God's primary name."[29] Chapter Seven presents the apophatic or negative way to God, basing itself on an extended text from *The Mystical Theology* of the Pseudo-Dionysius: "In this regard . . . little or no importance should be given to creation, but all to the creative essence, the Father, Son, and Holy Spirit, saying with Dionysius to God the Trinity: 'Trinity, superessential, super divine, and supereminent overseer of the divine wisdom of Christians, direct us into the super-unknown, superluminous, and most sublime summit of mystical communication.' "[30]

This rich heritage is drawn by Bonaventure into the universe of Francis as described in *The Canticle of Brother Sun*—thus bringing the range of human experience into the context of symbolic mysticism. Just as Francis's vision of the six-winged Seraph symbolized for Bonaventure the soul's journey into God, so all of creation and human experience symbolize God. Bonaventure expresses this universal symbolism through a cluster of images: the mirror, the book, the ladder, the stained-glass window:

> . . . the entire world is a shadow, a road, a vestige, and it is also a book written without. (Ex 2:9; Ap 5:1) For in every creature there is a shining forth of the divine exemplar, but mixed with darkness. Hence creatures are a kind of darkness mixed with light. Also they are a road leading to the exemplar. Just as you see that a ray of light entering through a window is colored in different ways according to the different colors of the various parts, so the divine ray shines forth in each and every creature in different ways and in different properties; it is said in Wisdom: *In her ways she shows herself.* (Wis 6:17) Also creatures are a vestige of the wisdom of God. Hence creatures are like a kind of representation and statue of the wisdom of God. And in view of all of this, they are a kind of book written without.[31]

CHRISTIAN NEOPLATONISM

The Franciscan view of universal symbolism was given a theoretical foundation on the philosophical-theological structure of Christian Neoplatonism. Developing it with his own genius, Bonaventure integrated into Christian Neoplatonism a distinctly Franciscan dimension. The Christian Neoplatonic tradition contains three principles, which impart to it its distinct form: emanation, exemplarity, and knowledge by participation and illumination. Bonaventure summed up his entire system with the statement, "This is our entire metaphysics: emanation, exemplarity, fulfillment, that is, to be illumined by spiritual rays and led back to the highest reality."[32]

This text is found at the center of a discourse on Christ the center, specifically on Christ as Son of the Father in the Trinity. This indicates the strategy of Christian theologians as they built these principles into their tradition. Although these principles are common to the pagan Neoplatonists, the Christians reshaped them for their own purposes, integrating them into their belief in Christ and the Trinity.

The principle of emanation was situated at the center of the doctrine of the Trinity, so that it became expressed in the processions of the Son and Holy Spirit from the Father. For Christians this emanation was consubstantial with the highest level of divinity itself. According to the Nicene-Constantinople creed, the Son and Holy Spirit were in every respect consubstantial with the Father. Within this context, Bonaventure develops his notion of the Father as the fountain-fulness of the divinity (*fontalis plenitudo*). In the Father the divinity possesses the fulness of perfection, the fulness of fecundity, the fulness of self-diffusing goodness. Drawing a principle from the *Liber de causis*, he applies it to the Father in the Trinity:

> . . . but the more primary a thing is, the more it is fecund and the principle of others. Therefore just as the divine essence, because it is first, is the principle of other essences, so the person of the Father, since he is the first, because from no one, is the principle and has fecundity in regard to persons.[33]

Later Bonaventure applies to the Father in the Trinity the principle of the self-diffusiveness of the good, derived from the Pseudo-Dionysius.[34] Out of this transposition of classical Neoplatonism, Bonaventure produces a notion of God as boundlessly dynamic and fecund, eternally communicating his divine perfection in a flow of creativity and love that begins with the Father, flows through the Son, and is completed in the Spirit.[35] Such a doctrine of God harmonizes eminently with Francis's religious experience.

The principle of emanation leads to the principle of exemplarity. When the Father out of his fecundity generates the Son as his Image and Word, he produces within the Son the eternal ideas, or archetypes of all that he can create. As Bonaventure says, "the Father generated one similar to himself, namely the Word, co-eternal with himself; and he expressed his own likeness and as a consequence expressed all the things that he could make."[36] Since this generation is eternal and the ideas are co-eternal with it, the world has an eternal existence in the divine mind, on the divine level itself. When God freely chooses to create, he selects from among these archetypes, producing creatures in space and time which express in a finite way the divine archetypes. Thus the Word in the Trinity is the Exemplar of creation. Just as the Word is the Image of the Father, so on the finite level, creatures are symbols of the Word. According to Bonaventure's imagery, the Word is the book written within the divinity, and the world is the book written without.

The generation of the divine ideas within the Word provides the ontological and theological base for the universal symbolism whereby creation reflects God. It is important to note that, in general, this principle of exemplarity forges a closer link between God and the world in the hands of Christian theologians than among their pagan Neoplatonic counterparts. For the Christians the Word is the consubstantial Image of the Father, but for the pagan Neoplatonists, the Nous is on a lower ontological level. Hence the material world is not so closely linked to the One as it is to the Father in the Trinity. Also even among the Christians, Bonaventure emphasizes the fact that God has ideas even of individuals and not merely of genera and species, thus providing an ontological base for Francis's love and concern for individual creatures, even the most lowly, like an earthworm.

This ontological exemplarism provides the basis for Bonaventure's doctrine of the vestige, which he derives from Augustine. The Latin term *vestigium*, meaning literally "footprint," was applied to the imprint of God on his creation. Since the act of creation proceeded from the Father, through the Son and was completed in the Holy Spirit, creation itself—because of emanation and exemplarism—bears the stamp of the power of the Father, the intelligibility of the Son, and the goodness of the Holy Spirit. Bonaventure sums up his vestige doctrine in the following quotation from *The Soul's Journey*, which we give in sense lines:

> For these creatures are
> shadows, echoes and pictures
> of that first, most powerful, most wise and most perfect
> Principle,
> of that eternal Source, Light and Fullness,
> of that efficient, exemplary and ordering Art.
> They are
> vestiges, representations, spectacles
> proposed to us
> and signs divinely given
> so that we can see God.
> These creatures, I say, are
> exemplars
> or rather exemplifications
> presented to souls still untrained
> and immersed in sensible things

so that through sensible things
which they see
they will be carried over to intelligible things
which they do not see
as through signs to what is signified.[37]

For the Christian Neoplatonists the entire created world is a vestige of the Trinity, but because of his subjectivity man reflects God
more closely. This leads us to the doctrine of man as image of God
and images of the Trinity and through this to the third Neoplatonic
principle, namely, knowledge by participation and illumination. The
epistemological counterpart to exemplarism is the Platonic doctrine
of knowledge by participation and the Augustinian doctrine of
illumination. According to the Platonic principle, our minds participate in the world of the forms; according to Augustine, God is
reflected in the depths of our soul as the light of eternity, truth,
goodness, and beauty. In Chapter Three of *The Soul's Journey*, Bonaventure bids us to enter into the temple of our minds. "Here," he
says, "the light of truth, as from a candelabrum, glows upon the
face of our mind, in which the image of the most blessed Trinity
shines in splendor."[38] At the depth of memory, intelligence, and
will, Bonaventure contemplates the reflection of God in the soul
like light in a mirror. It is by turning to this light that one is
assimilated into the likeness of the Exemplar; it is by following this
light that one proceeds on the soul's journey into God. Although
God's light is most intimate to the soul, penetrating the soul's very
fibers, as it were, it always remains reflected light and the soul
remains a mirror. The mirror of the soul is never absorbed into the
divine light.

The combination of Francis and Bonaventure can provide a single
paradigm for the Second Axial Period; for taken together, they
exemplify a form of consciousness that contains within itself the
integration of primal and First Axial elements. Francis provides the
immediate holistic spirituality that Bonaventure brings to reflexive
consciousness at the same time that the latter presents his own
holistic version of First Axial speculative mysticism.

ECKHART AND THE FEMININE

We turn now to another guide for the Second Axial Period: Meister
Eckhart, the German mystic, who flourished in the century after
Francis and Bonaventure. We have already seen the major resources
he offers for interreligious dialogue. I would like to explore here

the light he can throw on the emergence of the feminine in the
Second Axial Period. It is possible to view the coming of the Second
Axial Period as precisely the emergence of the feminine after its long
suppression. From this perspective the First Axial Period can be seen
as a breaking out of masculine energies from the more feminine,
holistic qualities of primal consciousness.

To explore the emergence of the feminine is a complex matter,
for it is not restricted to the biological female. The feminine can be
seen also as an energy existing in the psyches of all humans, female
and male; it has been perceived also as a metaphysical principle in
the cosmos, and as an aspect of the divinity itself. It is on this last
element that I will focus here, realizing that in so doing I will
not be ignoring the others. For according to the metaphysics of
exemplarism, God has imprinted his image on human beings and
the cosmos in his act of creation.

Christians, however, immediately encounter a problem—glar-
ingly manifested in the fact that I used the form "his" in speaking
of God. I was constrained to do so by a linguistic convention rooted
in over three millennia of patriarchy. Derived from its patriarchal
Jewish heritage, the Christian image of God is masculine. This
masculine conception is intensified by the archetypal images associated with the Hebrew God: king, warrior, lawgiver, priest. Unlike
members of archaic tribes or present-day Hindus, Christians cannot
draw from a rich tradition of goddesses and divine consorts. The
mother goddess of the Mediterranean world was suppressed by the
masculine sky god of ancient Israel. For Christians, the maleness of
the Jewish God was intensified by the fact that they believed his
unique incarnation occurred in the male Jesus of Nazareth, who
called God his father. This male image of God reached a peak in the
doctrine of the Trinity. It is here that patriarchy triumphed.
Although the doctrine of the Trinity introduced differentiations
within the divinity, instead of opening up the masculine-feminine
aspect of God it was formulated exclusively in the patriarchal terms
of Father and Son.

In the course of Christian history a number of attempts have
broken through this exclusively masculine image of God. For
example, both the divine Wisdom and the Holy Spirit have been
described as feminine. Because of their care and concern, God and
even Christ have been called mother. The most powerful feminine
image in Christianity has been Mary, the "mother of God."
Although this has offered some compensations for the dominant
masculine image, it has always been done on patriarchal terms, since
Mary, as a creature, is never subsumed into the divine level. At the
present time, when consciousness of the feminine is emerging in

many quarters, it is crucial for Christians to explore feminine aspects of the divinity and to see these in relation to the masculine.

PATRIARCHY AND THE TRINITY

In his essay entitled, "A Psychological Approach to the Trinity," C.G. Jung presents the Trinity as a primordial archetype, which in Pythagoras and Plato had a mathematical formulation involving the numbers one and three. In the Christian tradition it took on a concrete form through the patriarchal names Father and Son, and by the exclusion of the feminine. According to Jung, the form is concrete "in that the archetype is represented by the relationship 'Father' and 'Son.' Were it nothing but that, it would only be a dyad. The third element, however, the connecting link between 'Father' and 'Son,' is spirit and not a human figure." Jung draws out the implications of this for the exclusion of the feminine:

> The masculine father-son relationship is thus lifted out of the natural order (which includes mothers and daughters) and translated to a sphere from which the feminine element is excluded. In ancient Egypt as in Christianity, the Theotokos [the mother of God] stands outside the Trinity.[39]

After treating the male figures of father and son and the figure of spirit as life, Jung identifies this formulation of the archetype as distinctively patriarchal:

> Father-son-life (or procreative power), together with rigorous exclusion of the Theotokos, constitute the patriarchal formula that was 'in the air' long before the advent of Christianity.[40]

It would be interesting to speculate on what concrete formulation the Trinitarian archetype would have acquired in a matriarchal culture: for example, mother-daughter-life. It is possible also to penetrate patriarchy and matriarchy, to perceive in the Trinitarian archetype an inner dynamic which is imaged in the love between man and woman and in their procreation of offspring. I personally do not believe that there is only one manifestation or concretization of the Trinitarian archetype. I might note here that I am using the term "archetype," not in an exclusively psychological sense, but to mean an objective structure of reality which can be perceived by the psyche, especially the unconscious. If we are dealing with God as Trinity, then the divine reality—the divine Trinitarian archetype— in all its richness would provide the ground for many concretizations. In a correlative fashion, the mystery of the masculine and feminine is so rich that it can be realized in many modes, not only in the biological male and female.

With this as a preamble, I would like to focus on the central point of this investigation. I will not attempt to recast the patriarchal Trinitarian formula in matriarchal or masculine-feminine terms. Rather I will accept the patriarchal formula as expressing the masculine aspect of the divinity; but through the writings of Christian mysticism I will go beyond this masculine element to a primordial feminine ground of the Trinity. My position is that, in spite of its patriarchal dogmatic formulation, the Christian experience of God, in its deepest mystical states, is of a feminine ground of the divinity. It is of crucial importance for Christians to recover this feminine ground of the divinity because of the demands of our time in the dialogue of world religions and in recovering our rootedness in the earth. It is equally crucial that we not only recover this feminine ground but that we discover it as creatively related to the masculine aspect of the divinity.

THE TRINITY IN CHRISTIAN MYSTICISM

In his treatise *The Soul's Journey into God*, Bonaventure opens with a prayer which reflects the patriarchal Trinity: "In the beginning I call upon the First Beginning, from whom all illuminations descend as from the *Father of Lights*, from whom *comes every good and perfect gift*" (James 1:17). He continues with the formula: "I call upon the Eternal Father through his Son, our Lord Jesus Christ. . . ."[41] It is not surprising that Bonaventure should begin his treatise with an invocation to the Trinity, since he is one of the most explicitly Trinitarian theologians in Christian history. Throughout his writing he spells out his Trinitarian theology in great detail, not only in the inner divine life, but in its vestiges imprinted on creation. In Franciscan fashion he contemplates the reflection of the Trinity throughout the material universe.

For Bonaventure, however, the Trinity is not primarily concretized in the patriarchal names of Father and Son, nor in the mathematical pattern of three and one. As we have seen, for him, as for the mainstream Christian mystical tradition, the Trinity is primarily the archetype of divine emanation, expressed in the mystical symbol of the fountain. Bonaventure perceives the Father as an eternally flowing fountain of creative energy, generating the Son and resulting in the spiration of the Holy Spirit. He describes the Father as *fontalis plenitudo* (fountain-fulness).

There is reason to perceive this emanation archetype as a masculine

aspect of the divinity. It consists of power which flows out, expressing itself in intelligence or *Logos*, which is also the divine Word, as
the Son is designated. It is imaged as well in the mystical symbol
of light, shining out from its source, penetrating and illumining
darkness. Although a number of these archetypal qualities can be
associated with the feminine, I am focusing here upon their distinctive masculine aspect. From this point of view, then, the patriarchal
Trinity would coincide with the emanation archetype.

But the emanation archetype does not exhaust the divinity. There
is also the divine silence out of which the word is uttered, the divine
darkness out of which the light shines, the abyss out of which the
fountain flows. It is this silent, dark, fecund abyss of the divinity
that I would associate with the primordial feminine as the ultimate
ground of the divinity. Although there are hints of this dimension
in Bonaventure, the major articulator of it in the Christian West is
Meister Eckhart.

It is important to note that Eckhart did not ignore the patriarchal
Trinity nor the emanation archetype of fountain-fulness. However,
his more characteristic approach is to go beyond the Trinity to the
desert of the Godhead. This desert is the abyss out of which the
fountain-fulness flows, the silence out of which speech is uttered,
the darkness out of which light shines. Eckhart states:

> . . . it is stripped of matter that the soul attains to God. It is only thus
> that it succeeds in uniting itself to the Blessed Trinity. But its happiness
> can become even greater yet if the soul search out the naked Godhead,
> for the Trinity is only the manifestation of the Godhead. In the pure
> Godhead there is absolutely no activity. The soul attains to perfect
> beatitude only in throwing itself into the desert of the Godhead there
> where there are neither operations nor forms, to bury itself there and
> lose itself there in that wilderness where its ego is annihilated and where
> it has no more care than it had in the days before it existed.[42]

Eckhart evokes the mystical experience of the divine desert in the
following statement:

> I speak in all truth, truth that is eternal and enduring, that this same
> light [the spark of the soul] is not content with the simple divine essence
> in its repose, as it neither gives nor receives; but it wants to know the
> source of this essence, it wants to go into the simple ground, into the
> quiet desert, into which distinction never gazed, not the Father, not the
> Son, not the Holy Spirit.[43]

I believe that Eckhart has penetrated the other side of the Trinitarian archetype. If we accept Jung's principle of polarity, we can say
that this is the dark side, not in a destructive or evil sense, but in a
positive sense. If the emanation archetype, as presented by Bonaven-

ture, is that of light, then Eckhart's presentation is of darkness; if Bonaventure's is of fulness, then Eckhart's is of emptiness; if Bonaventure's is of speech, then Eckhart's is of silence; if Bonaventure's is of the patriarchal masculine Trinity, then Eckhart's is of the matriarchal feminine gound of the Trinity. I believe that we can associate the feminine with the abyss of the divinity, since it reflects the mysterious ground, the cave or abyss of the divinity, the undifferentiated mysterious hidden depths of the divine reality.

IMPLICATIONS OF THE DIVINE FEMININE

What are the implications of the feminine ground of the divinity? According to the principle that everything on the level of the divinity shares consubstantially in the divine nature, this feminine ground is fully divine. In fact, it has a certain primacy of order over the masculine Trinity, since it is the abyss out of which the Trinitarian processions flow. It is important to note that this ground is not a "fourth person" of the Trinity in a technical sense, for such has been excluded by the theological tradition, and rightly so, since it would merely subsume and transform the feminine element into the masculine Trinity. Rather, it stands as the presupposition and ground of the Trinity: the complementary other side of the Trinitarian archetype. It means that the masculine Trinitarian archetype alone is not the ultimate structure of reality and hence cannot subordinate the feminine to itself.

Where the Trinitarian archetype in its masculine form dominates, the feminine is identified with matter, which is relegated to the lowest level of the hierarchy of being. In the history of Christianity, the feminine principle has been imaged in the person of Mary the mother of God, through whom matter is given a new status. Jung has pointed out how Mary has been lifted up to produce a quaternity, which is the figure of completion. For Jung the Trinitarian three is incomplete without a fourth: "Medieval iconology, embroidering on the old speculations about the Theotokos, evolved a quaternity symbol in its representations of the coronation of the Virgin and surreptitiously put it in place of the Trinity." Jung saw the doctrine of the bodily assumption of Mary into heaven as the completion of the Christian quaternity:

> The *Assumptio Mariae* paves the way not only for the divinity of the Theotokos (i.e., her ultimate recognition as a goddess), but also for the quaternity. At the same time, matter is included in the metaphysical realm, together with the corrupting principle of the cosmos, evil.[44]

I agree with Jung that the quaternity manifests the ultimate completion of reality, but I do not believe that it can be achieved by assuming Mary and hence matter into heaven, because for Christians there always remains the infinite gulf between creature and creator. Therefore, to resolve the problem of the feminine aspect of the divinity through Mary is doomed to failure, for it subsumes the issue into the patriarchal hierarchy of being. While maintaining their patriarchal Trinitarian principles, Christians cannot admit into full consubstantiality with the divinity Mary, who is a creature, and matter, which is the lowest of creatures. On the other hand, if we locate the feminine aspect in the abyss of the divinity, we establish a quaternity in Jung's sense by situating the feminine at the very ground of the divinity.

Discovery of the feminine ground of the divinity challenges us to re-examine our understanding of matter. If viewed from the perspective of the patriarchal Trinity, matter stands at the lowest rung of being—below divinity and spirit. From the Greek philosophers, Christianity had assimilated the hierarchical structure of being. For example, Plato and Plotinus charted a spiritual path from matter to spirit to the divine. For Aristotle, matter was pure potentiality, open to a variety of specifications through form whereby it acquired intelligibility. Although matter is relegated to the lowest position in the patriarchal universe, it bears remarkable similarities to the feminine abyss of the divinity. Eckhart saw that in this abyss all differentiations fade and all hierarchies collapse. On the human level we see a reflection of this in the unconditional and undifferentiated quality of a mother's love. It may well be that there is a divine dimension of matter that lies undetected under the patriarchal archetype. If so, this would open to the theologian a feminine dimension in the Christian mysteries of creation, incarnation, redemption. A sign of the spiritual power of matter, hidden in the feminine abyss of the divinity, may be discerned in the paradoxical fact that the mystical symbols which reflect the loftiest level of the divinity are drawn from matter: water, light, darkness, abyss, ground.

This leads us to the questions of the relation between the masculine and the feminine in the Trinitarian archetype. I believe that they should be seen according to the coincidence of opposites of mutually affirming complementarity.[45] By this I mean that they are on an equal level, according to the Trinitarian principle of consubstantiality. By viewing the Trinitarian archetype as I presented it—with its masculine and feminine aspects—we avoid the problem of subordination, to which Jung has called attention in his treatment of Mary. The relation is complementary, not merely in a static way, but in a dynamic mutual affirmation of each other. The more feminine one pole is, the more it affirms its complementary masculine pole. In the history of Christian theology, the persons of the Trinity have been viewed as being constituted by their mutual relation. The foundation of this was laid by Augustine, was explored from the standpoint of human interpersonal relations by Richard of St. Victor, and brought to a climax by Thomas Aquinas' treatment of the divine persons as subsistent relations.[46] This rich theology of mutual relationship could be transposed to the feminine-masculine aspects of the Trinitarian archetype.

I have focused here on the divine archetype. How the divinity is or should be exemplified in human beings is a complicated issue. I do not believe that we can look at the divine reality and find there a photo-like model of relations between men and women; rather we can discover ultimate principles of and a divine grounding for such relations. I believe with Jung that these archetypes filter through the unconscious and cannot be analyzed in minute detail by the conscious mind. However, when the archetype is awakened from the unconscious—as I believe is happening at the present time in the case of the feminine side of the divine archetype—it works its way into consciousness and into social structures and personal lives. However, there is one point that should be made here. As Jung has abundantly illustrated, the masculine-feminine polarity is found within each psyche and is not relegated exclusively to the interrelation of the biological male and female. This means that Christians have the task of differentiating and assimilating in a new way the feminine divine archetype as this is imaged in their individual psyches.

VII

The Fulness of
the Mystery of Christ

As we move into the Second Axial Period, I would like to turn our gaze toward the future — toward the Christ of the twenty-first century. We began by grounding ourselves in the transition from primal to First Axial consciousness in the first millennium B.C.E. In the light of this we sought to view — from an astronaut's perspective — the major transformation that is occurring around the world at the present time: namely, the emergence of global consciousness. Then with the aid of theological models and spirituality, like dwarfs standing on the shoulders of giants, we sought to retrieve resources from the history of the Christian tradition. At the same time — guided by those who have already experienced the mutation — we attempted to move into the complex consciousness of the future by entering into the spiritual process of interreligious dialogue. As we moved forward, we drew resources from guides from the history of the First Axial Period who could point us in the direction of the emerging holistic spirituality. Now we turn directly toward the mystery of Christ as this is emerging on the eve of the twenty-first century.

Our methodology here will be a combination of the three approaches that we have taken throughout. In exploring the First Axial Period, we began with the historical method employed by Jaspers. Like him we bracketed out the Christian affirmation of Christ as axis of history and sought another axis which is common to several religions and which is accessible through an historical method. Then, having situated ourselves within Christian belief, we retrieved elements from the classical theological and spiritual tradition of Christianity, employing a textual-historical theological method. In describing the Second Axial Period in the first chapter, we used what I called a method of prophetic projection, extrapolating from data drawn from the past and present in a non-theological way. Now we will take our point of departure from Christian theology, situating ourselves within the context of the First and Second Axial Periods and drawing from the history of Christian theology and spirituality. From this context we will explore the fulness of the mystery of Christ.

THE FULNESS OF THE MYSTERY OF CHRIST

What do I mean by the fulness of the mystery of Christ? I can best answer this question by recounting my experience at the Christian ecumenical institute in Jerusalem called Tantur. During the academic year 1972–73, I had the privilege of living, along with my family, in the Ecumenical Institute for Advanced Theological Studies in Jerusalem. This Institute developed out of an initiative proposed by the Protestant observers at the Second Vatican Council to carry on the ecumenical spirit fostered at the Council and to channel it creatively into Christian theology. Living and working together that year were some thirty theologians, representing a wide spectrum of Christian traditions among which were Eastern Orthodox (Greek, Polish, and Rumanian), Roman Catholic, Anglican, Lutheran, Presbyterian, Reformed (Dutch, Belgian, and Swiss), Seventh Day Adventist. We were privileged to have in our community such leaders in ecumenism as Oscar Cullmann and Yves Congar. Rich as was our experience together in theology, our experience of Christian community was even richer.

Slowly through this year I began to become conscious of the deep bond that drew and held us together. It was our common grounding in the mystery of Christ. This was the case in spite of our differences—historical and doctrinal. I use the term "mystery of Christ" for this ground was experienced on a deep spiritual level—beyond that of doctrinal formulations. It was a mystery not merely in the sense that it could not be formulated adequately in abstract rational categories, but primarily in the sense that its reality was so vast and profound that it could never be fully drawn into reflexive awareness.

Even though we shared this common ground, this mystery had many facets. It was a single ground, it is true; but in our life together it was clear that no tradition had encompassed the whole. Our historical and cultural diversity had given to each tradition a grasp of this mystery that it could share with the others. It was only in this way that we could approximate the fulness of the mystery of Christ. For example, the Eastern Orthodox brought to our community their experience of the cosmic Christ; the Roman Catholics a devotion to the humanity and passion of Christ; the Lutherans Christ's redeeming grace; the Calvinists the power of Christ as revealed Word. Even if all the traditions had been at Tantur and had shared their entire riches, this heritage would not exhaust the mystery as it is being manifested in history. This is especially the case when we are moving into such a transformation of consciousness as that of the Second Axial Period.

We must begin with the awareness of the fact that the mystery of Christ is not limited to Christ's humanity, however rich this is. Rather it permeates all spheres of reality: the cosmos, the human community, and the divinity itself, as well as all of eternity and time. We will begin our exploration, then, with the cosmic Christ, drawing primarily from Teilhard; but we will even here not separate Christ from the Trinity, for we will explore Christ and the Holy Spirit in relation to the classical notion of the *anima mundi* or world soul. Then we will move into the sphere of the human, seeing Christ as the ground of the human person and of the fulness of the human: of male and female, and of human interpersonal love as a spiritual journey. Because Christ is the center, the microcosm, he is the ground of an integral, holistic spirituality. Finally, we will raise the question of Christ and world religions, drawing from classical and modern resources, but suggesting also a new approach through the anthropic principle that has begun to surface in astrophysics.

RECOVERY OF THE COSMIC

In the Second Axial Period the classical spiritual traditions of the First Axial Period must respond to the prophetic call of the earth and recover those dimensions lost at the transition into First Axial consciousness. This means not merely a recovery of the sense of cosmic sacrality of primal peoples, but the awakening of the spiritual significance of the material, biological, and cosmic dimensions of human existence as these express themselves in the political, social, and economic problems of our time. In other words, it is a spirituality that must recover its rootedness in the earth, in matter, in biology, discovering the spiritual significance of the total fabric of human life—as this has become vastly more complex in the Second Axial Period.

The recovery and transformation of these lost dimensions of spirituality offers a great challenge to all the traditions. For it is a creative task, to which each tradition must bring its distinctive resources, but which must at the same time be shared by all the traditions. We can already observe this process taking place. In the West many have turned to the primal peoples, such as the American Indians, to draw from their wisdom in resolving our ecological crisis. The women's movement, which began in the West but is now spreading around the world, can be seen as a sign of the re-emergence of the feminine principle and feminine consciousness which had been suppressed by the patriarchial consciousness of the First Axial Period. Since the last century Neo-Hindu movements have been attempting to relate classical Hindu spirituality to social, political, and economic problems. This was true of the Ramakrishna movement, in its social and educational concern, and in a striking way of Gandhi and his followers. Although many have looked upon this development as an assimilation by the East of Western social concerns, it can be viewed—in the larger context of the Second Axial Period—as a recovery in the realm of spirituality of the material dimensions of human existence. More recently within Christianity, liberation theology has dramatically drawn attention to the spiritual significance of the political, social, and economic dimensions of life. As this process continues, the future of the human race will largely depend on the success of the world's religions to develop an adequate spirituality of the Second Axial Period. Central in the development of this spirituality will be the dialogue between the primal peoples and the Axial religions.

More concretely, what is the role of the primal peoples in the emergence of Second Axial spirituality? I believe that they have a major—I would say even crucial—role. For they have possessed for countless millennia the fundamental form of spirituality which is emerging in the Second Axial Period and which is absolutely necessary for the very survival of the human race. They have been the womb out of which the Axial religions have been born, and have bequeathed to these offsprings a rich heritage of ritual and archetypal symbols which have nourished them for these twenty-five hundred years. In spite of the fact that in many cases they have been overpowered and even persecuted by the Axial religions, they have survived, with their identity and heritage, and are emerging as a major force among the spiritual traditions of the world.

Already they have been recognized by the Axial religions as the bearers of a rich wisdom and as prophets who must be listened to at this critical point in history. Their message is twofold: in their own persons and in their teachings they are making available a model and an ideal of a holistic spirituality that sees an organic interrelationship between the cosmos, the human, and the transcendent; and they bring to the world a very specific spiritual wisdom concerning the human relation to the earth at a time when our ecological crisis is the most profound and far-reaching problem confronting the human race.

What should be the response of the Axial religons and, I will add, of secular society? First of all, they should recognize the high value of the gifts offered by the primal peoples and receive them with respect and gratitude. I believe further that a fruitful dialogue can ensue in which all three participants—the primal, the traditional Axial, and the secular—will not only reach mutual understanding of each other but will inaugurate a spiritual process that can lead to the creative transformation from First Axial to Second Axial consciousness.

THE WORLD SOUL

As a topic of this dialogue, I would like to suggest the theme of the World Soul, which is one of the three divine principles in the Platonic-Neoplatonic tradition. I have chosen a theme from the First Axial Period that was developed at the very stage of transformation from its Pre-Axial antecedents. It first appeared in the fourth century B.C.E. in the dialogue of Plato entitled *Timaeus*. It became a classical element in the Platonic tradition, featuring in the synthesis of Plotinus in the third century C.E., in the Platonists of Chartres in the twelfth century, and again in Renaissance Platonism. Since the Neoplatonic tradition was assimilated by Christianity, Judaism, and Islam, it was drawn into these Axial traditions. I believe that the World Soul is the link between the primal spiritualities and the Axial traditions of the West. It stands in sharp contrast to the mechanism of Enlightenment science, and it has striking affinities with twentieth-century science and with the philosophy of organism of Whitehead, as well as with the Gaia hypothesis proposed by ecologists. The following quotation from the *Enneads* of Plotinus gives the essence of the doctrine of the World Soul in such a way that it resonates with the holistic, earth-centered spirituality of the primal peoples:

> Now to understand how life is imparted to the universe and to each individual, the soul must rise to the contemplation of The Soul, the soul of the world. The individual soul, though different from The Soul, is itself no slight thing. Yet it must become worthy of this contemplation: freed of the errors and seductions to which other souls are subject, it must be quiet. Let us assume that quiet too is the body that wraps it round—quiet the earth, quiet the air and the sea, quiet the high heavens. Then picture The Soul flowing into this tranquil mass from all sides, streaming into it, spreading through it until it is luminous. As the rays of the sun lighten and gild the blackest cloud, so The Soul by entering the body of the universe gives it life and immortality; the abject it lifts up. The universe, moved eternally by an intelligent Soul, becomes

blessed and alive. The Soul's presence gives value to a universe that before was no more than an inert corpse, water and earth . . .[1]

This passage is so holistic, one might wonder how it could come from the First Axial Period. In the complete Neoplatonic world-view, the World Soul emanates from a transcendent principle called the Intelligence, from which it receives the intelligible forms that it imparts to the material world; and the Intelligence itself emanates from the ultimate transcendent principle, the One. It is easy to see structurally how, with the First Axial impetus to transcendence, the World Soul could become fragmented off from the other principles and recede into the background. This is precisely what happened in the history of Christianity, where the World Soul was correlated with the Holy Spirit. This left the material world as an autonomous realm which could easily become the world machine of Enlighten-ment science, devoid of divine presence and its own organic vitality.

From a psychological viewpoint, Christians have experienced the Spirit primarily in the human sphere in their moral and spiritual life, and not in the geosphere and biosphere. The early Christians felt the power of the Spirit transforming their souls, imparting charisms, and uniting the community in a bond of love. The newness of life in the Spirit was so profound and overwhelming that cosmic dimensions received little stress. As the Church spread, the Christian experience of spiritual transformation encountered the Greek cosmic sense. The Greek Fathers gave expression to the cosmic dimensions largely through their development of the doctrine of the Trinity and its relation to creation. The cosmic dimension was also developed in Western medieval theology, especially among the Platonists of Char-tres and the Franciscans, but by the late Middle Ages certain juridi-cal, abstract, and individualistic tendencies in Western theology, tending to obscure the cosmic sense, gained ascendency. At the Reformation, of course, the burning issue was the justification of the Christian, and debate focused on whether the Spirit worked within or outside the rites and juridical structures of the Roman Church. Theologians saw Christ in his role of redeemer from sin, not in his relation to creation and the cosmic process. This period also saw the beginning of modern science, with its own methods of investigating the physical universe. While the religious controversy raged on the spiritual level, cosmic concern passed to the scientists, who had to struggle with the religious establishment in order to vindicate the autonomy of their method. There emerged a scientific interest in the cosmos that became increasingly secularized and divorced from religion: the result of this dichotomy was that when a man like Teilhard attempted to present a vision that encompassed both the physical sciences and the religious sphere, he was looked upon with suspicion by both camps.

In the history of theology, the doctrine of the cosmic Spirit is grounded in the doctrine of creation. Although there is a tendency in theology to relate creation to the Father, redemption to the Son, and sanctification to the Holy Spirit, there is another tradition, quite ancient, that sees the creation of the universe grounded in the processions of the persons in the Trinity. In this latter tradition, the three persons of the Trinity have a dynamic role in the creation of the universe. Creation begins with the Father, advances through the Son, and is completed through the Spirit. Gregory of Nyssa gives a concise formulation:

> . . . the fountain of power is the Father, and the power of the Father is the Son, and the spirit of that power is the Holy Spirit; and Creation entirely, in all its visible and spiritual extent, is the finished work of that Divine power . . . we should be justified in calling all that Nature which came into existence by creation a movement of Will, an impulse of Design, a transmission of Power, beginning from the Father, advancing through the Son, and completed in the Holy Spirit.[2]

Gregory was writing against a group that maintained that the Spirit had no part in creation. In a passage that contains a humorous overtone, he writes:

> For if the heaven, and the earth, and all created things were really made through the Son and from the Father, but apart from the Spirit, what was the Holy Spirit doing at the time when the Father was at work with the Son upon the Creation? Was He employed upon some other works, and was this the reason that He had no hand in the building of the Universe?[3]

Having been active in creation, the Spirit does not withdraw from the world, but acts as a dynamic presence throughout the universe. Gregory Nazianzen sees the Spirit as a universal presence in the world: "For He is the Maker of all these, filling all with His essence, containing all things, filling the world in His essence, yet incapable of being comprehended in His power by the world."[4] Although he is a universal presence and power in the world, he is also present in baptized Christians in a new way, but similar in its creative power; for he is "the Creator-Spirit who by Baptism and by resurrection creates anew; the Spirit that knows all things, that teaches, that blows where and to what extent He wishes."[5] Thus the Greek theologians can compare and yet contrast the two creations: the creation from non-being and the new creation into the divine life. They have no difficulty in linking the Spirit to both, without at the same time reducing the level of sanctification to that of the original creation. Behind this vision is a metaphysics of levels of perfection in the created universe, which allows the theologians to see the activity of the Spirit on each level proportioned to the perfection of that level.

While the concept of multi-leveled activity allowed the Christian theologians to see the Spirit operating throughout the universe, it also enabled them to tap the resources of Greek philosophy and integrate these into their Christian worldview. Hence they were able to attribute to the Holy Spirit the functions that Platonism and Neoplatonism had assigned to the *anima mundi*, or World Soul, a concept with deep roots in the history of religion and philosophy.[6] The World Soul idea emerges out of a primitive numinous awareness of the presence of the divine in nature, which in its early forms expressed itself in animism and polytheism, with cults of nature gods. This cosmic religious sense merged with the philosophical sense of the One in the thought of the Pre-Socratic Greek cosmologists. Aware of the unity of the cosmos, they sought to explore its rational structures. The Platonists called the unifying principle of the cosmos the World Soul, but balanced its immanent functions by its emanation from the transcendent realm. For the Neoplatonists the World Soul was the third hypostasis, emanating from Intelligence, which in turn, emanates from the One. Emanating from Intelligence, the World Soul goes out to form and order the material world and to act as an immanent principle of life and growth. Christian theologians were strongly influenced by these philosophical traditions.

It was in the context of Platonic and Neoplatonic thought that Christian theologians developed their doctrine of Trinitarian processions and the dynamic activity of the Trinity in the cosmic emanation and return. Against Neoplatonic subordinationism Christian theologians affirmed the consubstantiality of the Son and Spirit with the Father. At the same time they drew heavily from elements in the philosophical traditions. Writing on the doctrine of the World Soul, Tullio Gregory observes that "in general all the Greek theologians not only found in the first two hypostases of the Neoplatonic triad the representation of the Father and the Son, but they also completed the correlation by attributing to the Holy Spirit the functions of the *anima mundi*. . . ."[7] To link the World Soul with the Holy Spirit has significant theological results. It makes a bold affirmation of immanence and trancendence, bringing together the highest reality, a person of the Trinity, with the lowest level of matter. It thus forestalls any explicit or implicit dualism, which would conceive of the material world as basically alien or hostile to God. It also makes an emphatic affirmation of the unity of the cosmic process; for although the Spirit acts on each level in a way proportioned to that level, he acts in the same generic way throughout the universe—bringing order and form to creation and acting as a source of life and growth, leading creation to its fulfillment.

While the Greek theologians tended to relate the Holy Spirit to the World Soul, the Latins on the contrary hesitated to do so, although there were a few exceptions. Because of the strong Platonic influence in the twelfth-century school of Chartres, for example, it is not surprising to find William of Conches writing of the World Soul.[8] In a common medieval tradition flowing through Boethius, Pseudo-Dionysius, and John Scotus Erigena, William sees that the force energizing the cosmos is that of love.[9] He then identifies this cosmic love with the World Soul of Plato and links this with the Holy Spirit:

> The World Soul is the natural energy [*vigor*] by which some things merely move, others grow, others sense, others think. But we ask: What is that energy? Now as it seems to me, that natural energy is the Holy Spirit, that is the divine and benign harmony, which is that by which all things have being, move, grow, sense, live, think.[10]

William was not alone in linking the World Soul with the Spirit; this was common to a whole current of twelfth-century theology.[11] However, the movement did not gain momentum because of the criticism of William of St. Thierry and the condemnation of Abelard.[12] Also with the recovery of the text of Aristotle in the twelfth and thirteenth centuries there entered into the Western intellectual tradition an understanding of nature as autonomous, not requiring for its full functioning a transcendent principle like the World Soul.

TEILHARD AND THE WORLD SOUL

This background provides a perspective for some of Teilhard's own comments on the World Soul. In 1918 he wrote an essay entitled "The Soul of the World," printed in the volume *Writings in Time of War*.[13] Beneath the surface of our experience, he says, we can detect a soul of the world: "Whichever road we follow, we cannot withdraw from the superficial plane of day to day relationships without finding *immediately behind us, as though it were an extension of ourselves, a soul of the world*."[14] Throughout history, the true poets have felt its presence, "in the solitude of the deserts, in nature's fruitful breath, in the fathomless swell of the human heart."[15] The World Soul has "provided fuel for human enthusiasm and passion in their most intense forms."[16] Although its influence has been felt throughout history, it seems to be emerging with greater force and clarity:

> Even so, with the passage of time, its radiating influence seems to become progressively more distinctly recognizable, and more and more indispensable for our intellectual and emotional satisfaction. It will not be long before no structure of truth or goodness can be built up without a central position being reserved for that soul, for its influence and its universal mediation.[17]

The explorations of science into the energies of matter and the heightening of social awareness have directed attention to the Soul of the World, which "is gradually emerging all around us, as an absorbing and inevitable Reality."[18] In his religious perspective, Teilhard sees an intimate connection between the World Soul and Christ:

> Through the soul of the world, and through that soul alone the Word, becoming incarnate in the universe, has been able to establish a vital, immediate, relationship with each one of the animate elements that make up the cosmos.
> Through the soul, accordingly, and for all time, the humano-divine influence of Christ encompasses us, penetrates us, identifies itself with all the forces of our growth as individuals and as a social whole.[19]

In this essay Teilhard was expressing the same type of awareness and struggling with the same problems that have surrounded the questions of the World Soul in the history of philosophy and theology. Teilhard's World Soul combines the numinous awareness of the divine in the universe with the philosophical sense of unity. Furthermore, the World Soul is a vital, energizing force in the cosmos. Although he points out the relation between the World Soul and Christ, he does not associate the World Soul with the Spirit. Teilhard's later writings do not develop this outline of his concept of the World Soul, and in his later writings he does not develop this concept as a major theme, but associates the related themes more and more with the cosmic Christ. Nevertheless, this early essay provides a link in a chain of evidence giving support to the significance of a latent theology of the cosmic Spirit in Teilhard's thought.

We can now draw into focus his specific emphasis and evaluate his contributions for the Second Axial Period. The theology of creation, stemming from the Greek Fathers and moving through Western medieval theology, sees creation proceeding from the Father through the Son and completed in the Holy Spirit. Teilhard does not focus on the origin of things and develop what could be called a theology of the Father as ultimate source. Nor does he focus on the created world as reflecting back to its divine exemplar and develop a theology of the Son as archetype of creation as Bonaventure does. Rather he focuses on the movement of the cosmos towards its end. This is precisely the point of view of the Spirit; for in the theology of appropriation, finality is appropriated to the Spirit. Thus Teilhard's emphasis coincides with the theology of the Spirit, and specifically with the theology of the cosmic Spirit; for he studies fulfillment and finality not within the Trinitarian life, but within the cosmos itself.

What Teilhard sees as the immanent love energy of the cosmos, the theological tradition saw as the action of the transcendent Spirit, who is the love of the Father and the Son. Both Teilhard and the theological tradition affirm absolute immanence and transcendence. Although the transcendent is immanent in all levels of the cosmos — even in a speck of dust or an atom — the transcendent is not present in all levels in the same way, but according to the perfection of the level. The Spirit works in the plant kingdom as the ultimate source of vital energy, but is not present in his full personal reality because the plants are not persons and do not have the power to receive or give a personal response. They are, in the classical phrase, only vestiges of the Trinity. However, human beings can respond in a personal way since they are images of the Trinity. Finally, on the level of grace, the Spirit is present to human beings in a most personal way, transforming them into the likeness of the Trinity. This approach is based on two principles: (1) the immanence of the transcendent divinity in all levels of the universe; (2) varying degrees of divine presence based on the relative perfection of creatures. These two principles were the foundation of the cosmic theology of the Greek Fathers and of the Western medieval theologians, and they also form the basic structure of Teilhard's vision. For Teilhard sees the immediate action of Christ-Omega throughout the cosmos and at the same time maintains the graded perfection of the universe and hence the graded presence and action of Omega in the geosphere, biosphere, and sphere of human consciousness.

While Teilhard shares many elements with the classical theological tradition, he also makes an original contribution that is a result of his personal genius and his being a person of the twentieth century. In 1918 Teilhard wrote that "the soul of the world is gradually emerging all around us, as an absorbing and inevitable Reality."[20] Through advances in scientific knowledge, we have broken out of our static universe and enlarged our horizons. We no longer see ourselves as actors on a cosmic stage or as spectators of a cosmic drama. We are now part of the process and the process is part of us. We are turned towards an open future that awakens hope and anxiety. In an age in which evolution has become conscious of itself, we know that we have the possibility and the awesome responsibility of shaping the future structure of our universe. We have already extended our consciousness in all directions: into the energy of the subatomic world, by encircling the earth with a web of electronic communication, by establishing a foothold in outer space. All this is part of what Teilhard calls the process of complexification and planetization, leading to a new form of integral consciousness in which the highest powers of humanity will be integrated with the most elemental physical energy and channeled towards Omega. It is this modern experience that Teilhard has in mind when he speaks of the World Soul emerging. And it is this modern experience—so keenly perceived and so brilliantly expressed by Teilhard—that is the new dimension he adds to the tradition of the cosmic Spirit. The divine energy that flows from the Father through the Son to reach its creative completion in the Spirit is felt by the modern person in an extraordinary way. For the modern person feels there is nothing static in the universe since all is caught up in the process and the process is becoming conscious of itself. In the light of the emerging modern experience, then, we can see the divine energy acting in the universe in a way even more striking than classical theology had conceived.

The theology of the Holy Spirit is a key to Teilhard's cosmic evolution. It is true that Teilhard constantly points to Christ the Omega, who is the goal and motive force in evolution; but as a matter of fact, it is the process itself that he emphasizes. It is the movement, the dynamism, the openness to development that one senses in Teilhard's writings. For Teilhard sees the goal as inaugurating the process and as being achieved through the process. He makes us aware that we are not frozen in a static slot in the static world; rather we are moving in a dynamic process that sweeps along every particle of the universe. In Teilhardian vocabulary the central word is *genesis*; for he sees all levels of the universe caught up in a genesis, or process of becoming. It is this process of genesis that he describes in detail in *The Phenomenon of Man*.[21] It has been said that the modern person has discovered history and process. Using Teilhardian terminology, we can say that the nineteenth century discovered genesis in the sphere of consciousness, through Hegelian philosophy and the development of the tools of critical historical research. Darwin extended the awareness of genesis to the biosphere through his theory of the evolution of species. Twentieth-century physics and chemistry have explored the theoretical possibilities of genesis in the geosphere—in the inorganic and subatomic world. What Teilhard has done is to integrate all these levels of genesis into an organic process which he calls cosmogenesis and which reaches its fulfillment on the religious level in Christogenesis.

On the one hand, Teilhard brings the modern experience into the theology of the cosmic Spirit; on the other, his thought, seen in the context of the history of the theology of the Spirit, leads to the solution of certain theological problems at the same time that it raises others. For example, the presence of the Spirit in the universe overcomes any Gnostic or Manichaean dualism; for there is no realm of the universe where the Spirit is not present and working. Therefore, there is no autonomous nature that stands apart from God, as a Deist world-machine or a purely isolated mechanical process. For the Spirit works in electrons and atoms as well as in mystical ecstasy. Hence there are no purely natural laws. This does not introduce a supernaturalism or magic into the cosmic process; rather it means that what the scientist discovers as natural laws are manifestations of the energy of the cosmic Spirit. In this light, Darwin's principle of natural selection would be seen as a scientific way of charting the Spirit's selection of the species that will survive in the evolutionary process. Furthermore, the religious counselor cannot merely dismiss the findings of depth psychology as belonging to the "natural" realm; for even here in the depths of the unconscious, the Spirit works. In a theology of the cosmic Spirit, the theologian can see that at bottom there is no radical split between the sacred and the secular; for the Spirit works in the economic and political structures of society and in the on-going scientific enterprise.

A theology of the cosmic Spirit leads to a problem. Its inherent optimism might distract us from the problem of evil in the world. We must be open to the Spirit and confident in the Spirit's ultimate victory. But this does not free us from the struggle with evil or the need for discernment of spirits. We must cooperate with the Spirit in the midst of a universe that is emerging from imperfection and that is shot through with the force of evil. Teilhard was acutely aware of the destructive power of evil, in turning love into hate, destroying unity, and leading to fragmentation, thus holding back the evolutionary process. In our times there is great need for the gift of wisdom and the discernment of spirits. Teilhard was sensitive to this problem and tried to determine some norms for judgment and decision-making that would take into account the direction of evolution.[22]

I might illustrate the focus of our study by recasting the traditional hymn to the Holy Spirit *Veni Creator Spiritus* (*Come Creator Spirit*) in the context of Teilhard's cosmic evolution. Written by Rabanus Maurus in the ninth century, the hymn begins:

Come, Creator Spirit,
Visit the minds of your own;
Fill with divine grace
The hearts you have created.[23]

We can recast the hymn to reflect both the traditional theology of the cosmic Spirit and Teilhard's own articulation of the emerging modern experience:

Creative energy of the cosmos,
Love that unites atoms and humans
That through convergence
Creates new possibilities,
Fill human consciousness
With divine grace,
Creative love energy,
Infuse the divine milieu
With energizing love
And bring all creation
To the completion of Omega.

TEILHARD'S CHRISTOLOGY

In calling attention to the latent theology of the Spirit in Teilhard's thought, I do not imply that this dimension is more important than his Christology. Such a position would be anti-Trinitarian. I believe that in Teilhard the explicit Christology and the implicit theology of the Spirit are related precisely as classical theology has seen the relation between the Son and the Spirit. The persons of the Trinity are equal, but they differ in origin and hence in their personal properties as well as in their specific work in space and time. But while they remain distinct, they are yet intimately related and they interpenetrate. The reality of one is intimately tied up with the reality of the other. To affirm one is to affirm the other; to negate one is to negate the other. In Teilhard's cosmogenesis, the process and Omega are related in a similar way. Omega and the process are not identical; yet they are not completely separate. Omega implies the process and the process implies Omega. Like the persons of the Trinity, they interpenetrate; and like the persons of the Trinity, they are involved in a constant dynamic movement. While tending to remain hidden, the Spirit completes creation by causing it to be transformed into the image of the Son, who unites all things to the Father. Hence, in raising the question of the theology of the Spirit in Teilhard, we are really pointing to a deeper issue: that behind Teilhard's cosmic vision there is a Trinitarian archetype. Although for the most part implicit, this Trinitarian archetype provides the understructure for Teilhard's thought and operates throughout his writings. Teilhard himself did not develop a Trinitarian theology as such, either as an independent area or in relation to cosmogenesis, but he was not completely silent on the point; at times he refers to the Trinity and speaks of cosmogenesis as a kind of Trinitization.[24] In a text written in 1944, he gives a formal expression to his Trinitarian vision, interpreting the Trinity as the archetype of the cosmic process:

> To the sophisticated modern mind, the notion of one God in three persons undoubtedly appears to be something rather obscure, perhaps a bit bizarre, and at any rate superfluous. (Three Persons in God? What can that possibly mean?) Unfortunately this impression is only reinforced by the somewhat naive way in which certain of the faithful, for reasons of personal piety, tend to isolate in their devotional life either the Trinity from Christ or Christ from his Father and the Spirit. In point of fact, the trinitarian formulation, when properly understood, should rather serve to *reinforce* our appreciation of the divine unity by giving to it the kind of *structure* (or more accurately the kind of structural or constructed character) which we recognize to be the hallmark of every genuine and vital unity within the compass of our own experience. If God's life were not threefold (that is to say, if there were no interior relations within the divine life) we would be uanble to understand how he could subsist within himself independently of some created world. Furthermore, if God's life were not threefold, we would be at a loss to understand how he could create (and thereby incarnate himself) without becoming totally immersed in the world which he had brought into existence. From this point of view, the trinitarian nature of God is seen to be a conception not without relevance to the most pressing of our religious needs of the moment. Indeed the trinitarian character of God's life reveals itself to be the *sine qua non* condition of the inherent capacity of God to be the personal (and in spite of the Incarnation, transcendent) summit of a universe on the road to personalization.[25]

Commenting on another passage, in which Teilhard speaks of cosmogenesis as a process of Trinitization, Christopher Mooney makes an observation which can serve as a summary of Teilhard's Trinitarian perspective:

> In regard to the relationship of God to the material world, Teilhard begins by saying that creation is a reflection, an image of the life of the Blessed Trinity. This is what imposes upon it that metaphysical structure by which it must necessarily move from multiplicity to unity, and more precisely towards an ultimate unity with God.[26]

With a metaphysical structure, then, derived from its Trinitarian archetype, the world is moving from multiplicity to unity. It is moving towards a greater unity with God. However, it is very important to realize that for Teilhard the cosmos is moving toward union modeled on the Trinity—in which individuality is preserved and intensified in the union. Teilhard does not see individuality within the cosmos being swallowed up in the collectivity. Rather, he sees individuals having their autonomy deepened by a center-to-center union in which union and difference are maintained in absolute polarity and creative harmony.

PERSONALISTIC UNIVERSE

At the bottom of the evolutionary process, Teilhard sees a primal multiplicity that resembles in some respects the atomistic world of Democritus. Like Democritus' atoms, the particles are separate and distinct. But unlike the world of the Greek atomists, Teilhard's world contains an attractive force that draws the particles into genuine unions, not merely aggregates like grains of sand in a heap. Thus the particles do not remain forever in splendid isolation, nor do they eternally repel each other, nor enter into superficial unions. Rather they are drawn into ever more intimate and creative unions: from the atom to the molecule, to the cell, to the living organism, to the human person, to the human community, to the completion of union with Omega. However, in these various stages of union, the individual elements do not melt into the whole like drops of water in the sea.[27] At each stage of the way the union of elements is modeled on the Trinitarian union. This is what Teilhard means by the statement that cosmogenesis is in a process of Trinitization. The union that is sought at each level and at the end of the process is a union in which the particles retain their identity; in fact, their uniqueness is intensified in the union at the same time that they are brought together in a most intimate and creative way. Thus cosmogenesis reflects ever more perfectly the absolute and ineffable ideal of differentiated union which is the intimate life of the Trinity. Not only does each stage reflect the Trinitarian archetype, but the entire process is moving closer to its ideal in an ever greater participation in the Trinitarian mystery of differentiated union. For each stage marks a growth in interiority and consciousness, and this opens the possibilities of ever more intimate and creative unions. As cosmogenesis enters the sphere of human consciousness, creative union can be fully personal. In the *Sketch of the Personalistic Universe*, Teilhard describes in beautiful and profound terms how union among persons both unites them most intimately and at the same time reinforces the unique and incommunicable center of each person. It is here on

the level of interpersonal union that we have the highest approxi-
mation to the differentiated union of the Trinity:

> A person cannot disappear by passing into another person: because by
> nature, he cannot give himself *as a person*, except as he remains conscious
> of himself, that is, distinct. Even more, this gift which he makes of
> himself, we have seen, has the direct result of reinforcing that which is
> the most incommunicable in himself, that is of making him even more
> personal. 'Union differentiates.'[28]

When human persons transcend themselves in love for others and
at the same time affirm their own uniqueness, they are sharing—
within the limits of their finitude—in the ineffable Trinitarian
mystery in which distinction and union are had in absolute fulness.
This aspect of the Trinity has been explored by Augustine in Book
V of his *De Trinitate*. Commenting on Augustine's understanding
of the person in that passage, Father Paul Henry makes an observation that echoes Teilhard's concept of interpersonal union:

> This means that God is the perfect, in fact, the only perfect prototype
> of that which all love between persons tends to achieve—absolute unity
> and yet distinction—to be one with the other, not by losing one's identity
> but by perfecting it, even at the very source of one's being . . . That is
> why Divine existence is the ideal of all personal existence—to be fully
> oneself, but only in dependence upon, and in adherence to, another in
> the communion of unity.[29]

Having seen how Teilhard's cosmogenesis reflects and moves
towards the archetype of the Trinity, we can now examine how the
Spirit is related to his vision. In the history of Trinitarian theology,
the Spirit has been looked upon as the love that unites the Father
and the Son. He is called *amor* (love) and *nexus* (bond). Thomas
Aquinas gives a concise summary of this tradition in the following
paragraph:

> The Holy Spirit is said to be the bond of the Father and the Son,
> inasmuch as He is Love; because, since the Father loves Himself and the
> Son with one Love, and conversely, there is expressed in the Holy Spirit,
> as Love, the relation of the Father to the Son, and conversely, as that
> of the lover to the beloved. But from the fact that the Father and the
> Son mutually love one another, it necessarily follows that this mutual
> Love, the Holy Spirit, proceeds from both.[30]

Just as the Spirit is the love of the Father and the Son in the inner
life of the Trinity, so he is the person who engenders love within
human history. In his temporal mission, the Holy Spirit breathes
the fire of love in the hearts of human beings, uniting them in
mutual love among themselves, and finally, to Christ. The Spirit

draws human beings to know and love Christ and through Christ to be united to the Father. Being the consubstantial love of the Father and the Son, the Spirit enters human history and unites human beings in love after the pattern of the Trinity and sweeps them into the mystery of the Trinitarian life. In the Johannine account of the discourse at the Last Supper, Jesus tells his disciples that he is going to the Father and will send them the Holy Spirit. In the same context he enjoins upon his followers the new law of love and prays that they may be one as he and the Father are one and that the disciples may be one in the Father and the Son.[31] In the context of Trinitarian theology that sees the Holy Spirit as love, we can see the intimate connection between these themes of the Johannine discourse. From this point of view, the Spirit is seen as the divine love of the Father and the Son, sent into the world to draw human beings into intimate union and to lead them to an ever deeper participation in the mystery of the Trinitarian life.

Just as Teilhard does not develop a formal theology of the Spirit within the Trinity, neither does he develop a formal theology of the Spirit working within the Church. However, he does speak of a love energy, which permeates the entire cosmos and which performs functions similar to those assigned to the Spirit within the Church. For this love energy joins the particles in such a way that they unite in a Trinitarian model of differentiated union. At the same time the love energy, which emanates from Omega, unites the particles to Omega and simultaneously draws them forward to a higher level of union and participation in Omega.[32] Teilhard sees love energy permeating all levels of cosmogenesis and providing a key to understand the process of evolution: "The most expressive and at the same time the most profoundly accurate way to recount the story of universal evolution would undoubtedly be to retrace the evolution of love."[33] This love energy is such that it is the only thing capable of producing creative union: "Love alone is capable of uniting living beings in such a way as to complete and fulfill them, for it alone takes them and joins them by what is deepest in themselves."[34] This love energy acts throughout the entire sweep of cosmogenesis, uniting the particles of the universe in differentiated unions:

> Considered in its full biological reality, love—that is to say the affinity of being with being—is not peculiar to man. It is a general property of all life and as such it embraces in its varieties and degrees, all the forms successively adopted by organized matter. In the mammals, so close to ourselves, it is easily recognized in its different modalities: sexual passion, parental instinct, social solidarity, etc. Farther off, that is to say lower down on the tree of life, analogies are more obscure until they become so faint as to be imperceptible. But this is the place to repeat

what I said earlier when we were discussing the '*within* of things.' If there were no real internal propensity to unite, even at a prodigiously rudimentary level—indeed in the molecule itself—it would be physically impossible for love to appear higher up, with us, in 'hominized' form. By rights, to be certain of its presence in ourselves, we should assume its presence, at least in an inchoate form, in everything that is . . . Driven by the forces of love, the fragments of the world seek each other so that the world may come to being.[35]

THE MYTH OF ROMANTIC LOVE

Teilhard's cosmic Christ, within the context of the World Soul, provides a rich resource for a holistic Christian spirituality of the Second Axial Period. The love energy that permeates the universe integrates into an organic process the cosmic, the human, and the divine. We have seen how, in the evolutionary process, this energy draws into creative unions particles of matter on one level of the universe and human beings on another into creative unions. What does this suggest for a spirituality of love in the Second Axial Period—specifically for a spiritual path of love between man and woman? In order to place this in historical perspective, I will turn back to the twelfth century where there emerged in Western culture what can be called "the myth of romantic love."

The myth of romantic love is one of the most powerful and pervasive myths of Western culture. Born in France in the 12th century, the myth was shaped by poets and tellers of tales who sang the glory of the love between a man and a woman. This love—so powerful and so joy-producing—became the goal of one's quest in life. It became the center of a code of chivalry, a civilizing force that cultivated courtly manners and the gentle heart. It transformed the subsequent literature of Western civilization, as it permeated poetry, drama, and later the movies, television, and popular love songs. As it was progressively adopted by Western culture, it eventually superceded economic, social, and political considerations in contracting marriage. Romantic love became the only authentic reason for the choice of marriage partners. Now that the institution of marriage has been weakened by the divorce rate, romantic love has become even more significant. For instead of leading couples into lasting marriages, it now draws them into successive relationships of romantic love. To some extent, romantic love has in the twentieth century triumphed over marriage by supplanting it with successive romantic relationships.

Although the myth of romantic love has triumphed in Western

civilization, in itself it is an incomplete myth. In its popular form it lacks a spiritual dimension. It deals on the human level, with the love of intimacy between a man and a woman but does not give expression to the implications of this love for spirituality: in providing a spiritual path through the experience of mutual love, a path leading to union with God, with a corpus of spiritual wisdom and with accompanying spiritual disciplines and techniques. Although there were some attempts in this direction in the twelfth century and more successfully in the fourteenth century in Dante, the spiritual dimension of this love did not find a permanent place in the romantic love traditions of Western culture.

This was unfortunate especially because the twelfth century produced a rich body of spiritual writing precisely on the spiritual significance of intimate mutual love. Bernard of Clairvaux composed his sermons on the Song of Songs, extolling the mutual love of the bride and the bridegroom, employing this love as a symbol of the love between the soul and God. His eighty-six sermons contain a fully developed spirituality of love, with extended analyses of the dynamics of love and the stages of the spiritual journey through love. Richard of St. Victor studied the mutual love of friendship as a participation in the love of the persons of the Trinity. Aelred of Rievaulx wrote a treatise entitled *Spiritual Friendship*, in which he explored the spiritual possibilities of close ties of friendship within monastic communities.

Although historians perceive some interaction between the monks who wrote on spiritual themes and the secular poets and writers of romances, the two streams never fully converged.[36] Hence neither significantly enriched the other. As a long-range effect, the myth of romantic love has remained an incomplete myth even to this day in Western culture. The major exception to this was Dante, who in his *Divine Comedy* transformed the romantic love of the twelfth-century troubadours into a full-fledged spiritual path. Through his love for Beatrice, he was led up the heavenly spheres to an ecstatic vision of God. Yet even Dante's transformation of romantic love did not produce a complete myth. For in the tradition of the Neoplatonism of the First Axial Period, his love for Beatrice drew him from the material and personal to the spiritual and the universal. This time the balance was tipped in the direction of the spiritual. The physical side of love was left behind.

This raises a number of questions. Is it possible to have a myth of romantic love that opens to the spiritual dimension without abandoning the physical? If sexual love is not evil or degraded, is it more than humanly noble? Can it lead to spiritual fulfillment? In other words, can there be a complete and integral myth of romantic love? I wish to propose that there can, especially in the holistic spirituality of the Second Axial Period. However, we cannot turn to classical sources for such a myth, for in this area our culture is deficient. Nevertheless we can draw elements from the twelfth-century courtly love traditions, from the twelfth-century monastic writings on love, and from Dante's *Divine Comedy*. Yet these elements have not been integrated into a whole. I will draw from Dante's *Divine Comedy* taking (1) the myth of romantic love as this is presented in the episode of Paolo and Francesca in the *Inferno*. (2) I will describe Dante's transformation of this myth through his love of Beatrice in the *Purgatorio* and the *Paradiso*. (3) I will treat the current of monastic writings on the spirituality of love as this was expressed by Bernard of Clairvaux. Finally, I will propose a transformation of these several strands into an integral spirituality of love which has special significance on the eve of the twenty-first century.

PAOLO AND FRANCESCA

In Canto V of the *Inferno*, Dante tells the story of the love of Paolo and Francesca. Although written in the fourteenth century, it presents in essence one of the forms of romantic love cultivated in the twelfth century. It can be seen as setting the stage for Dante's subsequent transformation of the myth of romantic love in his treatment of Beatrice in the later portions of the *Divine Comedy*. The incident is based on historical fact, but we do not know with certainty any details beyond the general outlines of the story. Out of political considerations Francesca's father arranged for a marriage between her and the brother of Paolo. While living at the brother's castle, Francesca and Paolo fell in love, were discovered by the brother, and stabbed to death. In his fictional journey in the *Divine Comedy*, Dante meets them and speaks with Francesca in the circle of the lovers shortly after entering the Inferno. Eager to learn their tragic story, Dante requests Francesca to speak. In what has become a famous statement of the laws of romantic love, she tells of how her beauty enkindled love in Paolo's gentle heart (a technical term in romantic love literature). Once awakened, this love required— according to the canons of romantic love—that she love him in return. The two of them were so gripped by their love that for all eternity they remain in its embrace. So far the dynamics of romantic love are positive. But in a flash comes the tragic note: this love brought them to death. Love, which by its very nature should bring happiness, fulfillment, and the enrichment of life, instead brings death—a tragic, violent death followed by an eternity of suffering

in the Inferno. Dante has Francesca tell the story, beginning each
section with the word "love":

> Love, which is quickly enkindled in a gentle heart,
> Seized this one for the fair form that was taken from me—
> and the way of it afflicts me still.
>
> Love, which absolves no loved one from loving,
> seized me so strongly with delight in him,
> That, as you see, it does not leave me even now.
>
> Love brought us to one death.[37]

Francesca's words move Dante greatly, urging him to make the
following request: "Francesca, your torments make me weep for
grief and pity; but tell me, in the time of the sweet sighs, by
what and how did Love grant you to know the dubious desires?"[38]
Francesca gives the following response:

> One day, for pastime, we read of Lancelot,
> how love constrained him;
> we were alone, suspecting nothing.
>
> Several times that reading urged our eyes to meet
> and took the color from our faces,
> but one moment alone it was that overcame us.
>
> When we read how the longed-for smile
> was kissed by so great a lover, this one,
> who never shall be parted from me,
>
> kissed my mouth all trembling.
> A Gallehault was the book and he who wrote it;
> that day we read no farther in it.[39]

In this passage Francesca and, through her, Dante are criticizing
romantic love, at least in the form that has come through the tales
of Lancelot's love of King Arthur's wife, Guinevere. For it was by
reading of this incident that Paolo and Francesca were drawn into
the romantic love that lead to their death. Francesca calls the book
they were reading a Gallehault, which in the context means pan-
derer, for Gallehault was the name of the man who secretly brought
Lancelot and Guinevere together. Yet Dante's feelings are mixed,
for here—and through the *Divine Comedy*—he has enormous respect
for romantic love. When he hears these words from Francesca, he
faints out of compassion: "While the one spirit said this, the other
wept, so that for pity I swooned, as if in death, and fell as a dead
body falls."[40] What is the basis of Dante's admiration for and

criticism of romantic love? Although the issue is complex, we can get some clarification from the *Purgatorio*, where he gives his philosophy of love. There he claims that all love is natural and in itself good. However we must exercise our freedom, choosing according to the order presented to ourselves by reason.[41] Applying this to the case of Paolo and Francesca, we can see that Dante perceives the awakening of their romantic love as good in itself, but their pursuit of it goes counter to the right order of marriage relationships since it violates Francesca's marriage with Paolo's brother.

DANTE'S LOVE OF BEATRICE

After Dante leaves the ambiguous romantic love of Paolo and Francesca, he proceeds down the circles of the Inferno and up the terraces of the mountain of Purgatorio. At the summit of the mountain, in the earthly paradise, Beatrice appears. In real life Dante had first met Beatrice in Florence when he was nine years old. Overwhelmed by her beauty, he fell deeply in love with her. When Beatrice died at an early age, Dante was thrown into a state of depression. As he eventually recovered and began writing the *Divine Comedy*, he made Beatrice his chief spiritual guide. It was his love for her that drew him into God. Of necessity, however, this was a purely spiritual love, with no physical component and without the emotional intimacy of an earthly relationship.

At the outset of the *Divine Comedy*, when Dante has lost his way in the dark forest, it is Beatrice who comes to Virgil in limbo, saying to him:

> Go now, and with you fair speech
> and with whatever is needful for his deliverance,
> assist him so that it may console me.
>
> I am Beatrice who send you.
> I come from a place to which I long to return.
> Love moved me and makes me speak.[42]

Saved from his confusion by Beatrice's love, Dante follows Virgil through the Inferno and up the mountain of Purgatorio. At the summit of the mountain Beatrice appears to him in heavenly splendor:

> A lady appeared to me, girt with olive
> over a white veil, clothed under a green
> mantle with the color of living flame.

And my spirit, which now so long
had not been overcome with awe
trembling in her presence,

without having more knowledge by the eyes,
through hidden virtue that came from her,
felt the old love's great power.[43]

When Beatrice appears, Dante feels his old love for her surge again. In the following sequences, that love has to be purified so that he can make the ascent with her to God. It is through his love for her and hers for him that his ascent is accomplished. As they climb up the heavenly spheres in Paradiso, the divine wisdom and love are mediated to him, especially through her eyes and smile. For example, in the sphere of Mars Dante sees a heavenly light flash across the heavens:

Thus the light; wherefore I gave my heed to it,
then I turned back my sight to my lady,
and on this side and that I was amazed,

for in her eyes was blazing such a smile
that I thought with mine I had touched the limit
both of my beatitude and of my paradise.[44]

At each level of the ascent, it is Beatrice who radiates the divine love to Dante until she draws him into the highest heaven. The divine truth, goodness, and beauty shine through her person and awaken the reflection of the divine in Dante's soul. She is, therefore, the archetypal symbol, in the terms of C.G. Jung's psychology, of Dante's own soul as an image of God. She is his contrasexual feminine aspect, his *anima*, which contains the treasures of all nobility—a nobility that not only awakens the human qualities of the gentle heart, according to the code of courtly love, but a nobility which far surpasses that for it enkindles the divine spark within the soul. But Beatrice is even more than Dante's *anima*, for in her appearance in Purgatorio she is symbolically depicted as a Christ figure. In this she transcends the horizons of the *anima*, taking on even more profound cosmic functions of mediating the divine to Dante. It is through her, and their love, that Dante experiences the Christ mystery in its fulness. As *anima* and Christ figure, Beatrice leads Dante to the dazzling light of the beatific vision depicted at the climax of Paradiso. In her, romantic love has reached the height of its spiritual potential. And yet this spiritual ascent has left behind the human, the physical, the sexual dimensions. Although it took its point of departure from an interpersonal encounter between the youthful Beatrice and Dante, when it began its spiritual journey,

Beatrice was already a beatified soul in heaven. Whatever permanent value there is in Dante's spiritual transformation of the myth of romantic love, it does not provide a spiritual path through the physical, the emotional, and the sexual aspects of love between a man and a woman. Ironically the resources for such a spiritual path are found rather in the monastic tradition, where celibate monks of the twelfth century meditated on the erotic imagery of the Song of Songs as a symbol of the soul's union with God.

BERNARD ON THE SONG OF SONGS

The classical treatment of erotic imagery in a spiritual context is found in the sermons of Bernard of Clairvaux on the Biblical text of the Song of Songs. In the twelfth century Bernard preached a series of eighty-six sermons in which he interpreted the love between the bride and the bridegroom, described in sensuous and erotic terms in the Song of Songs, as an allegory of the love between the soul and Christ and, on another level, as an allegory of the love between the Church and Christ. Throughout, Bernard treats explicitly such vivid physical details as the kiss of the mouth and the breasts of the bride and the bridegroom. In contemporary psychological categories, the imagery deals primarily with oral rather than genital sexuality, although the latter is implied. In his explicit treatment of erotic material Bernard stands far removed from Dante, who deals exclusively with the spiritual aspects of his love for Beatrice.

In an eloquent passage Bernard gives a striking eulogy of love and specifically the love between a man and a woman. He begins by quoting the first verse of the Song of Songs: "Let him kiss me with the kiss of his mouth." Who is it, he asks, who makes that statement? It is the bride. "But," Bernard asks, "why bride? Because she is the soul thirsting for God." He then compares the bride-groom relationship with other basic human relationships. "Fear motivates a slave's attitude to his master, gain that of wage-earner to his employer, the learner is attentive to his teacher, the son is respectful to his father. But the one who asks for a kiss, she is a lover." For Bernard, love is primary: "Among all the natural endowments of man love holds the first place, especially when it is directed to God, who is the source whence it comes." At this point Bernard emphasizes the intimacy of this love, which is profoundly expressed in sexual union. "Between these all things are equally shared, there is no selfish reservations, nothing that causes division. They share the same inheritance, the same table, the same home, the same marriage-bed. They are flesh of each other's flesh."[45]

For all of its depth and beauty, Bernard's treatment of the love of man and woman merely underscores the problem raised above, namely, that Western culture lacks a complete myth of romantic love. In general, the early romantic poetry and tales did not explicitly incorporate the spiritual ascent. Dante transformed the early tradition by drawing it into a spiritual journey, but in so doing, left out of the journey the physical aspect of romantic love and its rich emotional life of interpersonal intimacy. Bernard, on the other hand, blends the spiritual with the erotic, but the erotic becomes only a subjective image of the spiritual and not an objective stage of the journey. Is it possible to have a myth of romantic love in which all of the elements are united into an integral whole: the sexual, the interpersonal, and the spiritual? I believe that it is possible and especially called for at this stage of history with the emergence of the Second Axial Period.

It has been conventional to distinguish between Eros and Agape, with Eros described as sexual desire and Agape as spiritual love. In *The Power of Myth*, Joseph Campbell followed this line of thinking but added a third kind of love which he called Amor, a term which he took from the courtly love tradition and which Dante had Francesca use in her description of falling in love with Paolo. Campbell considers Eros and Agape as universal loves and Amor as highly personal. "Eros," he says, "is a biological urge. It's the zeal of the organs for each other. The personal factor doesn't matter. Agape is love thy neighbor as thyself—spiritual love. It doesn't matter who the neighbor is. . . . But with Amor we have a purely personal idea. The kind of seizure that comes from the meeting of the eyes, as they say in the troubadour tradition, is a person-to-person experience."[46]

It is this personalized Amor that is the heart and center of the holistic interpersonal love I am proposing. It is eminently passionate, but with a spiritual passion—a passion for each other as persons. But since the two are also sexual persons, their erotic passion can be drawn into the flame of their mutual personal passion. And the single flame of love that they share at the depths of their persons can mount and burst into the infinite flame of divine love, as it did for Dante and Beatrice. To include this final phase, we must add a fourth to the three types of love that Campbell identified: namely, passionate Amor between the human person and God and between God and the human person. This is the kind of spiritual-mystical love that Bernard of Clairvaux experienced and expressed through the image of the bride and the bridegroom. The mutual flame of love between the human lovers thus integrates not only their mutual Eros and Amor but the divine Amor as well. This integration is not static nor the breakthrough of a single moment, but the very energy of a spiritual journey which progresses in the total unfolding of a life together that is simultaneously a journey into the fire of divine love. In the fulness of their human love they are drawn together into the fulness of the mystery of Christ, the passionate bridegroom of their souls.

THE COSMIC PERSON

In conclusion I would like to focus on an archetypal image that can draw together the various strands of this book and synthesize them around the fulness of the mystery of Christ in the Second Axial Period. It is the archetype of the Cosmic Person. This is the image of a human being who links the cosmos, humanity, and the divine. The archetype expresses not merely a universal cosmic principle that permeates the cosmos, but it expresses the human as well. Essential to it is the image of an individual human being who is linked to the cosmos as microcosm to the macrocosm. This human being joins the human also to the divine.

This archetype is found in primal traditions and in the religions of the First Axial Period. In Christianity it is present in the doctrine of the cosmic Christ, but this must include not only the universal presence of the divine Logos in the cosmos but the incarnate Christ as well. This archetype brings together two strands of Christian theology and spirituality: the awareness of the Logos, as second person of the Trinity permeating creation and the focus on the humanity of Christ, so graphically depicted in the gospels and culti- vated in the spirituality of Western Christianity in the meditations on the life of Christ. It is sometimes expressed theologically in the pre-existence of the humanity of Christ and the primacy of Christ in creation.

A classical source for this understanding is the cosmic hymn in Colossians (1:15–17), in which Christ is called "the image of the invisible God, the first-born of all creation; for in him all things were created, in heaven and on earth, visible and invisible, whether thrones or dominions or principalities or authorities—all things were created through and for him. He is before all things, and in him all things hold together." This was a favorite text of Teilhard and the major scriptural source for his formulation of his understanding of the cosmic Christ. Although throughout his writings he constantly emphasized the cosmic dimensions of the mystery of Christ, he repeatedly affirmed the importance of the incarnation and Christ's human existence. I believe that this presents strong evidence for the fact that Teilhard's cosmic Christ was indeed the archetype of the cosmic person, as described above, and not merely the presence of the divine throughout the cosmos.

This archetype of the cosmic person contains all the essentials of the fulness of the mystery of Christ, for it includes his life, death, and resurrection as part of the redemptive Paschal mystery. This is indicated in the continuation of the text from Colossians: "He is the head of the body, the church; he is the beginning, the first-born from the dead, that in everything he might be pre-eminent. For in him all the fulness of God was pleased to dwell, and through him to reconcile to himself all things, whether on earth or in heaven, making peace by the blood of his cross." (18–20)

If we return to that aspect of the archetype that links the human to the cosmos, we may discern a striking emergence of the archetype of the cosmic person in contemporary science. Over the last several decades scientists have amassed evidence to support the big bang theory of the origin of the physical universe. According to this theory some fifteen billion years ago there occurred an enormous explosion which set in motion the transformation of matter from a gaseous state to solids, to stars, planets, galaxies, and life as we know it on earth. The original explosion also set in motion a force that is propelling the galaxies away from one another at an enormous velocity in what is called the expanding universe. Recently some scientists have been struck by what they call the anthropic principle.[47] Derived from the Greek term *anthropos*, meaning human being, this term highlights the place of the human in the universe. The original explosion was so great and the heat generated was so intense that if it had varied by being hotter or cooler even infinitesimally, the universe as we know it would not have developed. This is especially the case in regard to the human species. Although scientists do not think in terms of purpose or final causality in the universe, they have taken cognizance of the extraordinary proportion between the original explosion and the emergence of human life in the universe. This leads one to think that the human species brings the process to a level of fulfillment, for the great cosmic drama can be known through human consciousness. From the perspective of the archetypal imagination, one can conjecture that if the anthropic principle is imprinted in the very matter and energy of the universe, it would come to consciousness in the archetypal image of the cosmic person.

Since a substantial part of this book was devoted to interreligious dialogue, I would like to suggest that the archetype of the cosmic person be made the focus of a new level of interreligious dialogue. This archetype can bring together primal and First Axial religions and may even draw together some First Axial religions in one of the most difficult areas of dialogue: namely, their claims concerning the unique role of their founders, for example, the Buddha, Christ, and Muhammed. If we were to see these founders not only in their historicity as teachers of wisdom, but in some way linked to the archetype of the cosmic person, we may bring a new level of sophistication and clarification into the dialogue.

I would like to close with one of the most powerful expressions of the cosmic person in Christian spirituality: Dante's mystical vision at the climax of the *Divine Comedy*. It is drawn from the First Axial consciousness, but can be a focal point for integrating the dimensions of pre-Axial consciousness. It is by its nature holistic for it integrates the cosmic, the human, and the divine. As is often the case with the archetype of the cosmic person, it manifests itself in a mandala design, whose significance for the differentiation and integration of opposites has been explored by C.G. Jung. The mandala—with its circle, center, and square or cross—symbolizes the ultimate harmony of opposites that is the goal of the spiritual journey—both individual and cosmic. This vision of Dante echoes several mandala images explored in this book, especially Francis's vision of the Six-winged Seraph in the form of Christ crucified.

The last canto of Dante's *Divine Comedy* captures in poetic form some of the most profound metaphysical and mystical insights into harmony. The *Comedy* is, in many respects, a *summa* of Western thought, integrating classical and medieval culture and foreshadowing the Renaissance. Although our cosmology has changed since the fourteenth century, Dante's insights penetrate to a universal level and illumine the issues of harmony as we encounter them today. In his journey through Inferno, Purgatorio, and Paradiso, Dante marvels at the harmonies of the Ptolemaic universe, the progress of history and the stages of the soul's ascent into God. And he anguishes over the lack of harmony in his own city of Florence, in the human community at large, in the crimes of individuals and in his own struggle for virtue. With the aid of his guides—Virgil, Beatrice, and Bernard of Clairvaux—Dante comes progressively to understand the patterns of harmony that integrate love and justice, desire and will, life and death, multiplicity and unity, the divine and the human.

Finally in the final Canto xxxiii of the Paradiso, when Dante has reached the summit of his journey, he is given a vision of three modes of harmony at the very heart of reality. Here the multiplicity of created forms in the universe is reconciled with unity in the divine mind; divine opposites are reconciled within the divinity; the human person is reconciled with God and harmonized within himself or herself and with the universe. In the first of these harmonies Dante sees reconciled the multiplicity of creation with unity and simultaneously creation reconciled with the Creator. When Dante gazes upon God's infinite goodness, he exclaims:

> O abounding grace, by which I dared to fix my look on the Eternal Light so long that I spent all my sight upon it! In its depths I saw that it contained, bound by love in one volume, that which is scattered in leaves through the universe, substances and accidents and their relations as it were fused together in such a way that what I tell of is a simple light. I think I saw the universal form of this complex, because in telling of it I feel my joy expand.[48]

Dante here echoes a long metaphysical tradition that sees the unity of all things in the divine mind. In the depth of the divinity he perceives the ultimate harmony of the universe: "the universal form of this complex." All the disharmonies he had encountered in his journey are resolved in a higher divine harmony such that creation appears as a book whose meaning is now clear, for he sees precisely how it expresses God.

In the divine light Dante is given a further vision, this time of the harmonies within the divinity:

> In the profound and clear ground of the lofty light appeared to me three circles of three colors and of the same extent, and the one seemed reflected by the other as rainbow by rainbow, and the third seemed fire breathed forth equally from the one and the other . . . O Light Eternal, that alone abidest in Thyself, alone knowest Thyself and, knowing, lovest and smilest on Thyself![49]

For Dante, the Christian, this is a vision of the Trinity, in which the unity of the divine nature is harmonized with the diversity of persons. This vision reflects a more universal metaphysical tradition in which divine opposites are harmonized: the divine ground with divine dynamism, the divine being with divine knowledge, divine justice with divine love. This balance of opposites within the inner realm of the divinity is the basis for all harmony in the universe.

One would think that Dante, after having penetrated into the harmonies of the universe and the divinity, would have completed his journey. But there still remains another harmony to be grasped: namely, the relation of humanity to the divinity. While gazing upon the divine light, Dante sees that it takes on human form: as Dante says, "painted with our image."

> That circling which, thus begotten, appeared in Thee as reflected light, when my eyes dwelt on it for a time, seemed to me, within it and in its own color, painted with our likeness, for which my sight was wholly given to it. Like the geometer who sets all his mind to the squaring of the circle and for all his thinking does not discover the principle he

needs, such was I at that strange sight. I wished to see how the image was fitted to the circle and how it has place there.[50]

Again Dante responds as a Christian, for the human form within the circling divine light is Christ, the God-man. However, this specifically Christian image reflects a larger metaphysical tradition that grounds the nature of the human person in his or her relation to the divinity. According to this tradition human persons are most in harmony with themselves and the universe when they harmonize themselves at the depth of their being with God, who is their source, exemplar, and goal. This is precisely how Dante concludes his *Comedy*. In wonder he "wished to see how the image was fitted to the circle," that is how the human is harmonized with God. As the geometer trying to square the circle, his mind was "smitten by a flash wherein came its wish;" the tensions within his own person were harmonized—those tensions of virtue and vice, of will and desire, so vividly depicted in the *Inferno* and *Purgatorio*. The *Comedy* closes with Dante's achievement of harmony within himself, with the universe, and with God: "Now my desire and will, like a wheel that spins with even motion, were revolved by the Love that moves the sun and the other stars."[51]

NOTES

CHAPTER I

1. Karl Jaspers, *Vom Ursprung und Ziel der Geschichte* (Zurich: Artemis, 1949), pp. 19–43.
2. Ibid., p. 19; trans. Michael Bullock, *The Origin and Goal of History* (New Haven: Yale University Press, 1953), p. 1. For the ongoing academic discussion of Jaspers' position on the Axial Period, see *Wisdom, Revelation, and Doubt: Perspectives on the First Millennium B.C., Daedalus* (Spring, 1975); and *The Origins and Diversity of Axial Age Civilizations*, ed. S.N. Eisenstadt (New York: State University of New York Press, 1986).
3. Pierre Teilhard de Chardin, *Le Phénomène humain* (Paris: Editions du Seuil, 1955); see also *L'Activation de l'énergie* (Paris: Editions du Seuil, 1962) and *L'Energie humaine* (Paris: Editions du Seuil, 1962). For a more detailed study of Teilhard's thought in relation to the second Axial Period, see my paper "Teilhard de Chardin and the Religious Phenomenon," delivered in Paris at the International Symposium on the Occasion of the Centenary of the Birth of Teilhard de Chardin, organized by UNESCO, September 16–18, 1981, UNESCO Document Code: SS.82/WS/36.
4. Teilhard, *Le Phénomène humain*, pp. 268–269.
5. Ibid., p. 292; trans. Bernard Wall, *The Phenomenon of Man* (New York: Harper and Row, 1965), p. 262.
6. Ibid.
7. On the concept of dialogic dialogue, see Raimundo Panikkar, *Myth, Faith and Hermeneutics* (New York: Paulist Press, 1979), pp. 241–245; see also *The Intrareligious Dialogue* (New York: Paulist Press, 1978).
8. Jaspers, *The Origin and Goal of History*, p. 1.
9. Anselm of Canterbury, *Cur Deus Homo*, prologue.

CHAPTER II

1. Bernard of Chartres, as cited by John of Salisbury, *Metalogicon*, III, 4; *P.L.* CXCIX, 900 "Dicebat Bernardus Carnotensis nos esse quasi nanos, gigantium humeris incidentes, ut possimus plura eis et remotiora videre, non utique proprii visus acumine, aut eminentia corporis, sed quia in altum subvehimur et extollimur magnitudine gigantea."
2. Jean Leclercq, lecture delivered at Fordham University, November 30, 1976, unpublished.
3. *Julian of Norwich: Showings*, trans. Edmund Colledge and James Walsh (New York: Paulist Press, 1978).
4. Augustine, *De Trinitate*, VII-XV.

5. *A Book of Showings to the Anchoress Julian of Norwich*, ed. Edmund Colledge and James Walsh, 2 vols. (Toronto: Pontifical Institute of Mediaeval Studies, 1978).

6. Thomas Berry, "Contemporary Spirituality—Its Global Content, Its Historical Dimensions, Its Future Vision," *Riverdale Studies* 1(1975), 1.

7. John Dunne, *The Way of All the Earth: Experiments in Truth and Religion* (Notre Dame: University of Notre Dame Press, 1972), p. ix; Raimundo Panikkar, *Myth, Faith and Hermeneutics* (New York: Paulist Press, 1979), pp. 241–245; see also *The Intrareligious Dialogue* (Paulist Press, 1978).

8. Peter Berger, *The Other Side of God: A Polarity in World Religions* (Garden City, N.Y.: Anchor Books, 1981).

9. See Donald Rothberg, "Contemporary Epistemology and the Study of Mysticism," in *The Problem of Pure Consciousness: Mysticism and Philosophy*, ed. Robert K.C. Forman (New York: Oxford University Press, 1990), pp. 163–211.

10. Karl Jaspers, *The Origin and Goal of History*, trans. Michael Bullock (New Haven: Yale University Press, 1953), p. 3.

11. *Chāndogya Upanishad*, VI, ii, 1–2; trans. R.C. Zaehner, *Hindu Scriptures* (London: J.M. Dent & Sons, 1966), p. 105.

12. Ibid., VI, viii, 4; trans., p. 108.

13. Ibid., VI, viii, 7 ff.; trans., p. 109.

14. Augustine, *Confessions*, VII, 9; trans. Rex Warner, *The Confessions of St. Augustine* (New York: New American Library, 1963), p. 147.

15. Ibid.

16. Origen, *De Principiis*, 4.2.4.

17. Gregory the Great, Ezekiel 2, 9, 8.

18. Augustine of Dacia, OP, cited in New Catholic Encyclopedia S.V. "Exegesis, Medieval."

19. Ps. 114:1–2.

20. Dante, Epistle to Can Grande della Scala, trans. Nancy Howe in Mark Musa ed. *Essays on Dante* (Bloomington: University of Indiana Press 1964), p. 37.

21. Thomas of Aquinas, *Summa Theologiae*, I, q. 1.

22. Bonaventure, *Breviloquium*, Prologue.

23. Richard of St. Victor, *The Mystical Ark*. I, 1; iv, 17–21.

24. Bonaventure, *The Soul's Journey*, VI.

25. R.E.L. Masters and Jean Houston, *The Varieties of Psychedelic Experience* (New York: Holt, Rinehart, and Winston, 1966).

26. Stanislav Grof, *Realms of the Human Unconscious* (New York: Viking Press, 1975).

27. Masters and Houston, *The Varieties*, p. 308.

28. Ibid., p. 181.

29. Ibid., p. 207.

30. Ibid., pp. 218–219.

31. Grof, *Realms*, p. 147.

32. Masters and Houston, *The Varieties*, p. 308.

CHAPTER III

1. Ewert Cousins, "Models and the Future of Theology," *Continuum*, VII (1969), pp. 78–92.

2. Ian G. Barbour, *Myths, Models and Paradigms: A Comparative Study in Science and Religion* (New York: Harper & Row, 1974); B. Kazemier and D. Vuysje, eds., *The Concept and the Role of the Model in Mathematics and Natural and Social Sciences* (Dordrecht: D. Reidel, 1961), p. 334; Max Black, *Models and Metaphors* (Ithaca: Cornell University Press, 1962); Mary Hesse, *Models and Analogies in Science* (Notre Dame: Notre Dame University Press, 1966). For a presentation of the various types of models used in the sciences, see L.

Apostel, "Towards the Formal Study of Models in the Non-Formal Sciences," in Kazem-ier and Vuysje, eds., pp. 1–37.

3. See especially Ian Ramsey, *Religious Language* (London: SCM Press, 1957); *Freedom and Immortality* (London: SCM Press, 1960); *On Being Sure in Religion* (London: Athlone Press, 1963); *Models and Mystery* (London: Oxford University Press, 1964); *Religion and Science* (London: SPCK, 1964); *Christian Discourse* (London: Oxford University Press, 1965); See also John McIntyre, *The Shape of Christology* (London: Westminster Press, 1966); Frederic Ferré, "Mapping the Logic of Models in Science and Theology," *The Christian Scholar*, XLVI (1963), 99–39; William Austin, "Models, Mystery, and Paradox in Ian Ramsey," *Journal for the Scientific Study of Religion*, VII (1968), pp. 41–55.

4. Ramsey, *Models and Mystery*, pp. 1–21.

5. Ibid., p. 210.

6. Avery Dulles, *Models of the Church* (New York: Image Books, 1978); *Models of Revelation* (Garden City, NY: Image Books, 1985).

7. Theological systems have other functions besides the expression of religious experience, such as establishing the validity of belief, defending a position against objections, establish-ing the coherence and reasonability of the structures of belief. Yet even these functions presuppose a level where the systems are giving expression to religious experience.

8. Rudolf Otto, *The Idea of the Holy* (New York: Oxford University Press, 1958, pp. 12–40.

9. William James, *The Varieties of Religious Experience* (New York: University Books, 1963).

10. Otto, op. cit.

11. Mircea Eliade, *Patterns in Comparative Religion* (New York: Sheed & Ward, 1958); *The Sacred and the Profane* (New York: Harcourt, Brace, 1959); *The Myth of the Eternal Return* (New York: Pantheon Books, 1954).

12. C. G. Jung, *The Collected Works of C. G. Jung* (New York: Pantheon Books, 1960).

13. R. E. L. Masters and Jean Houston, *The Varieties of Psychedelic Experience* (New York: Holt, Rinehart and Winston, 1966); Stanislav Grof, *Realms of the Human Unconscious* (New York: Viking Press, 1975).

14. Much work has been done as a basis for studying Anselm with the model method: see, for example, A. Harnack, *History of Dogma*, Vol. VI (Boston: Dover Publications, 1961); J. Riviere, *The Doctrine of the Atonement*, Vol. II (St. Louis: Herder, 1909); G. Aulen, *Christus Victor* (New York: Collier, 1986); G. Williams, *Anselm: Communion and Atonement* (St. Louis: Concordia, 1960). For a listing of further pertinent research, see Williams, op. cit., pp. 5–9.

15. Otto, op. cit., p. 53, n. 1.

16. Ibid., pp. 50–59; P. Tillich, *Systematic Theology*, Vol. II (Chicago: University of Chicago Press, 1957), pp. 172–173; C. Anstey, "St. Anselm Demythologized," *Theology*, LXIV (1961), p. 18. For a study of redemption from the standpoint of the experiential models of depth psychology, see P. Pruyser, "Anxiety, Guilt, and Shame in the Atonement," *Theology Today*, XXI (1964), pp. 115–133.

17. Aristotle, *Metaphysics*, pp. 1016–1017, 1048, 1070; for a study of Aristotelian analogy in the context of scientific models, see Hesse, op. cit., pp. 130–156; Plato, *Republic*, VI, pp. 506–511; Otto, op. cit., pp. 45–49, 140–142; Ramsey, *Models and Mystery*, pp. 9–10.

18. See W. T. Stace, *Religion and the Modern Mind* (Philadelphia: Lippincott, 1952), for an analysis of the effect of changing cosmological models on modern religious attitudes.

19. On the Sky-God and Earth-Mother, see Eliade, *Patterns in Comparative Religion*, pp. 38–153, 239–264.

20. Pierre Teilhard de Chardin, *Œuvres de Pierre Teilhard de Chardin* (Paris: Editions du Seuil, 1955).

21. See C. Mooney, *Teilhard de Chardin and the Mystery of Christ* (New York: Harper & Row, 1966), pp. 67–145.

22. For a comparison of Teilhard's cosmic Christology with that of the New Testament and

the Greek Fathers, see G. Maloney, *The Cosmic Christ from Paul to Teilhard* (New York: Sheed and Ward, 1968); on Teilhard in relation to the medieval Franciscan cosmic experience, see my own study, "Teilhard de Chardin and Saint Bonaventure," in M. Meilach, ed., *There Shall Be One Christ* (Saint Bonaventure, NY: Franciscan Institute, 1968).

23. The devotion to the humanity of Christ, cultivated by Bernard of Clairvaux and the early Franciscans, can be traced in such writings as Bonaventure's *Lignum Vitae* and the *Spiritual Exercises* of Ignatius of Loyola. Both of these include lengthy meditation on the virtues displayed by Christ in his earthly life, presented as models to be imitated by the Christian.

24. See Aulen, op. cit., but in conjunction with the criticism of McIntyre, *St. Anselm and his Critics*, pp. 197–200.

25. Such elements are found in the existential emphasis on individuality, authenticity, anxiety and guilt; see J. Macquarrie, *An Existentialist Theology* (London: Macmillan, 1955).

26. Augustine, *De Trinitate*, V–VII; see H. Wolfson, *The Philosophy of the Church Fathers*, Vol. I (Cambridge, Mass: Harvard University Press, 1964), pp. 350–359. For a pioneering study of the differences between the Western and Eastern approaches to the Trinity, See Théodore de Régnon, *Études de théology positive sur la Sainte Trinite*, 4 vols. (Paris: Retaux, 1892–1898). Although Augustine shaped the characteristic model of Western theology, this was not the only model he employed: see O. du Roy, *L'intelligence de la foi en la Trinité selon Saint Augustin* (Paris, Études Augustiniennes, 1966).

27. Karl Rahner, "Remarks on the Dogmatic Treatise; 'De Trinitate,' " in *Theological Investigations*, Vol. IV (Baltimore: Helicon Press, 1966), pp. 77–102.

28. On the history of this model, see de Régnon, op. cit.; on its significance in Eastern theology, see V. Lossky, *The Mystical Theology of the Eastern Church* (London: J. Clarke, 1957), pp. 44–66; in contemporary theology, see Karl Barth, *The Doctrine of the Word of God* (Edinburgh: T. & T. Clark, 1936), pp. 339–399; Tillich, *Systematic Theology*, Vol. I (Chicago: University of Chicago Press, 1951), pp. 249–252; Karl Rahner, "Theos in the New Testament," in *Theological Investigations*, Vol. I (Baltimore: Helicon Press, 1961), pp. 79–148; "The concept of Mystery in Catholic Theology," and "The Theology of the Symbol," in *Theological Investigations*, Vol. IV (Baltimore: Helicon Press, 1966), pp. 36–73, 221–252.

29. An example of this experiential model can be found in Eckhart's dynamic, "Gothic" mysticism, as described by Rudolf Otto in *Mysticism East and West* (New York: Meridian Books, 1957), pp. 183–206.

30. An example of this experiential model can be found in Bonaventure, *Itinerarium Mentis in Deum*, VI. p. 3.

31. Paul Henry, *Saint Augustine on Personality* (New York: Macmillan, 1960), pp. 8–11.

32. Ibid.; see also Mother Mary Clark, "The Human Person and God," *The Downside Review*, LXXXIV (1966) p. 15–30; B. Fraigneau-Julien, "Réflexion sur la signification religieuse du mystère de la Sainte Trinité." *Nouvelle revue théologique*, LXXXVII (1965), p. 6743–87.

33. Pierre Teilhard de Chardin, *The Phenomenon of Man* (New York: Harper & Row, 1965), pp. 260 ff.

34. See especially Teilhard's *Introduction à la vie chrétienne* (unpublished), p. 45; see Trinitarian references in Mooney, op. cit., p. 287.

35. For a discussion of complementary models, see Austin, op. cit.

36. See, for example, Augustine, *De Trinitate*, VIII–XV, and Bonaventure, *Itinerarium Mentis in Deum*.

37. For the similarities between the inward way in Christian and Hindu thought, see Otto, *Mysticism East and West*, pp. 57–104. For an extensive treatment of the image of God see G. Ladner, *The Idea of Reform* (Cambridge: Harvard University Press, 1959). For a detailed analysis of the image of God doctrine in Augustine and Thomas Aquinas, see J. Sullivan, *The Image of God: the Doctrine of St. Augustine and its Influence* (Dubuque: Priory Press, 1963).

38. See Sullivan, op. cit., pp. 49–69, 136–148, 216–272.

39. See Sullivan, op. cit., pp. 49–69, 136–148, 216–272.

40. See Jean Leclercq, *The Love of Learning and the Desire for God: A Study of Monastic Culture*, trans. Catharine Mistahi (New York: Fordham University Press, 1974), pp. 233–286.

41. Louis Bouyer, *History of Christian Spirituality*, Vol. I: *The Spirituality of the New Testament and the Fathers*, trans. Mary P. Ryan (New York: Seabury Press), p. 212.

42. Origen, *17th Homily on numbers*, 4; cited in Bouyer, op. cit., p. 297.

43. See the chapter heading of Bonaventure's *Itinerarium Mentis in Deum*, and the note on speculation in my translation: *Bonaventure: The Soul's Journey into God, The Tree of Life, The Life of St. Francis* (New York: Paulist Press, 1978), p. 59.

44. Augustine, *The Confessions*, VII, 10; trans. Rex Warner, *The Confessions of St. Augustine* (New York: Mentor Book), p. 149.

45. Ibid., VII, 9.

46. Ibid., VII, 10; trans., p. 149.

47. Ibid., VII, 17; trans., pp. 153–154.

48. Ibid., IX, 10; trans., p. 201.

49. Augustine, *On the Teacher*, 14.

50. Leclercq, op. cit., pp. 233–286.

51. Ibid., p. 233.

52. Ibid., p. 245.

53. Ibid., p. 264.

54. Loc cit.

55. Ibid., p. 275.

56. Ibid., p. 278.

57. Ibid., p. 266.

58. Bernard of Clairvaux, *Sermons on the Song of Songs*, 2–4.

59. Song of Songs, 1:1.

60. Bernard of Clairvaux, op. cit., 3:1; trans. Kilian Walsh, *The Works of Bernard of Clairvaux*, Vol. II: *Song of Songs I* (Kalamazoo: Cistercian Publications, 1979), 16.

61. Ibid., 7:2; trans., pp. 38–39.

62. Ibid., 74:6f; trans., xxi.

63. Bonaventure, op. cit., Prologue 3; trans., pp. 54–55.

64. Bonaventure, *Hexaemeron*, I, 17; the English translation is my own.

65. *Hexaemeron*, I, 24.

CHAPTER IV

1. Ewert H. Cousins, "Process Thought on the Eve of the 21st Century," The inaugural address of the Alfred P. Stiernotte Lecture Series, Quinnipiac College, Hamden, Connecticut, September 18, 1984, published as a booklet.

2. Raimundo Panikkar, *The Vedic Experience: An Anthology of the Vedas for Modern Man* (Berkeley: University of California Press, 1977).

3. *The Unknown Christ of Hinduism* (London: Darton, Longman and Todd, 1964).

4. Idem, *The Trinity and the Religious Experience of Man* (Maryknoll, N.Y.: Orbis Books, and London: Darton, Longman and Todd, 1975); this is a revised edition of *The Trinity and World Religions* (Madras: The Christian Literature Society, 1970).

5. Idem, *The Intrareligious Dialogue* (New York: Paulist Press, 1979).

6. Idem, *Myth, Faith, and Hermeneutics* (New York: Paulist Press, 1979).

7. Karl Barth, *Church Dogmatics*, 4 vols. (Edinburgh: T. and T. Clark, 1936–1969); Paul Tillich, *Systematic Theology*, 3 vols. (Chicago: The University of Chicago Press,

1951–1963); Karl Rahner, *Theological Investigations*, 14 vols. (New York: Seabury Press, 1971–1976).

8. See Teilhard de Chardin, op. cit.; also *The Divine Milieu* (New York: Harper and Row, 1965); *Science and Christ*, trans. René Hague (New York: Harper and Row, 1968); *Christianity and Evolution*, trans. René Hague (New York: Harcourt, Brace Jovanovich, 1971). On process thought, see Alfred North Whitehead, *Process and Reality: An Essay in Cosmology* (New York: Macmillan, 1929); John B. Cobb, *A Christian Natural Theology: Based on the Thought of Alfred North Whitehead* (Philadelphia: Westminster Press, 1965). On the theology of hope, see Jurgen Moltmann, *The Theology of Hope: On the Ground and the Implications of a Christian Eschatology*, trans. James W. Leitch (New York: Harper and Row, 1967). On the theology of liberation, see Gustavo Gutierrez, *A Theology of Liberation*, trans. Sister Caridid Inda and John Eagleson (Maryknoll, New York: Orbis Books, 1973).

9. Heinz Robert Schlette, *Towards a Theology of Religions*, trans. W.J. O'Hara (New York: Herder and Herder, 1966).

10. On the developement and structure of the *summa* genre, see M.D. Chenu, *Toward Understanding Saint Thomas*, trans. A.M. Landry and D. Hughes (Chicago: Henry Regnery, 1964), pp. 297–322.

11. Jn. 1:1–18; Col. 1:15–20. See also Phil. 2:6–11; Heb. 1:1–4.

12. Justin Martyr, *Apologia*, I, 46. Unless otherwise noted, the translations are my own.

13. Clement of Alexandria, *Stromata*, V, 5, 29.

14. Augustine, *De Magistro*. 11, 38.

15. Bonaventure, *Hexaemeron*, coll. I; *De Reductione Artium ad Theologiam*.

16. Pierre Teilhard de Chardin, *Œuvres de Pierre Teilhard de Chardin*, 9 vols. (Paris: Editions du Seuil, 1955–65). See Christopher Mooney, *Teilhard de Chardin and the Mystery of Christ* (New York: Harper and Row, 1966), George Maloney, *The Cosmic Christ: from Paul to Teilhard* (New York: Sheed and Ward, 1968).

17. On nirvana, see Thomas Berry, *Buddhism* (New York: Hawthorn Books, 1967), pp. 23–29; on Advaitan Hinduism, see Heinrich Zimmer, *Philosophies of India*, ed. Joseph Campbell (New York: Pantheon Books, 1951), pp. 455–463.

18. Raymond Panikkar, "Toward an Ecumenical Theandric Spirituality," *Journal of Ecumenical Studies*, V (1968), pp. 522–533.

19. Ibid., p. 522.

20. Ibid., p. 527–528.

21. Ibid., p. 509.

22. Examples of this tendency can be seen in the Middle Ages in the theology of Thomas Aquinas and in the twentieth century in the theology of Karl Barth. Although Thomas held a vestige doctrine based on appropriation (*Summa Theologiae*, I, q. 39, a. 7), he gave it a weak interpretation (*Summa Theologiae*, I, q. 32, a. 1), and did not make it central to his theological enterprise as did his contemporaries the Augustinians. Karl Barth has severely criticized the vestige doctrine in *The Doctrine of the Word of God: Prolegomena to Church Dogmatics*, Vol. I, Part I, trans. G.T. Thomson (New York: Scribners, 1936), pp. 383–399. Since Barth holds the exclusive revelation of the Trinity in Christ, he believes that to take the vestiges seriously is to run the risk of admitting a second source of the revelation of the Trinity.

23. Augustine, *De Trinitate*, VI, 10, 11–12; VIII–XV.

24. Robert Grosseteste, *Dictum 60: Omnis Creatura Speculum Est*, ed. Servus Gieben, in "Traces of God in Nature According to Robert Grosseteste," *Franciscan Studies*, XXIV (1964), pp. 154–155.

25. Bonaventure, *Itinerarium Mentis in Deum*, c. 1, n. 14.

26. Bonaventure, *Breviloquium*, p. 2, c. 12, n. 1.

27. Bonaventure, *Itinerarium*, c. 3, n. 5, trans. Philotheus Boehner, *Saint Bonaventure's Itinerar-*

ium Mentis in Deum, Vol. II of *Works of Saint Bonaventure*, ed. Philotheus Boehner and Sr. M. Frances Laughlin (Saint Bonaventure, N.Y.: Franciscan Institute, 1956), p. 69.

28. Bonaventure, *Itinerarium Mentis*, c. 3, n. 5, trans. Boehner, op. cit., p. 69.

29. Augustine, *De Trinitate*, VIII, 10, 14; *Tractatus in Ioannem*, XIV, 99; XXXIX, 5; Richard of St. Victor, *De Trinitate*, III; Alexander of Hales, *Summa Theologica*, I, n. 304; Bonaventure, *Itinerarium Mentis*, c. 6, n. 2.

30. On the foreshadowing of the Trinity in the Old Testament, see Augustine, *De Trinitate*, II, 10, 18, 35; Bonaventure, *Quaestiones Disputatae de Mysterio Trinitatis*, q. 1, a. 2, concl. On the reflection of the Trinity in Greek philosophy, see Augustine, *Confessions*, VII, 9, 13–15; Thomas Aquinas, *Summa Theologiae*, I, q. 32, a. 1; Bonaventure, *I Sent.*, d. 3, p. 1, a. un., q. 4; on the World Soul, see Tullio Gregory, *Anima Mundi* (Florence: Sansoni, 1955).

31. Athanasius, *Ad Serapionem*, epist. III, 5.

32. Basil, *Liber de Spiritu Sancto*, 16, 38.

33. Gregory of Nyssa, *Sermo de Spiritu Sancto adversus Pneumatomachos Macedonianos*, 13. English trans. from *Gregory of Nyssa, Nicene and Post-Nicene Fathers*, 2nd Series, Vol. V (Grand Rapids, Mich.: Eerdmans, 1953), 320.

34. Gregory Nazianzen, *Oratio XXXI: De Spiritu Sancto*, 29. English trans. from *Gregory Nazianzen, Nicene and Post-Nicene Fathers*, 2nd Series, Vol. VII (Grand Rapids, Mich.: Eerdmans, 1955), 327.

35. Hilary of Poitier, *De Trinitate*, I, 2, 1.

36. Augustine, *De Trinitate*, V; VII, 4; see Eugène Portalié, "Augustin (Saint)," *Dictionnaire de Théologie Catholique*, Vol. I (Paris: Librairie Letouzey et Ané, 1931), 2346–48.

37. Augustine, *De Trinitate*, V, 8, 9.

38. On Abelard, see Victor Murray, *Abelard and St. Bernard* (Manchester: University Press, 1967); see *Enchiridion Symbolorum*, ed. Henricus Denzinger-Adolf Schönmetzer, 34th ed. (Barcelona: Herder, 1967), 721 [368] ff. On appropriations, see Richard of St. Victor, *De Tribus Appropriatis Personis in Trinitate* (PL 196, 991–94); see A. Chollet, "Appropriation aux Personnes de la Sainte Trinité," *Dictionnaire de Théologie Catholique*, Vol. I, 1708–100.

39. Thomas Aquinas, *Summa Theologiae*, I, q. 39, a. 8; Bonaventure, *Breviloquium*, p. 1, c. 6.

40. Bonaventure, *I Sent.*, d. 3, p. 1, a. un., q. 4.

41. See a discussion of this in the light of the Christian Trinity by John Chethimattam, *Consciousness and Reality* (Bangalore: Bangalore Press, 1967), pp. 233–40.

42. For example, in the Middle Ages, Alanus de Insulis held that the appropriations were purely verbal: *Theologiae Regulae*, XLIX (PL 210, 642); Thomas Aquinas held that appropriations were more than merely verbal, but did not give them a strong interpretation or make them thematic in his system (see n. 22, above); Bonaventure, on the other hand, gave them a strong interpretation and made them central to his vision: see *Itinerarium Mentis in Deum*.

43. The Westerner is inclined to have a special problem here because of his understanding of the categories of being and non-being. He or she is likely to interpret nirvana—and the silence of the Father—as non-being in a Western sense. Since the Christian identifies God and Being, such an interpretation would seem atheistic and nihilistic. However, the identification of God and Being is presently being questioned in the West: see Raymond Panikkar, "The God of Being and the 'Being' of God: an Exploration," *Harvard Divinity Bulletin*, I (1968), 12–16; also Leslie Dewart, *The Foundations of Belief* (New York: Herder and Herder, 1969), pp. 396–425.

44. Ignatius of Antioch, *Magn.* 8:2. On the variant reading of this text, see Robert M. Grant, *The Apostolic Fathers: a New Translation and Commentary*, Vol. 4: *Ignatius of Antioch* (London: Thomas Nelson & Sons, 1966), 62.

45. In his letter to the Ephesians, 19:1, Ignatius speaks of "the stillness of God" (ησυχία).

On alternate interpretations of *Magn.* 8:2, see Virginia Corwin, *St. Ignatius and Christianity in Antioch* (New Haven: Yale University Press, 1960), p. 127.

46. See Corwin, op. cit., pp. 116–153.

47. See Corwin, op. cit., p. 141; Grant, loc. cit.

48. Augustine, *De Trinitate*, XIV; see Bonaventure, *Itinerarium Mentis in Deum*, c. 3.

49. Étienne Gilson, *The Christian Philosophy of Saint Augustine*, trans. L.E.M. Lynch (New York: Random House, 1960), p. 299.

50. Titus Szabó, *De Trinitate in Creaturis Refulgente Doctrina S. Bonaventurae* (Rome: Herder, 1955), p. 70.

51. Panikkar, op. cit., p. 524.

52. Théodore de Régnon, *Études de théologie positive sur la Sainte Trinité*, première série (Paris: Retaux, 1892).

53. See Gregory Nazianzen, *Oratio II*, 38.

54. Basil, *Homilia XXIV, Contra Sabellianos et Arium et Anommoeos*, 4.

55. Pseudo-Dionysius, *De Nominibus Divinis*, 2,7.

56. John Damascene, *De Fide Orthodoxa*, I, 12.

57. Tertullian, *Adversus Praxean*, 8.

58. Creed of the Eleventh Council of Toledo, 675; see Denzinger-Schönmetzer, op. cit., 525 [275].

59. Bonaventure, *I Sent.*, d. 27, p. 1, a. un. q. 2, ad. 3; on the *coincidentia oppositorum* in Bonaventure, see my studies: "The Coincidence of Opposites in the Christology of Saint Bonaventure," *Franciscan Studies*, XXVIII (1968), 27–45; "La Coincidentia Oppositorum' dans la théologie de Bonaventure," Actes du Colloque Saint Bonaventure, in *Études franciscaines*, XVIII (Supplément annuel, 1968), 15–31.

60. See Bonaventure, *I Sent.*, d. 27, p. 1, a. un. q. 2.

61. See below pages 126–129.

62. Pseudo-Dionysius, *De Mystica Theologia*, 1, trans. Elmer O'Brien, *Varieties of Mystic Experience* (New York: Holt, Rinehart and Winston, 1964), pp. 78–79; I have altered the punctuation in transcribing the text since the English original was printed colometrically.

63. Raimundo Panikkar, "La secularisation de l'herméneutique: Le cas du Christ: Fils de l'homme et fils de Dieu," in *Herméneutique de la secularisation*, ed. Enrico Castelli (Paris: Aubier, 1976), pp. 213–248.

64. Charles T. Tart, "Science, States of Consciousness and Spiritual Experience: The Need for State-Specific Sciences," in *Transpersonal Psychologies*, ed. Charles T. Tart (New York: Harper and Row, 1975), pp. 9–58.

CHAPTER V

1. Huston Smith, *The Religions of Man* (New York: Perennial Library, Harper and Row, 1965).

2. Ibid., p. ix.

3. John S. Dunne, *The Way of All the Earth: Experiments in Truth and Religion* (Notre Dame: Notre Dame University Press, 1978), p. ix.

4. Ewert Cousins, "Models and the Future of Theology," *Continuum*, 7(1969), 78–92.

5. Rudolf Otto, *The Idea of the Holy: An Inquiry into the Non-Rational Factor in the Idea of the Divine and Its Relation to the Rational*, trans. John W. Harvey (New York: Galaxy, Oxford University Press, 1958).

6. See Rudolf Otto, *The Idea of the Holy*.

7. Raimundo Panikkar, *The Trinity and the Religious Experience of Man* (New York: Orbis Books, 1973).

8. Raimundo Panikkar, *Myth, Faith and Hermeneutics* (New York: Paulist Press, 1979), 242–243.

9. William James, *The Varieties of Religious Experience* (New York: Longmans, Green, and Co., 1902).

10. Richard Woods, ed., *Understanding Mysticism* (Garden City, New York: Dobuleday, 1980); Steven T. Katz, ed., *Mysticism and Philosophical Analysis* (New York: Oxford University Press, 1978); *Mysticism and Religious Traditions* (New York: Oxford University Press, 1983).

11. Peter L. Berger, *The Heretical Imperative: Contemporary Possibilities of Religious Affirmation* (Garden City, New York: Doubleday, 1980), pp. 143–172.

12. Peter L. Berger, ed., *The Other Side of God: A Polarity in World Religions* (Garden City, New York: Doubleday, 1981).

13. Ewert H. Cousins, *Global Spirituality: Toward the Meeting of Mystical Paths* (Madras: University of Madras, 1985).

14. Rudolf Otto, *Mysticism East and West: A Comparative Analysis of the Nature of Mysticism*, trans. Bertha L. Bracey and Richenda C. Payne (New York: Macmillan, 1960).

15. See Steven T. Katz, "Language, Epistemology, and Mysticism," in Steven T. Katz, ed., *Mysticism and Philosophical Analysis* (London: Sheldon Press, 1978); see also Katz's "Conservative Character" in *Mysticism and Religious Traditions*, pp. 4–5.

16. On Eckhart and Śankara, see n. 14, above; on Rāmānuja and Bonaventure, see John Plott, *A Philosophy of Devotion: A Comparative Study of Bhakti and Pratatti in Visist Advaita and St. Bonaventure and Gabriel Marcel* (Delhi: Motilal Banarsidass, 1974).

17. The English translations of these works are taken from The Classics of Western Spirituality: *Bonaventure: The Soul's Journey into God, The Tree of Life, The Life of St. Francis*, trans. and ed. Ewert Cousins (New York: Paulist Press, 1978), pp. 53–116; and *Meister Eckhart: The Essential Sermons, Commentaries, Treatises, and Defense*, trans. and ed. Edmund Colledge and Bernard McGinn (New York: Paulist Press, 1981), pp. 177–208. These translations have been made from the critical texts: *Doctoris Seraphici S. Bonaventurae opera omnia*, edita studio et cura pp. Collegii a S. Bonaventura, X volumnia (Quaracchi: Collegium S. Bonaventurae, 1882–1902) and *Meister Eckhart: Die deutschen und lateinischen Werke*, herausgegeben im Aufträge der Deutschen Forschungsgemeinschaft (Stuttgart and Berlin: W. Kohlhammer, 1936).

18. Bonaventure, *The Soul's Journey into God*, Prologue, 2–3; trans., p. 54.

19. Ibid., VI, 2; trans., p. 102.

20. Ibid., trans., p. 103.

21. Bonaventure, *I Sent.*, d. 27, p. 1 a. un., q. 2 (I, 214–216).

22. Otto, *The Idea of the Holy*, pp. 1–40.

23. Bonaventure, *The Soul's Journey*, VII, 1; trans., p. 111.

24. Ibid., 4; trans., p. 113.

25. Ibid., 6; trans., p. 115.

26. Eckhart, *German Works: Sermon 52*; trans., pp. 199–200.

27. Ibid.; trans., p. 200.

28. Ibid., *Sermon 53*; trans., p. 205.

29. Ibid., *Sermon 48*; trans., p. 198.

30. Ibid., *Sermon 83*; trans., p. 206.

31. Ewert H. Cousins, "Fulness and Emptiness in Bonaventure and Eckhart," *Dharma*, 6(1981), 59–68; see also my study, *Bonaventure and the Coincidence of Opposites* (Chicago: Franciscan Herald Press, 1978).

CHAPTER VI

1. After a year of preparation the first phase of this research program culminated in a conference at the East-West Center, June 10th to 14th, 1991, An Exploration of Contemporary Spirituality: "Axial Age Civilizations" and "Primal Traditions."
2. Ewert Cousins, "Preface to the Series," in Bernard McGinn and John Meyendorff, eds., *Christian Spirituality I: Origins to the Twelfth Century* (New York: Crossroad Publishing Company, 1985), p. xiii.
3. Lame Buffalo, *Native Spiritual Voices*, privately published, p. 1.
4. On Francis and nature, see the seminal article by Lynn White, "The Historical Roots of Our Ecological Crisis," *Science* 155(1967), 1203–1207.
5. Bonaventure, *Legenda maior*, IX, 1; trans. Ewert Cousins, *Bonaventure: The Soul's Journey into God, The Tree of Life, The Life of St. Francis* (New York: Paulist Press, 1978).
6. For the critical text of *The Canticle of Brother Sun*, see *Die Opuscula de Hl. Franziskus von Assisi: Neue text Kritische Edition*, ed. Kajetan Esser (Grotta Ferrata: Collegium S. Bonaventurae, 1976), pp. 122–133; trans. Cousins, op. cit., pp. 27–28.
7. Bonaventure, *Legenda maior*, VIII, 6.
8. Ibid., X, 7.
9. Ibid., I, 5.
10. Ibid., XIII, 3.
11. *Legenda Perugina*, 43; for the text of the *Legenda Perugina*, I am using *Scripta Leonis, Rufini et Angeli Sociorum S. Francisci*, ed. and trans. Rosalind B. Brooke (Oxford: Clarendon, 1970).
12. Ibid.
13. Ibid.
14. Ibid.
15. Ibid.
16. C.G. Jung, *Memories, Dreams, Reflections*, ed. A. Jaffe (New York: Pantheon, 1963), p. 205.
17. On the psychological aspects of alchemy, see Edward F. Edinger, *Anatomy of the Psyche: Alchemical Symbolism in Psychotherapy* (La Salle, IL: Open Court, 1985).
18. See Bonaventure, *Collationes in Hexaemeron*, I; John Duns Scotus, *Re. Par.*, lib. 3, d. 7, q. 4: *Op. Ox.*, lib. 3, d. 7, q. 3, dub. 1.
19. See Bonaventure *I Sent.*, d. 27, p. 1, a. un., q. 2.
20. Bonaventure, *Soul's Journey*, Prologue 2.
21. Ibid.
22. Ibid.
23. Ibid., Prologue 3.
24. Ibid.
25. Ibid., I, 13.
26. Ibid., II, 10.
27. Ibid., III, 4.
28. Ibid., IV, 3.
29. Ibid., V, 2.
30. Ibid., VII, 5.
31. Bonaventure, *Hexaem*, XII, 14.
32. Ibid., I, 17.
33. Bonaventure, *I Sent.*, d. 2, 1. un., q. 2.
34. Bonaventure, *Soul's Journey*, VI, 2; See also Pseudo-Dionysius, *De caelesti hierarchia*, IV, 1, *De divinis nominibus*, IV, 1, 20.
35. Ibid.
36. Bonaventure, *Hexaem.*, I, 17.

37. Bonaventure, II, 11.

38. Ibid., III, 1.

39. C.G. Jung, "A Psychological Approach to the Trinity," in *Psychology and Religion East and West: Vol. 11 of The Corrected Works of C.G. Jung*, 2nd ed., trans. R.F.C. Hull (Princeton: Princeton University Press, 1969), p. 132.

40. Ibid., p. 133.

41. Bonaventure, *Soul's Journey*, Prologue, 1.

42. This quotation is from the sermon *Expedit vobis*, which is printed as #76 in *Meister Eckhart*, ed. Franz Pfeiffer (Göttingen: Vandenhoeck and Ruprecht, 1924). Although previous editors considered this sermon to be Eckhart's, it was not listed by Joseph Quint among Eckhart's authentic works in his critical edition (see note 43, below); yet it is from the Eckhart school and represents in a concise fashion the essence of his position.

43. Eckhart, *German Works: Sermon 48*; translation from *Meister Eckhart: The Essential Sermons, Commentaries, Treatises, and Defense*, trans. and ed., Edmund Colledge and Bernard McGinn (New York: Paulist Press, 1981), p. 198. This translation has been made from the critical text: *Meister Eckhart: Die deutschen und lateinischen Werke*, herausgegeben im Aufträge der Deutschen Forschungsgemeinschaft (Stuttgart and Berlin: W. Kohlhammer, 1936–).

44. C.G. Jung, "A Psychological Approach to the Trinity," pp. 170–171.

45. For a study of this form of the coincidence of opposites, see my book, *Bonaventure and the Coincidence of Opposites* (Chicago: Franciscan Herald Press, 1978).

46. See Augustine, *De Trinitate*, V; Richard of St. Victor, *De Trinitate*, III; Thomas Aquinas, *Summa Theologiae*, I, q. 29, a. 4. corp.

CHAPTER VII

1. Plotinus, *Enneads*, V, 1, 2; English translation by Elmer O'Brien, *The Essential Plotinus* (Indianapolis: Hackett Publishing Company, 1986), pp. 92–93.

2. Gregory of Nyssa, *On the Holy Spirit Against the Followers of Macedonius* [Eng. trans., *Gregory of Nyssa, Nicene and Post-Nicene Fathers*, 2nd Series, Vol. V (Grand Rapids, Mich.: Eerdmans, 1953), p. 320].

3. Ibid. [Eng. trans., p. 319].

4. Gregory Nazianzen, *Oratio*, 31 [Eng. Trans., *Gregory Nazianzen, Nicene and Post-Nicene Fathers*, 2nd Series, Vol. VII (Grand Rapids Mich.: Eerdmans, 1955), p. 361].

5. Ibid.

6. On the history of the concept of the World Soul, see Tullio Gregory, *Anima Mundi* (Florence: Sansoni, 1955), pp. 123 ff.

7. Ibid., p. 126. Gregory points out that in making this correlation the theologians at times fell into expressions that smacked of subordinationism.

8. Ibid., pp. 15–16; 41 ff; 123 ff. See Peter Dronke, "L'amor che move il sole e l'altre stelle," *Studi Medievali*, 3rd Series, 6 (1965), 401–413.

9. Dronke, op. cit., pp. 339 ff.

10. William of Conches, *In Boethium*, cited in Gregory, op. cit., p. 15; see also Dronke, op. cit., p. 410.

11. Dronke, op. cit., p. 410; Gregory, op. cit., pp. 133 ff.

12. William of St. Thierry, *Epistola de Erroribus Guillelmi de Conchis, Patrologia Latina*, 180, 333–340. On the condemnation of Abelard, see *Enchiridion Symbolorum*, ed. Henricus Denzinger-Adolf Schönmetzer, 32nd edition (Rome: Herder, 1963), 722 (370). See Gregory, op. cit.., pp. 3, 17, 116 ff., 243 ff.; Dronke, op. cit., pp. 411–413. The force of the objection of William of St. Thierry was directed against the technique of appropriation and the vestige doctrine. Yet this tradition continued to flourish in the thirteenth century.

13. Teilhard, "L'Ame du monde," in *Écrits du temps de la guerre*, pp. 221–232 [Eng. trans., "The Soul of the World," in *Writings in Time of War*, pp. 175–190].

14. Teilhard, *Writings in Time of War*, p. 182.

15. Ibid.

16. Ibid., p. 183.

17. Ibid.

18. Ibid.

19. Ibid., pp. 186–187.

20. Ibid., p. 183.

21. Teilhard, *Le Phénomène humain*, Vol. I of *Œuvres de Pierre Teilhard de Chardin* (Paris: Editions du Seuil, 1955) trans., *The Phenomenon of Man*, revised edition (New York: Harper and Row, 1965).

22. On the question of evil in the world, see Teilhard, *Le Phénomène humain*, pp. 345–348 trans., pp. 311–313; *Le Milieu Divin*, Vol. IV of *Œuvres* (Paris: Seuil, 1957), pp 71–102 trans., *The Divine Milieu* (New York: Harper and Row, 1960), pp. 45–68].

23. Rabanus Maurus, *Veni Creator Spiritus, Patrologia Latina*, 112, 1957:
    > Veni, Creator Spiritus
    > Mentes tuorum visita.
    > Imple superna gratia
    > Quæ tu creasti pectora.

24. Christopher Mooney, *Teilhard de Chardin and the Mystery of Christ* (New York: Harper and Row, 1966), p. 287; and Donald Gray, "Creative Union in Christ in the Thought of Teilhard de Chardin," unpublished dissertation (Fordham University, Theology Department, 1968), pp. 3 ff.

25. Teilhard, *Introduction à la vie chrétienne* (unpublished), pp. 4–5 [Eng. trans., Gray, op. cit., pp. 4–5].

26. Mooney, op. cit., p. 173; Father Mooney is commenting on a text of Teilhard from *Comment je vois*, pp. 18–19.

27. Teilhard, *Le Phénomène humain*, pp. 291 ff. [Eng. trans., pp. 262 ff.].

28. Teilhard, *Esquisse d'un univers personnel*, in *Œuvres*, VI, pp. 84–85.

29. Paul Henry, *Saint Augustine on Personality* (New York: Macmillan, 1960), p. 10; see Augustine, *De Trinitate*, V, 3, 4–5, 6.

30. Thomas Aquinas, *Summa Theologiae*, I, q. 37, a. 1, ad 3 [Eng. trans., *Basic Writings of Saint Thomas Aquinas*, Vol. I, ed. Anton Pegis (New York: Random House, 1945), p. 355]. See Augustine, *De Trinitate*, VI, 5, 7; XV, 17, 31; Bonaventure, *I Sent.*, d. 10, a. 2, q. 1.

31. Jo. 14–17.

32. Teilhard, *Le Phénomène humain*, pp. 293 ff. [Eng. trans., pp. 264 ff.].

33. Teilhard, *L'Esprit de la terre*, in *Œuvres*, VI, p. 41.

34. Teilhard, *Le Phénomène humain*, pp. 295 [Eng. trans., p. 265].

35. Ibid., pp. 293–94 [Eng. trans., pp. 264–65].

36. See, for example, Jean Leclercq, *Monks and Love in Twelfth-Century France* (Oxford: Clarendon, 1979).

37. Inferno, v, 100–106. The English translation of Inferno and Paradiso is by Charles Singleton, *The Divine Comedy* (Princeton: Princeton University Press, 1975).

38. Ibid., 116–120.

39. Ibid., 127–138.

40. Ibid, 139–142.

41. See Purgatorio, xvii, xviii.

42. Inferno, ii, 67–72.

43. Purgatorio, xxx, 31–39. The English translation is by John Sinclair, *The Divine Comedy of Dante Alighieri* (New York: Oxford University press, 1961).

44. Paradiso, xv, 31–36.

45. Bernard of Clairvaux, *On the Song of Songs*, 7:2. English translation by Kilian Walsh, *On the Song of Songs* (Kalamazoo, Mich.: Cistercian Publications, 1979).

46. Joseph Campbell, with Bill Moyers, *The Power of Myth*, ed. Betty Sue Flowers (New York: Doubleday, 1988), pp. 186–187.

47. John Barrows and Frank Tipler, *The Anthropic Cosmological Principle* (Oxford: The Clarendon Press, 1986).

48. Paradiso, xxxiii, 82–93; translation of this and the following passages from Paradiso are by Sinclair.

49. Ibid., 115–120; 124–26.

50. Ibid., 127–138.

51. Ibid., 140–145.